In Praise of
C-SPARK

The case for strategic workforce education has never been presented in a more compelling way. *C-Spark* is a reminder to CEOs of large organizations about the unique responsibility and opportunity they have to grow their companies through a sincere commitment to investing in their employees' education. A great read in a very relevant world.

URSULA BURNS, former CEO, Xerox;
Board Member, American Express, Exxon and Nestlé

C-Spark is an invaluable guide to both the purpose and the practice of workforce education. Moreover, it is a testament to the value of embracing the "And"— understanding that incorporating positive social impact leads to stronger, more sustainable business performance. With *C-Spark*, Vivek has illuminated a path for CEOs to make a real difference in the lives of their employees and the legacy of their business.

JIM COULTER, Executive Chairman and a Founding Partner, TPG

The future will be seized by CEOs who see the genius of the "And" and not the tyranny of the "Or." For CEOs who see their employees as an asset to invest in, *C-Spark* provides a practical toolkit to strategically use workforce education for their organization's needs, both for today and for the future.

GREG CREED, former CEO, Yum! Brands;
Board Member, Aramark and Whirlpool

C-Spark champions the idea that a CEO's future workforce can be found within their own organization. The U.S. military successfully employs this idea every year with thousands of military personnel being educated and trained in new skills. Corporate America and stalwart CEOs now have the chance to do the same, thanks to the availability of high-quality workforce education. Even the military could benefit from the ideas discussed in this book.

ERIC FANNING, former Secretary, U.S. Army;
President & CEO, Aerospace Industries Association

Corporate boards and C-suite executives are discovering that what makes a great company is being completely redefined. The decades-old stakeholder model is being transformed at a head-spinning pace by a values-driven societal expectation of change. The "Age of And" is here and *C-Spark* offers a path to navigate these choppy waters and ensure your employees are truly part of these history-making changes.

ROBIN HAYES, CEO, JetBlue Airways

As business leaders, we must challenge ourselves to create organizations with purpose that goes beyond the pursuit of profit. We must reimagine the future to include breakthrough approaches and investments in a workforce that will unlock value for all stakeholders and our collective future. In *C-Spark*, Vivek Sharma poses some critical questions about the universal opportunity to elevate workforce education as a strategic lever in organizations. This book is a valuable toolkit of tangible lessons and inspiring anecdotes for growing and engaging a workforce that drives both business impact and meaningful social impact.

KEVIN JOHNSON, President & CEO, Starbucks

Being born the same year as Brown v. Board of Education, I was raised to work for the best education possible and then give back to my community. As one of the few Black female CEOs, I made sure my employees were coached, educated and promoted. *C-Spark* is the codification of what I inherently knew was important — education — with corporate America being an important ally in that goal. Every CEO should read this book and incorporate its tenets into their business in order to keep the "And" in our ever-changing global landscape.

DEBRA LEE, former CEO, BET Networks;
Board Member, AT&T, Burberry, Marriott and Procter & Gamble

Successful leaders who have embraced the concept of strategic workforce education appreciate the power of their people to drive corporate growth. *C-Spark* challenges every CEO to make a commitment to ongoing education of their employees — and by doing so, reap the rewards of their increased engagement.

RON SUGAR, former CEO, Northrop Grumman; Chairman of the Board, Uber;
Board Member, Apple, Amgen and Chevron

C-Spark is truly an ignition guidepost that captures the best of leadership and workforce engagement — starting with C-Suite recognition and commitment. Through new and enduring engagement practices, *C-Spark* reinforces the principle that human capital is the foundation of successful companies. If you are an "employee first" leader, this book is a must read! You'll refer back to it often for insights and wisdom.

MAGGIE WILDEROTTER, former CEO, Frontier Communications; Board Chair, DocuSign;
Board Member, Costco Wholesale Corporation, HPE and Lyft

C-SPARK

CEO-led Workforce Education
for the AGE *of* AND

VIVEK SHARMA

Foreword by Meg Whitman

Printed in the United States of America
First Edition, August 2021

ISBN 978-1-7356223-5-4 (Paperback)
ISBN 978-1-7356223-4-7 (Hardcover)
ISBN 978-1-7356223-3-0 (Ebook)

Published by Sairya, LLC
Cover design by Ontes Creative

Dedication

To Saina, Arya and Deepika

न चोरहार्यं न च राजहार्यं
न भ्रातृभाज्यं न च भारकारि।
व्यये कृते वर्धते एव नित्यं
विद्याधनं सर्वधनप्रधानम्॥

No one can steal it and no state can snatch it;
It cannot be divided and it's not heavy to carry;
It increases as one spends and expands as one shares;
Education is the best wealth among all.

A Sanskrit shloka on education

Contents

Acknowledgments

This book would not have been possible without the help of many mentors, colleagues and friends. When I explained that I wanted to address the pressing need for strategic workforce education to a CEO-level audience in a compelling and entertaining manner, there was never any hesitation. Instead, I was bestowed with relevant notes and research, gracious amounts of time and unique perspectives based on years of corporate experience. I am grateful to all of you for your generosity and endless support.

First, thanks to George Barrett, Jason Baumgarten, Daniel Casse, Dominic Casserley, Tammie Chen, James Citrin, Dr. Michael Crow, Barbara Desoer, Lynne Doughtie, Steve Ellis, Mark Fields, Doug Haynes, David Hoverman, Tsun-yan Hsieh, Secretary Ray Mabus, Teri McClure, Amy Miles, Dr. Phil Regier, John Rogers, Chuck Rubin, Brad Smith, Ken Smith, Sara Spiering, Tom Staggs, Ron Sugar, Maggie Wilderotter, David Wilkie and David Windley for sharing your valuable insights for this book. Special thanks to Meg Whitman for a thoughtful and elegant foreword.

To Jim Alessandro, Sean Flynn, Jonathan Lau and Michelle Westfort, I am grateful for your thought leadership and research support for "strategic enterprise education" and your willingness to share your personal stories as well.

To Daniel Altobello, Rocio Alvarez, Nori Barajas, Elizabeth Brown, Rebecca Friendly, Nicole Garcia, Mitch Gordon, Rodney Grover,

Martha Hopkins, Ryan Johnson, JT Kim, Ray Lutzky, Tarun Malhotra, Colleen Monaco, Annette Neu, Gabriel Perez, Neil Petty, Court Picciolo, Brendan Riley, Jake Siegler, Nisha Smales, Eugene So, Maryam Sohraby, Courtney Sulzberger, Garry Thaniel, Ryan Tritch, Stephanie Tsales, Betsy Tucci and Regan Turner — thank you for sharing your perspectives and for your help.

Thanks to Scott Blue for serving in a unique role as thought partner and editor; to Brian MacDougall, for unwavering support in helping move quality work forward; to Nicole Stephens, for your scheduling magic that freed up time for writing this book; and to John James Nicoletti, for helping to see this book through to its completion.

C-Spark is a call to action for CEOs of large organizations to leverage strategic enterprise education™ (SEE) to usher in the *Age of And* — a new age of similar gravity as the Atomic Age, Space Age and Information Age. The *Age of And* is an era that combines, coordinates and delivers colinear outcomes — business *And* social impact, the employee *And* the learner, the customer *And* the community, the shareholder *And* society, the good fiduciary *And* the good citizen, doing well *And* doing good.

Foreword

My way into Vivek's book is pretty simple. Talent and education are topics that have always been important to me. My education and my eagerness to continue learning have proven significant to my personal and professional journey.

Fresh out of Harvard's MBA program, I started as a brand assistant at Procter & Gamble. At that time, P&G took learning seriously because it knew that senior leadership and the next CEO were going to come from inside the company. If you were in marketing, you went to copy college, and there you would learn to assess and analyze advertising copy. If you were a chemist working on a new hand soap formulation, P&G would practically give you an advanced degree in chemistry. They were among the first to tie executive compensation to how well a given leader prepared their employees.

When I was 26 years old, Bain & Company believed in me, and I became a consultant and, ultimately, a partner. Today, Bain and the other leading strategy consulting firms make education a core priority in the career trajectories of their people. At the time I worked there, Bain's philosophy was to recruit the top 5% of talent from leading business schools and take their hunger and raw talent to mold them into world-class consultants. This effort to mentor and train up consultants was initially dependent on the office geography or practice area — it was a tribal and disparate effort. Then, about halfway into my tenure, we figured out that whenever we encountered a new engagement in one office, we'd have to make a call across the company to see if anyone else had ever worked on a similar strategic problem or initiative. We knew we had to codify the learnings and begin making them accessible more readily as we grew and evolved to refine incoming raw talent more quickly. In other words, we had to quickly educate consultants on a new project on what their colleagues from a previous project already knew.

All that I learned at P&G, Bain and later at The Walt Disney Company was then tested mightily at eBay as we grew it from 30 people to a 15,000-person company. At eBay, we experienced hockey stick growth at a compounded monthly rate of 70%. This continued for nearly four years as we went from $4 million in revenues to $40 million to $400 million and then to $4 billion. Think about it. When I joined eBay, everything was changing. It was 1998, and people were still figuring out email (remember the Tom Hanks and Meg Ryan movie, *You've Got Mail?*).

All the new technologies facilitated new rates of change and a new pace of work. My workforce had to integrate constant learning into their day-to-day work life just so they could continue to make decisions they needed to make, no matter their level in the organization — whether it was frontline customer service or software developers. Each year, upskilling people for new technologies, more velocity and scalability was a critical priority to ensuring we grew quickly and smartly. My subsequent leadership experiences as CEO of Hewlett-Packard, as board director and as a candidate running for governor of California further forced me to examine the workforce and education from an ever-widening set of variables and perspectives.

As a longtime investor in and board chair of Teach for America, I am passionate about re-energizing the teaching profession, recruiting high-potential talent among those ideally suited for it, yet who would have never considered standing before a group of 5- to 18-year-old kids. I believe that by getting these fair-minded individuals into classrooms, a difference can be made in public schools, the communities they serve and among all the individuals who are touched by the organization. More students are finishing high school. More students are matriculating to college.

However, if you're familiar with college graduation rates at all, you know it can't stop there. The future of America, American education, American business and American leadership rests in and very much beyond K-12 education.

It means CEOs have to take much more responsibility for ongoing education of their workforce. Howard Schultz did this at Starbucks through the Starbucks College Achievement Plan (SCAP). When he went all in on educating his partners (employees), many of us took a step back and wondered if it would work. But Howard proved that it was a great decision for his company, his people and his customers. He was way ahead of his time with SCAP, a program which Kevin Johnson, the current CEO, has very wisely expanded and accelerated. His employees see a commitment, and they stay at Starbucks in record numbers. He saved the company time and energy connected to hiring, retention and knowledge transfer.

Additionally, Howard demonstrated that workforce education was not just a pioneering one-off move. It's an essential move with a long view and, as Vivek demonstrates in *C-Spark*, a move that delivers powerful outcomes for businesses and their employees. With technology as a driving force in everything from fashion to agriculture, the ability to commit to people by offering them meaningful educational opportunities will make the difference for CEOs across industries and markets. Workforce education helps you address some of your most fundamental and strategic priorities — growth, agility, recruitment and retention, diversity and inclusion, corporate responsibility and even brand strength. Furthermore, as this approach reaches critical mass, you can do your part to ensure that America, as it did time and time again in the 20th century, remains at the forefront of business and innovation leadership globally.

If you're a CEO stuck in quarter-to-quarter mentality — and believe me, I know that world wherein within three months you get very publicly evaluated — and you won't somehow make this wise and competitively advantageous move on behalf of your company or the people in your company, you need to do it for your country. We live in a time and place that has shown us that American democracy is incredibly fragile. Truth, justice and the American way — yes, the very foundation of Superman — is in danger.

America's future and way of life depends on an educated workforce. It depends on people being able to read and write and think critically and listen to different points of view and discern the truth. As you probably know firsthand, we have an education system that isn't delivering all of that to all of our people. Think back to the 20th century, when public school hit its stride and families had access to all sorts of institutions such as Boy Scouts, Girl Scouts, 4-H and religious communities of faith. Undeniably, they supported an educational ideal and contributed to the building of an educated workforce. These institutions play a less prominent role in

American life today, and in many cases, they have been shaken to their core.

It is now up to CEOs like you and companies like yours to pick up the mantle of those institutions and become a vital link in the lives of your people and your community. It will make a tangible difference in the lives of your employees and the towns, cities and regions in which you operate. It will improve the performance of your company, and it will impact the strength and vitality of America itself for years to come.

In *C-Spark*, Vivek gives you the path you need to make it happen. It's a path poised to equip you to change lives, grow your company and make an impact that will ensure a lasting, memorable legacy. I sincerely hope that you take this path.

With my best wishes,
Meg Whitman
Telluride, Colorado
August 2021

Introduction

This book is for CEOs of large organizations. If you're one of them, you probably already understand this simple statement of fact: workforce education isn't working. Your workforce — the most educationally diverse in history — has found itself in a ditch. Despite deep investments in legacy workforce-education modalities, too many of your people find themselves disengaged, overmatched, struggling with agility, unproductive, inefficient or, to make matters even worse, leaving you in droves.

As CEO, your natural inclination is to dive into the ditch, demonstrate your leadership abilities and show everyone the way out. But, for many reasons, you can't — and you shouldn't — at least not until after you've read further. The reason is simple. Current thinking has reduced workforce education to a limited tool operating in the lower reaches of your organization or has buried it as a siloed strategic function designed to address challenges or opportunities flying below the level of your corporate objectives. Today, the crisis has found its way to the corporate level — to your level. It's now, officially, your problem.

The solution to this problem is in the title of this book. It's called the C-Spark. It offers the first and only approach to workforce education that redefines it as a strategic tool worthy of delivering authentic impact on corporate trajectory.

C-Spark, as its name implies, hinges on your strategic acuity and your leadership alone. It is not a pipe dream or a theoretical musing.

It's empirical and evidence based. It first ignited when a leading global research–based public university and a beloved, multinational retailer sat down for a cup of coffee. Michael Crow, president of Arizona State University, and Howard Schultz, Starbucks CEO at that time, were both members of the Markle Foundation National Commission called Rework America.

"Howard was the co-chair, and I was the sub-chair of the part focused on the individual, and so we happened to be there at the same time," said Crow. "Neither of us could have anticipated the lightning bolt relative to what we might do together as we sat down at a retreat center in Tarrytown, New York."

Lightning struck when Schultz offered a thought.

"Howard said, 'You know, at the end of the day companies have to start taking responsibility for all of their capital, their human capital — their financial capital and their natural capital. Think of that as things related to the environment and natural resources that are driving the company,'" recounted Crow.

It was a conversation that permanently changed workforce education, and in 2014, Arizona State University (ASU) and Starbucks collaborated to launch the Starbucks College Achievement Plan (SCAP). Starbucks recognized that the linchpin of its future rested in its partners — the baristas who pull the espresso and deliver the frontline in-store and online experience that keeps customers coming back for more. Crow, named among *Fortune's* World's 50 Greatest Leaders, has personally led the charge on innovation leadership at ASU. In doing so, he has sought to bridge the gap between the current state of public-private partnerships while finding ways to upend the traditional way institutions of higher education approach, tailor and deliver learning. It aligns with many pathbreaking initiatives ASU has pursued. Its ability to spread its mission to ever-growing nontraditional student populations is altering higher education's two-centuries-old role and has earned ASU the number one *Most Innovative School* ranking by *U.S. News & World Report* for more than six years.

The two entities teamed up, developed a customized program based on Starbucks' set of strategic challenges and opportunities and established the platform for its delivery. SCAP was born. As of 2018, SCAP was enrolling more than 12,000 Starbucks partners. More than 2,400 partners had completed their bachelor's degree since the program launched. Since implementing SCAP, Starbucks enjoyed the highest employee retention rate in retail while continually raising the bar on customer connection. SCAP participants were also being promoted three times faster than the Starbucks corporate average. However, anyone who completed the program was free to leave Starbucks. In doing so, they remained loyal alumni of the company, burnishing its brand halo. The program also impacted recruiting, with more than 20% of applicants pointing to SCAP as a motivating factor in pursuing jobs at the company.

With the SCAP program's success, a natural question followed: How could this type of impact be replicated across the entirety of corporate America? It would require building an entrepreneurial organization that would translate corporate objectives into strategic workforce education partnerships in cooperation with like-minded, leading global universities. It would also require a company that could translate between corporate and university environments at scale, ensuring differences were bridged and that preexisting challenges tied to the speed, structure and culture proved irrelevant to facilitating the smooth delivery of a precision-built and custom workforce-education program. It would also necessitate significant upfront capital to launch a new business from ground zero.

Enter TPG's The Rise Fund. As part of TPG, a global investment firm with more than $103 billion in total assets under management across 14 global offices, the $11 billion Rise Fund invests in growth-stage, mission-driven companies that have the power to change the world. Jim Coulter, Executive Chairman and a Founding Partner of TPG, has been a vocal champion of the *Age of And* and the necessity for large corporations to think beyond business growth. As he shared with the World Economic Forum in 2020:

> The world has reached a critical juncture in the relationship between industry and society. We are no longer in a period where, as Milton Friedman said, "the only social responsibility of business" is to continually increase its profits. The idea that impact investing must generate lower financial returns than traditional investment strategies is a misconception. We have found the opposite to be true. Accelerating our portfolio companies' impact meaningfully contributes to their growth.

TPG's The Rise Fund saw the approach and extraordinary impact of SCAP and found them perfectly aligned with its mission. By that time, Kevin Johnson was named Starbucks CEO. Steve Ellis, managing partner, TPG, and co-managing partner, The Rise Fund, points to Johnson's rhetoric as a critical factor that inspired TPG:

What does Kevin talk about when he talks about SCAP? He doesn't start with retention. He doesn't start with all the commercial benefits that are accruing to Starbucks in the context of the human capital impact. He talks first and foremost about how it transforms the customer experience. And you know, an education program that leads to improvement in the customer experience is absolutely, spot-on and 100% aligned with what is in the best interest of the enterprise, right?

Around that time, I was a senior executive at The Walt Disney Company and, through earlier stints at Yahoo! and McKinsey & Company, had experienced firsthand the workforce education and skill challenges in large corporations. I had also maintained my window into higher education as an adjunct professor of data science at the University of Southern California's Marshall School of Business. This gave me a unique vantage point of being able to look at corporate America as a professor and at universities as an executive. Here were two leading ecosystems that had so much to offer to each other yet, with rare exceptions like SCAP, had not found a sustainable and scalable way to partner. The solution, I was convinced, was a boundary-spanning organization across these two ecosystems that could effectively work with different cultures, different clock speeds, different key performance indicators (KPIs) and different stakeholders; and this organization would be focused on driving business impact for the corporation through workforce education for its employees.

In 2018, we launched InStride, with me as CEO and the first "InStrider" — the term we use for our employees. Like most startups, I started in my home office and then quickly moved to a four-desk,

WeWork-based office in downtown Los Angeles. Armed with a unique set of lenses through which to view the market opportunity, three things became immediately apparent for the success of the InStride movement — leveraging workforce education to deliver on the strategic priorities of CEOs, partnering with leading global universities for outcome-oriented online education and building a scalable digital platform to deliver a seamless learner and corporate experience.

Today, InStride serves as a public-benefit company whose mission is to provide life-changing strategic enterprise education to its employees in partnership with the highest quality global academic institutions. As of June 2021, we serve nearly 40,000 employees from more than 40 leading employers through 1,700 online degrees, certificates and credentials, and we have helped our learners avoid $350 million in student debt. In 2020, InStride was recognized with *Inc.'s Best in Business* award and as one of *Fortune's Impact 20* companies globally.

This book expands on the vision and serves as my invitation to you: join the movement. Know that it will speed momentum of American corporate growth and impact such that it will once again be recognized, felt and revered across the world. And throughout your career as a CEO, it will ensure that your strategic agenda will succeed today and long into the future. Broken into four parts, *C-Spark* covers the following:

Part I establishes why the C-Spark is necessary. It lays out the problem and core challenges as a nation, within the corporate sector and throughout higher education. It also reviews why workforce education in its current operating models persists in its inefficacy and inadequacy.

Part II lays out the journey to and through the C-Spark and what results once it's ignited. It's a powerful tour de force of each step toward C-Spark ignition and what happens immediately following that event.

Part III illustrates how companies are modeling and embodying the C-Spark, leveraging it as a strategic tool that is directly and effectively affecting corporate trajectory, and what it means for learners' lives.

Part IV visualizes the path forward in light of the C-Spark, arming you with calls to action among workers, education partners, government and other leaders within your industry.

As of this book's writing, we are hopeful of emerging from the worst global lifetime event imaginable — COVID-19. It is a tipping point for the workforce. Brick-and-mortar closures have led to dramatic levels of unemployment. Technology has supplanted some jobs that may never return, while driving a dire need for employee upskilling and reskilling.

It is an event that has quickened my urgency in getting this manuscript to press, because I believe that the careful and strategic deployment of workforce education and a revisioning of educational design established over an entire life is the only path forward. It's critical to the future of work and the future of global business, economic prosperity and equality worldwide.

I believe only the corporate sector is innovative enough to make this happen. Government will not take it on. Existing institutions of higher learning cannot take this on. Businesses strategically innovating from within is the only way.

To all CEOs, take it from this CEO: you are the linchpin upon which that innovation hinges.

In service,
Vivek Sharma
Los Angeles
August 2021

PART I

The American workforce is in Crisis. It's a crisis with a capital C because, like the term C-Spark, it has ascended to the level of you, the CEO. It's your crisis. It's industry agnostic and — backed by the most recent U.S. Census data, which reveals an aging, shrinking population — it's not going away.

Because of it, you're forfeiting revenue.

You're sacrificing business agility, missing opportunities and witnessing an erosion of market share due to workers who hold mastery in an obsolete skillset and need to expand or shift it.

You're spending millions to recruit workers for all levels and roles.

You're losing millions when you can't retain them.

You're struggling to hire your way to acceptable — let alone ideal — levels of diversity, equity and inclusion. You know solving for DE&I through recruiting alone is just impossible.

Your corporate citizenship doesn't ring true.

Your brand — the culture it creates and the experience it delivers — suffers because of unengaged, disconnected workers who feel little loyalty and no sense of a future under your employ.

In all of these cases, you, the CEO, set the agenda, build the team and drive your unique KPIs across the firm. In this endeavor, it always comes down to your people. If they execute, ideate, anticipate and solve problems; gain fluency across skillsets; and find their work deeply satisfying — all of which fulfill the promise of your corporate objectives — you win.

You're doing all of this in a world that is changing. As consumers find new ways to shop, their needs are evolving, and the terms of marketing and selling are shifting. As you go to market across borders, you find some countries oriented toward globalism and others devoted to protectionism. You've witnessed a pandemic that has shifted how work and business get done. Your business continuity and planning must account for climate-borne disasters that have increased in frequency and severity. These factors are foregrounding and accelerating the promised rise of digital technology and automation across the organization. Additionally, they create job losses while disrupting and quickly transforming how you set, manage and fulfill objectives. They are bringing you back to your people; you must rely on their creativity and dexterity to exploit new opportunities and surmount new challenges.

You may also be part of an increasing number of executives who see the need for change in the way people learn on the job. You know that many of your employees have started an associate or bachelor's degree and did not finish that education. There are 36 million such employees in the United States alone, and most of them have a solid reason for leaving. They lost interest. They sought a career first. They couldn't shoulder the heavy financial burden amid the ever-increasing rise in tuition, books and fees.

In this growing populace, you see potential, and you've built programming or sought partners who offer them a learning opportunity. You've likely created a chief learning officer or head of learning and development position, and your company is part of the annual

$180 billion global spend in workforce education. However, most likely, you've lived through the disappointing or unclear results and a low return on that investment. You're not alone. Companies like yours have found that less than 2% of their workforce participates in traditionally configured and deployed workforce education and tuition reimbursement programs. Even fewer graduate. Those who do rarely find that the education they received boosts their career prospects. So, traditional workforce education isn't solving the problem or achieving the desired outcome. It doesn't work. It's time to discover why, with thoroughness and empathy. Along the way, you'll begin to pick up on why you are the exact solution to the problem you're trying to solve.

Chapter 1

The Rise, the Fall and the Call

July 16, 1945. It's 5:30 a.m. in the New Mexico desert. A spark ignites inside a giant orb. In a split second, a violent, inconceivable flash exceeds daylight. A cloud of flame and smoke extends eight miles into the sky. Shockwaves ripple for nearly 100 miles. The moment prompts lead physicist Dr. J. Robert Oppenheimer to reflect on a quote from the Hindu scripture, Bhagavad Gita:

If the radiance of a thousand suns were to burst at once into the sky, that would be like the splendor of the Mighty One.

The Manhattan Project was successful and the Atomic Age born.

Oppenheimer's culminating moment began six years earlier when he was appointed to helm the Manhattan Project. Initiated out of fear that Germany was advancing the development of an atomic bomb, the project sought to win the arms race and end World War II. In creating the atomic bomb, the United States employed 130,000 people and invested the modern equivalent of $23 billion. It marshaled the work of scientists, engineers, and manufacturing, safety and transportation specialists. It mobilized companies such as Monsanto and Chrysler and employed top-secret sites throughout the United States and Canada.

It also ushered in a "golden age" of American higher education worldwide. Recruited from a diverse array of public and private institutions, Manhattan Project collaborators included Columbia University, the University of California at Berkeley, the University of Chicago, Cornell, Princeton, MIT, the University of Illinois, the University of Rochester, Stanford University, the University of Tennessee-Knoxville, Washington University and the University of Wisconsin. In doing so, it placed U.S. educational and commercial firepower — and the potency of their partnership — on the map.

On July 16, 1969, just 24 years after crossing the nuclear threshold, Americans awoke to the ignition of five F-1 rocket engines lifting Apollo 11 astronauts toward the moon. The decisive moments of the American moonshot were underway. Roughly 100 hours later, Neil Armstrong announced, "Tranquility Base here. The Eagle has landed."

Apollo 11 had fulfilled its objective. The Space Age was born.

In taking his "one giant leap for mankind," Armstrong fulfilled President John F. Kennedy's goal of landing on the moon within a decade. In surmounting the president's ambitious challenge, and throughout the Apollo program, NASA invested the modern equivalent of $175 billion and enlisted thousands of industrial partners, including Grumman, Lockheed, Martin Marietta and Playtex (Playtex designed the space suits). It also partnered with a core of renowned universities. Rice University donated land for NASA's "Manned Spacecraft Center" (now known as Johnson Space Center). The MIT Instrumentation Lab built the Apollo Guidance Computer and navigational software. The University of Arizona mapped the moon's surface in preparation for the moon landing. The California Institute of Technology (CalTech) and Stanford designed and performed experiments on lunar specimens. This cooperative achievement showed that America had solidified its place as the global leader in collaborative higher education. It has also led to enduring and ongoing partnerships between NASA and these schools, even as it almost singlehandedly created Silicon Valley. In 1955, William Shockley, a co-inventor of the bipolar transistor, opened up a Mountain View, California-based "factory" to produce the innovation. Two years later, eight employees left Shockley Transistor Company to begin Fairchild Semiconductor. Two employees from Fairchild eventually founded Intel. From South San Francisco to Cupertino, the valley rose.

Another 25 years later, a more subtle yet no less epic kindling of innovation emerged. This time the spark was a simple, subtle double-click. On October 13, 1994, anyone with a personal computer could download the initial release of Netscape Navigator, formerly known as Mosaic, and begin browsing the Internet.

The tipping point for easy-to-use digital communication had reached its threshold. The Information Age was born.

American universities led the way, and the worldwide web transcended its computer-science origins, with limited, text-only email and the occasional message board. Integral to its rise were Silicon Graphics founders Jim Clark and Marc Andreessen. Andreessen developed the graphical user interface for the Navigator browser, which emerged from his work at the National Center for Supercomputing Applications (NCSA) at the University of Illinois, Urbana-Champaign.

NCSA was a part of the National Science Foundation's drive to develop a series of supercomputer centers throughout the United States. It paved the way for unique and powerful collaborations between venture capitalists, establishing technology companies and countless universities in service to the commercialization and mainstreaming of personal computing that forged America's leadership role in creating and disseminating information technology.

By this point in the late 20th century, America's unique partnerships between the corporate and university sectors were the gold standard worldwide. American university research led the way. The military's GI Bill and a healthy public university system made the promise of a college degree fiscally accessible and requisite. Enrollment and graduation rates climbed. In 1940, 5% of Americans earned a bachelor's degree. By 2019, that total increased to more than 35%.

The High-Water Mark

Higher education is one of America's most valuable assets and one of its largest exports. *The New York Times* reported that the value of education is equal to twice the revenue of America's top agricultural export, soybeans. In total, education's export value — when you add others, including food, transportation, clothes, tuition and student spending — actually rivals that of pharmaceuticals and automobiles. International students see a tremendous amount of value in America and American education, because it translates very clearly into better workplace outcomes and social status outcomes. For them, the delta is very clear.

The mystique of American higher education has made it an ascendent portal to the American dream. For international students seeking undergraduate and graduate degrees, it has been the global dream. In this way, American higher education built a pipeline and emerged as a prime importer of talent, slotting valedictorians from every continent into the American workforce. The future has seemed infinitely powered by this well-honed calibration between higher education, government and industry. In *Fear and Loathing in Las Vegas*, Hunter S. Thompson wrote of the American psyche fueling the age in this way:

> You could strike sparks anywhere. There was a fantastic universal sense that whatever we were doing was right, that we were winning. We had all the momentum; we were riding the crest of a high and beautiful wave . . . So now, less than five years later, you can go up on a steep hill in Las Vegas and look West, and with the right kind of eyes you can almost see the high-water mark — that place where the wave finally broke and rolled back.

In 2013, the Institute for Public Policy Research (IPPR) saw this ebbing wave as an avalanche and foretold a clear delta in peril. According to IPPR, the full flowering of the 20th century university had come, and its time was over. Like packed snow majestically at rest on a mountainside, higher education gave the appearance of stability. Underneath, decades of shifts were applying intolerable pressure to the university's fundamental structure. It cited global economic change. It pointed to tuition that was rising faster than inflation. It illustrated that the value of a traditional degree for the cost was slipping. Meanwhile, universal, digital connectivity was making content ubiquitous, transforming learning.

Snowmelt & Digital Change

Today, as a CEO, you might ask, "What snowpack?" It's gone. In 2020, half of U.S. universities previously listed in the Top 100 slipped away. Between 2011 and 2017, government investment in university research as a percentage of GDP slid by a quarter, while state investment in universities had decreased by 79%. Undoubtedly, if you've sought to engage with a university on a partnership of any type, you've also felt something else. While you've spent the last decade transforming and innovating every corner of your business, universities have faced an existential crisis. You have trended toward speed and automation. Higher education has been navigating many barriers to maintain its pace with business.

Since 2010, corporate-led digital change has hit a magnificent inflection point. Think about your firm 10 to 12 years ago. Most functions were executed on traditional platforms — administrative, sales, manufacturing, supply chain, marketing and customer relationship management. Then came total digital transformation. Internet and cellular bandwidth increased. Cloud computing came into its own. Application programming interfaces (APIs) proliferated. Big data. Machine learning. Artificial intelligence. Supply chains. Digital currency and financial technology. Robotics. The Internet of things. Virtual and augmented reality. Now, even the talk of quantum computing is reaching the mainstream. Quantum R&D, the front end of innovation, isn't happening only at MIT — it's happening more at IBM. And more at Google. And within niche players such as Atom, ColdQuanta and D-Wave.

These innovations are revolutionizing your business with near-term shock, awe and long-haul momentum. In turn, they have shifted your strategic calculus, your business operations, how you build and propagate your brand and its culture and your pure velocity relative to the new clock speed of the corporate world. It's also wreaking havoc with how you build your workforce. While universities have also shifted inside the digital reality, at the end of the day, their current approach still relies on siloed structures based on a centuries-old culture and pace. Ask yourself, "How can they ever expect to keep up?" They can't, and this has become a problem — your problem.

You need an educated workforce. As job qualifications shift and evolve with uncompromising frequency and companies like yours spend billions in recruiting backed by the promise of benefits and training, more than 60% of employers find it challenging to hire the right talent, and 50% attribute the difficulty to a mismatch in training, relevant experience and education. Meanwhile, research and advisory firm Gartner found that 70% of the workforce does not believe they have the skills required to do their jobs today. Let's take a moment to see how this plays out on the ground.

If you're a technology firm focused on software development, you've witnessed how AI and machine learning are shifting the role of the software developer. Software has begun writing itself. Legacy developers and new graduates don't carry the skills necessary to mind automated development and tweak the algorithms.

Another industry caught in the crosshairs of this transformational period is financial services. Getting cash, trading stock, even applying for a loan are now self-serve activities. Banks and other financial firms have been trying to keep pace with moving from physical to digital money. New technology-based monetary systems such as Bitcoin are disrupting entire financial markets. "Bankers" of the future will need a much different view of money and a much different skill set to bring meaning to any currency exchange model.

Many first jobs came via the ubiquitous quick-service restaurants that dot every corner of the country. Franchises have been trying to maintain their customer-centric approach to serving millions of people. These days, "Do you want fries with that?" is no longer the primary question to ask, as franchisees have automated everything, including drive-through greetings, point-of-sale video boards, mobile app-based ordering options and robotic burger-flippers. These staples of the American workforce and American diet also have grasped the need to automate their systems efficiently, but it's an industry that still needs people. Recent McKinsey research found that productivity improved by up to 25% when employees were "connected."

COVID-19 & The Call

When COVID-19 hit in the spring of 2020, the symphony of workforce challenges hit a crescendo. A chasm between the top and lower half of the employment pyramid widened. The tech sector, best represented by FAANG — Facebook, Amazon, Apple, Netflix and Google — grew. Digitally attuned members of the workforce worked from home and weathered the storm. Conversely, most other sectors, including industrial, hospitality, travel and retail, had to adapt, temporarily close or simply go out of business. Frontline workers suffered, either through layoffs or increased risk of exposure to the virus. The resulting socioeconomic gap threatens the economy, while millions of workers find themselves in a career freefall. The future of the workforce — your workforce — is in peril.

"The whole U.S. political economy was like a giant preexisting condition," said Richard V. Reeves, a senior fellow at the Brookings Institution, in an interview with *Inside Higher Ed*. "And COVID-19 came along and exposed it all."

The article went on to say that "initial data suggest that lower-income students and those from minority groups may leave higher education, perhaps permanently."

Herein lies the menace. A cumulative impact of an undereducated, insufficiently trained workforce will negatively impact profits, create competitive disadvantages and pose a grave threat to corporate America. It's why Amazon, GE, Intel, Disney, Microsoft and Google have made attempts to develop corporate universities from scratch. As we'll learn later in this section, these forays, which cost billions annually, are suboptimal. In the meantime, universities, for all of their shortcomings, barriers, challenges and lack of corporate savvy, still hold the keys to American progress in the 21st century. What, then, is the answer?

It's time for a new spark.

It's a spark no less epic or ambitious than the ones that harnessed nuclear energy, space and the information superhighway. It's a spark that recognizes companies of the future must drive growth toward both revenue and social impact. It's a spark that will reignite ambition, energy and creativity in the interest of global leadership. It's a spark that will reclaim the university as a critical natural resource for business.

It's the C-Spark. It calls upon CEOs like you to recognize, wield and deploy workforce education as a primary strategic tool in close partnership with leading global colleges and universities. By placing education at the forefront, the C-Spark innovates and unifies leadership, management, sales, production and supply chain. Its newfound strategic utility informs and expands national conversation — from political discourse to high-level CEO-focused forums shaping policy such as the Business Roundtable. It will equip America to overcome the existing challenges facing the workforce and higher education while supplanting a set of heavy, awkward and unworkable legacy solutions. Like Chrysler, Monsanto, Lockheed and Playtex in previous "ages," corporations like yours must rise to the occasion. You must execute the C-Spark with precision. In doing so, you will reestablish yourself as a company that "does well by doing good." Importantly, this isn't a Pollyanna call to altruism. It's a business opportunity grounded in precedent.

In 1942, the United States faced a different workforce crisis. Employees were off to war, creating a labor shortage. Economists within the government worried that bidding wars for the best job applicants would drive ever-higher salaries and cause runaway inflation. In response, President Franklin Delano Roosevelt signed Executive Order 9250. It authorized the creation of an Office of Economic Stabilization, which froze wages. Companies had to pivot to attract and retain employees, debuting a form of compensation called "benefits." At the forefront were a collective of CEOs who saw an immediate, strategic need for action while holding the long view. They created what is now the bundle of workforce perks known as benefits. Health insurance was at the core of these new benefits packages. Health insurance, the province of the affluent and a rare luxury, was going mainstream. More than any other benefit, health insurance was a competitive chip in the workforce recruitment battle. It also wisely and compassionately anticipated the return of wounded soldiers from the war, ensuring those veterans received affordable care as they reentered the workplace. With that, a philosophy emerged that healthy employees were good for business and the community. This work of a few visionary CEOs triggered public policy and regulation. Today, failure to offer insurance to full-time employees is illegal. Social impact became a societal imperative.

The same forces that shaped the history of benefits and healthcare align with a pattern that ensues when business strives toward corporate and social good. Visionary leaders take a bold first step that, at the time, appears anachronistic. Undaunted, they persist, guided by their values and vision. Over time, their vision captures the imagination of the many. Followership emerges. Adoption ensues, leading to public acceptance and, over time, expectation. Eventually, it bubbles up into the body politic. Policy discussions take place, and a legislative and regulatory journey takes hold.

And so, what of the C-Spark? What will it yield? It will travel on a similar path. And in doing so, the byproducts of the partnerships that blossom, restoring corporate and educational cooperation, will birth a new Age. Instead of resulting in a single noun such as the Atomic, Space and Information Ages, it will be distinguished by the word "and," a coordinating conjunction that befits the moment. This new age, known as the *Age of And*, will create colinear impact wherein achieving simultaneous, values-driven goals is no longer optional, and not doing so rings like a hollow excuse. It's also an age marked by not just one but many *"Ands"*:

The Age of Business *And* Social Impact.
The Age of the Employee *And* the Learner.
The Age of the Customer *And* the Community.
The Age of the Shareholder *And* Society.
The Age of the Good Fiduciary *And* the Good Citizen.
The Age of Doing Well *And* Doing Good.

In each case, both sides of the *And* build on each other. And to get there, we must first thoroughly examine the challenges in play driving the desperate need for a C-Spark.

Chapter 2

The U.S. Workforce:
An Apollo 13 Moment

Each "Age" described in the last chapter can be seen through the lens of the Hero's Journey outlined in Joseph Campbell's *The Hero with a Thousand Faces*. "Act 1" of that journey not only includes a call to something new, it also forces a confrontation with "what is" in the form of enemies, allies and obstacles. Leaning into that notion, let's return to the Space Age for a brief moment.

"Houston, we've had a problem."

Apollo 13 Commander James A. Lovell's words reinforced the initial call to mission control by crewmate Jack Swigert. A damaged wire in the spacecraft's service module ignited Teflon insulation on an oxygen tank. The ensuing fire built up too much pressure in the tank, and an explosion occurred. The crew in space and on the ground mobilized, engineering one of the most daring rescues in human history. Using primitive tools and technology, from T squares to duct tape, NASA's team could assess, imagine, formulate and deliver a precise response set to a seemingly chaotic and complex set of challenges. Apollo 13 splashed down safely in the South Pacific. With its drama and high stakes, the mission captivated the world, and the space program advanced with an even greater emphasis on the well-being of its most valuable resource: people.

Your business, amid digital and global transformation, is moving at a high velocity. In *Thank You for Being Late*, Thomas Friedman, a *New York Times* columnist and best-selling author, argues the pace at which we're moving is sowing unprecedented change. He then discusses Moore's Law. Developed by Gordon Moore, who co-founded Intel, a technology company responsible for most processors inside today's digital devices, Moore's Law states that computer processing transistors (and thus, computer processing speed) would double every 18 to 24 months. The original projection covered a time frame between 1965 and 1975, and yet it continues validating itself to this day. Friedman argues that technology across the centuries has gained boundless, exponential momentum. In our current context, its Mach-level speed is colliding with two other forces that upsurge digital potency: global markets that more thoroughly network the world together and the urgent reality of climate change.

"We have no choice but to learn to adapt . . . It will be harder and require more self-motivation — and that reality is surely one of the things roiling politics all over America and Europe," writes Friedman.

The Workforce Crucible

What does this mean for you? We're in a workforce Apollo 13 moment — a crucible that, if navigated successfully, will ensure corporate America's leadership well into the 21st century while supporting an evolution into the *Age of And*. Alternatively, failure to surmount this challenge will force a "tripping point." If your people are inadequate to the moment, unable to adapt, underqualified or not predisposed to flexibility and agility, decline is inevitable. Failure is probable.

Perhaps it's stating the obvious. After all, using legacy best practice, you're trying to do everything you can to stem the tide, reinvigorate your team and charge hard into global markets moving at warp speed. Maybe you've been attempting to innovate how you deliver workforce education and training. You might have even partnered with individual institutions. You're already a part of the annual $180 billion investment in workforce education, and you're at your wit's end because it's not delivering. Either participation is low, or it seems you're spinning your wheels. As you walk your halls, your factory floor, your labs, your cubes or your stores and showrooms, you begin to understand that you are attempting to inspire and prepare the most educationally and culturally diverse set of individuals in the history of work.

If you're a Fortune 1000 company, the complexities of this reality deepen because you employ somewhere between tens of thousands and half a million workers. They range in age between 25 and 65. Most know they must work for a long time — maybe up to 60 years of their lives. They expect their current job will vanish because of digital innovation. Over their lifetime, they will unexpectedly pivot toward new and not-yet-created positions at some or many points throughout their career. The World Economic Forum validated the accuracy of this hunch. Its 2018 Future of Jobs Report projects that the ratio of automated tasks grows approximately 20% per year. By 2022, machines and algorithms will have "increased their contributions to specific tasks by 57%."

Many of your employees work from home and may know you only "digitally" via Zoom or Google Hangouts. By nature, they are insecure and untrusting. They get that amid economic fluctuations, a shift in global culture and the trend toward digital transformation, drastic change is a reality they will live with across their careers. Job security is tenuous. They arrive at your company optimistic, but in the back of their minds, they consistently evaluate their tenures and wonder if they should head to greener pastures. When combined with the approximately 70% of them who don't feel qualified in their current position, insecurity is a daily reality. Older, more experienced members of your workforce understand that the education they received at 25 will not carry them to retirement. In 2020, John Richards and Chris Dede asserted in an *Educause Review* article titled "The 60-Year Curriculum: A Strategic Response to a Crisis" that the "requirement to prepare for a lifetime of changing employment is not optional."

Still, accessing additional education the traditional way — offline and on-campus — is daunting and feels unrealistic for most of your workforce to pursue seriously. These sociological and psychological factors create difficulties for you, but they compound when we begin examining critical data around their educational paths.

Your Team: Carrying Unmet Aspirations for Education

Across your team, some individuals started but did not finish an associate or bachelor's degree. In total, this represents roughly 36 million working adults nationwide. They probably understand the consequences of that choice, deepening insecurity and affecting their career outlook. More than likely, they know their decision has also impacted their wallet. On average, they make about half their degreed counterparts (approximately $41,000 versus $74,000 annually).

They left school for many reasons. Maybe it was simple economics. Total student loan debt in the United States is estimated at

$1.5 trillion. Eighteen-year-olds in the United States are encouraged to access hundreds of thousands of dollars in loans to attend school; many of those who forgo higher education may have begun to count the costs. They've seen peers take on staggering amounts of debt that will require at least 20 years to liquidate.

Despite the income disparity between graduates and nongraduates, some dropouts in your ranks believe that a college degree doesn't necessarily guarantee return on investment. At the current rate of change based on Friedman's thesis, some of those entering the workforce from college find that their degrees are soon obsolete. The combination of financial inaccessibility and perceived or actual lack of return makes the value of a college degree difficult for them to understand.

According to the U.S. Bureau of Labor Statistics through monthly U.S. Census Bureau survey data pulled from more than 60,000 households, this populace — those who started but did not finish a postsecondary education — compose the majority of your workforce. It is followed, in statistical order, by high school graduates, those who completed an undergraduate degree, those who have attended graduate school and those who have pursued less than a high school diploma. In short, you have a primary workforce who have attempted but not finished school, have an education that may or may not be serving them or have no education or training at all. Analyzing and preparing this tapestry of workers for what you need them to do and how you need them to think becomes even more complex.

Moving down to the individual amplifies the intricacy and messiness of what you face. On the ground, you begin to witness the mixed reality of your workforce at the intersection of your corporate strategy. The following anecdotes emerged from an InStride effort to canvas hundreds of American workers, uncovering insights around their wants, needs and desires as adult learners while tracing their path to workforce education. Through them, the complexity of the workforce as a learning cohort emerges.

Consider Sarah. She's one of 50 million frontline workers in the United States. Sarah has an associate degree and quickly rose to lead teller at a branch of a leading U.S. bank. Then she hit a career wall and her frustration built. The professional development roadmap that promised advancement seems like a farce. Sarah feels ignored, and she has witnessed a wave of external hiring above her with no commitment to internal promotion.

"[The roadmap] is a checkmark for them. It's a joke," said Sarah. To her, the gap between her demonstrative, sincere interest in and pursuit of management's development criteria versus management's lack of commitment to her roadmap prompted a severe reaction. Sarah is on her way out.

Tenisha offers a wholly different picture from the frontline. She went to trade school after discovering that a four-year degree was not for her. She frames her decisions as not wanting to "waste time . . . sitting there. And studying is such a pain. I just wanted to get to something. I have all these plans, and school really slows you down."

Tenisha pursued ultrasound as a career and is proficient in two different modalities. Furloughed by her hospital in March of 2020 because of COVID-19, she was shell-shocked. She believed that being in healthcare was a safe bet for her career. She went three months without a job as she and her husband dipped into their savings to survive. She has big dreams of starting a family and buying a house. Going back to school feels like a setback to Tenisha. While her company would pay for her to get training in a different, in-demand modality, it's just not motivating enough. To Tenisha, there's no guarantee that she'll remain employed and have a stable career path.

Kevin is a knowledge worker. Peter Drucker defined knowledge workers in his 1959 classic, *The Landmarks of Tomorrow*, as higher-level workers who apply theoretical and analytical knowledge to deliver a product or service. The most common examples are nurses, software developers, consultants and lawyers. Kevin is a customer service representative at a risk management organization. He admits he's antsy for something new at work. While he may be at the same company for ten years, he's usually never in the same position for longer than a year.

He earned an associate degree in human resources "because every company has an HR department." Now, he wants to go after a bachelor's degree in business because it might open more doors. Along the way, Kevin has been passed up for a position for which he was qualified, but someone with more seniority beat him out. Even if the person was a better fit, Kevin is already looking elsewhere. He seeks a company that will value his experience and enable him to pursue his education. He says he wants to "learn and earn."

Terique, our final individual, is an aspiring leader. He manages customer service representatives at an insurance carrier. He tried to go to college three times, but he felt the clock ticking. He didn't want to get stuck making a low-to-median income in his hometown, so he moved to a city where he landed his insurance job.

However, Terique isn't progressing in his job. He thrives on coaching his team members individually and having the whole team be successful, but in his career development, his manager isn't as engaged as he had hoped. He watches his peers get full support from their managers in their career development and feels disregarded. He's resentful and resigned. He seeks promotion to a customer service manager, but when he researched other CSMs, he discovered they all had bachelor's degrees. Not having a degree, coupled with the lack of support from his manager, leaves Terique actionless.

This albeit tiny survey of individual employees foregrounds the crisis up close. Perhaps you and those you manage face similar states of cynicism, confusion, inaction or maybe all three. In all cases, navigating the future rests in evolving your culture.

The Costs of This Moment

On the one hand, dealing with a workforce crisis is about being prepared for evolving toward what's next every day. On the other, you're incurring costs and losses that prove a frustrating and significant barrier to growth and productivity, all while impacting market share and competitive advantage. But how?

Let's start with the most pressing cost: recruitment. You may be a CEO who just can't find the right people — or keep them. Your number one issue is attracting and retaining talented people. You know that the right talent will drive revenue and profit, and that demands recruiting a diverse and skillful set of people.

Once they're in your doors, you then have to keep them engaged even as you find a way to keep their skills up to date. That means once an employee receives their orientation, the cost of recruitment becomes the cost of retention. In some industries, this cycle is high stakes. Even before COVID-19, the healthcare industry faced a shortage of close to half a million registered nurses in an industry where the attrition rate is somewhere between 20 to 30%, and each departing nurse costs between $40,000 and $65,000, possibly more if you factor in a given worker's depth of experience and years on the job.

This is not a problem that's limited to healthcare. Retail operations experience an annual turnover rate of 60%. A 10,000-person retail operation that values and hires several hourly wage workers invests $22 million a year in recruiting and retention. This issue is further complicated as automation replaces many traditional jobs and creates new opportunities that require different skill sets. Turning back to the technology industry offers a case in point. It has some of corporate America's highest attrition rates. Yet more concerning is the need among traditional software developers for instant, endless upskilling.

These examples reinforce the fact that when it comes to the workforce of the future, you have to keep them, and you have to keep them learning.

The Rise of Social Impact

You're also feeling the millennials big time. This new generation of workers seeks meaningful jobs and expects their employers to embrace social responsibility. They make up 30% of the workforce, and by 2025, they will make up 75% of the workforce. Today, nearly three-quarters of millennials would take a pay cut to work for a socially responsible company, would consider a company's social and environmental commitments before deciding where to work and won't take a job if a potential employer doesn't have strong social responsibility.

"If you're a large corporation," said David Hoverman, a partner at Bain & Company, "customers and employees now expect that you're going to make some sort of societal contribution in terms of the collective productivity and gainful career development of the workforce. And so, I think that expectation is a societal shift in mindset that's been well documented by social scientists: This is what millennials expect from companies versus what Gen-Xers like me expected from companies, which is that they would send me a paycheck."

Millennials have an unlikely supporter in this quest that is also impacting your strategic mix. Over the last five years, institutional investors and corporate shareholders, while still committed to Milton Friedman's statement "the business of business is business," began rejecting the notion that this maxim was incompatible with social purpose activities. In 2018, Harvard Law School's Forum on Corporate Governance reporting on the double emphasis on business as business and business as a purveyor of social good wrote that it:

> [builds] on a series of significant trends related to corporate social purpose in recent years: the growing significance of corporate social impact activities, as 90% of public companies now practice some form of social purpose, the repositioning of social purpose as a viable strategy for building competitive advantage, and a virtual explosion of investor interest — including significant interest by "mainstream" investors — beginning in 2016, and continuing into the 2018 annual meeting season.

The report discusses how, in 2016, shareholder proposals on social responsibility hit an inflection point, becoming the second-most prevalent genre of proposal that year. The number grew in 2017. By 2018, mainstream investors were "taking a new and prominent interest in social purpose as a means to sustainable, for-profit operations. There have been recent high-profile and significant calls to action, highlighting the need for CEOs to deliver both strong financial performance as well as positive social impact to be strong performers in the long-term." A 2018 Edelman survey focused on institutional investor trust found that 67% of investors expected companies to take a stand on public issues, 69% care about how a company treats its employees and 82% say trust is essential when considering whether to invest in a company. Among the most significant priorities tied to social responsibility? How companies hire, train and pay their employees. The workforce was entering the investor equation. Business Roundtable, an association of chief executive officers from America's leading companies, thrust it more thoroughly into corporate discourse.

Business Roundtable promotes a thriving U.S. economy and expanded opportunity for all Americans through sound public policy. In 2019, it redefined corporate purpose to "better reflect a free-market economy that serves all Americans," extending it beyond the traditional mantra of shareholder value. Adding to the principle of corporate purpose, the roundtable participants proclaimed a newly articulated "shared, fundamental commitment to all of our stakeholders." They then detailed five commitments: delivering value to customers and exceeding their expectations, investing in employees and supporting them with training and education, dealing fairly and ethically with suppliers, supporting communities in which they work and generating long-term value to their shareholders.

Jamie Dimon, chairman and CEO, JPMorgan Chase & Co. and the chairman of Business Roundtable, said:

> The American dream is alive but fraying. Major employers are investing in their workers and communities because they know it is the only way to be successful over the long term. These modernized principles reflect the business community's unwavering commitment to continue to push for an economy that serves all Americans.

Along with Dimon, 181 CEOs signed and endorsed the evolved definition, including Jeff Bezos, founder and executive chairman, Amazon; Tim Cook, CEO, Apple; John Stankey, CEO, AT&T; and Satya Nadella, CEO, Microsoft Corporation.

As a direct result of investors and shareholders — mainstream, activist and otherwise — corporate social responsibility has become the domain of boards of directors at a time when boards wield significant power. More than likely, you're held accountable to a corporate social responsibility strategy, how that strategy stacks up next to the competition and how that strategy gets communicated to stakeholders. Even if you're not yet experiencing this from an *Age of And* perspective, you may have a board member tapping you on the shoulder about skill obsolescence. She tells you that she believes a rapid upskilling revolution is just what your workforce needs.

As a CEO, you face myriad obstacles in your quest to adequately empower your workforce and make it go amid the G-forces of the current age. You are in the Apollo 13 crucible. Successfully navigating it is paramount to survival and leadership. Whether we look at your frontline employees or your investors and shareholders, what we see is that challenges at the ground level of your workforce weave their way across your entire enterprise. They create obstacles that make ushering in the *Age of And* seemingly impossible.

However, you have strong allies in your quest. They are the leading U.S. colleges and universities. As we'll discover next, they may need you just as much as you need them.

Chapter 3

CEO.edu:
A Corporate Campus Tour

What challenges face chief executives at institutions of higher learning? For this chapter, you'll walk in the shoes of a university president.

Cross the threshold into the academy, CEO.com. You are now the CEO.edu, helming a massive, complex web of purpose — equal parts nation-state, corporation, educator, research center, nonprofit service provider and foundation. From your corner office, you look beyond the glimmering emerald lawn dotted with plots of tulips or roses arranged in the logo of your school. Emerging from sun-splashed trees, streams and frisbee-catching dogs, you can see a small city's worth of architecture that composes your campus headquarters. On your wall, among images of your most successful alumni — most likely Nobel laureates — hangs a stylized map of your satellite campuses. You established them in urban centers or rural outposts domestically and abroad to further your mission or exploit a perceived market opportunity.

Your role as president is to successfully grow this university, serve your communities of influence, thoroughly master the roles of visionary and politician and raise billions of dollars while directing a head-spinning array of business units. The core of the business is knowledge: its discovery and propagation. You execute this core across mediums and channels in the United States and through affiliates, partnerships and campuses that cross borders. It's a multinational enterprise that relies on a unique collaboration between your workforce and your customers, who engage in a spiral of dialogue, research and new knowledge creation. As we'll see later, this co-creative energy walks a delicate balance as you at once teach and leverage the expertise of your most valuable resource: students.

The University Business Model and Economic Drivers

Within your business model, two main sub-offerings roll up under knowledge creation. They are pedagogy and research. These services get packaged in two ways. First, there is a brick-and-mortar-based personal learning experience. It underscores the value of living, learning and exploring through in-person community to varying degrees of on-site commitment. Second, there is a relatively nascent (the last two decades) online experience that attempts to translate the essence of your brand and your team through a digital environment to deliver the same quality of in-person learning to anyone you choose, anytime, anywhere.

In addition to the core, there are several other revenue channels that come to mind. They vary based on your size, geography and philosophy. For example, you may oversee a tradition-rich sports program — one of 65 National Collegiate Athletic Association (NCAA) Division I Football Bowl Subdivision schools — and you are reaping millions of dollars in bottom-line growth through inter-collegiate athletics. That means you'll take a share of the $7.6 billion annual haul from apparel licensing, corporate sponsorships, video deals and gate receipts. You'll reinvest most of it into a recruiting arms race, coaches' salaries and a consistent regimen of facility upgrades — all while running multiple sports franchises.

When it comes to residential and commercial real estate, you're all in. You depend on buildings for accommodating or advancing growth, so you build them, add to them and remodel or restore them. You make strategic real estate investments for flipping or leasing. You run parking facilities.

In addition to your role as a realtor and real estate developer, you are also a retailer. You engage in diverse partnerships and ventures across vertical industries. You might run one or multiple hotels and restaurants. Your bookstore is a marketplace of required academic resources, casual reading, university-driven apparel, collectibles, dishware, periodicals and digital technology. Your recreation and entertainment offerings include facilities with gyms, bowling alleys, tennis courts, swimming pools, hockey rinks, golf courses, arcades and cinemas. Your teaching hospital is also a business, delivering healthcare to the communities you serve and an array of diagnostic or specialty clinics in your college town and beyond.

Still, your core business model is grounded in your primary offerings. As a rule, your institution over-relies on an annual subscription approach (tuition), accounting for more than 45% of revenue at most public universities. Your subscriber universe is governed by standards you set for vetting and selecting your populace. It is usually a mix of high school grade point average, service- and athletic-based achievement, standardized test scores and Google job interview-like "intangibles" around why a given prospect wants to subscribe to your institution. You walk a line between revenue generation and perception of precious opportunity and selectivity among your subscriber base. It comes with an imperative: you must live up to the promise of the very best knowledge industry firms, maintaining high standards that are constantly improving to justify your price even as you expand your customer base to increase volume. It's a tricky balance that only a few of your premium-equivalent peers can claim.

Again, depending on your philosophy, tier and geography, subscription pricing varies, but most complain that the price of what you offer is outrageous. It has to be. There are three reasons for this. First, if you're a public university, you have an investment group mercilessly decreasing funding across the board: your state government. *Inside Higher Ed* has reported that "state funding nationwide is nearly 9% below pre-Great Recession levels and 18% below where it was before the 2001 tech bust. Per-student education appropriations increased 2.4% between fiscal year 2018 and fiscal year 2019, but 2019 marks the 'likely end' to post-recession recovery funding," the report states. It forces you to rely on tuition and fees like never before, as you've done in previous downturns, but your success isn't guaranteed.

Second, if you're private, you have very little cash flow to rely upon outside of fundraising, grants and your endowment in the face of continually shrinking federal dollars. Lastly, in both cases, you're at the whim of the market and a regulatory environment that shifts almost year to year. For example, if immigration policy suddenly limits your ability to enroll international students, this could severely downgrade your annual class size and further degrade subscription revenue. In the summer of 2020, that number was zero due to the COVID-19 pandemic. At that time, there were complaints and withdrawals of U.S.-based students who, along with their parents or guardians, were dissatisfied with the fact they would be spending $40,000+ per year on virtual, Zoom-based learning from home without the richer, on-campus experience.

In selling the future one student at a time, your second key avenue to growth is through fundraising — called development. It poses a challenge all its own. In fiscal year 2020, giving was down 10%. That number doesn't consider that only a handful of institutions were churning out annual million-to-multimillion-dollar general fund, capital campaign or targeted gifts. Even fewer had thriving endowments. COVID-19 cut deeply into your development plans. *Inside Philanthropy* reported 83% of university fundraisers had canceled or postponed some or all of their solicitations through the outbreak. In the same survey, University of Wisconsin-Madison Chancellor Rebecca Blank asserted, "My expectation is, there's going to be a number of schools going out of business as a result of this."

Compounding your challenges is the fact that, though you are the size of a Fortune 500 company — at times the single largest employer in the town or city you call home — you reliably struggle to design and execute an adequate Fortune 500 go-to-market strategy. The academic and marketing vision are often in conflict, with marketing seen as a necessary evil and unnecessary flourish. The sheer number of stakeholders involved in making go-to-market decisions often dilutes the final strategy anyway — boards, committees, alumni and usually understaffed internal marketing organizations sometimes seek, and take blindly, the third-party advice of consultants and agencies. Suddenly, the future of your enrollment hinges on an art nouveau shot of a student eating miniature textbooks out of a cereal bowl with the caption, "College: Eat It Up."

Even though you work with elements most consumer brands would die for — tradition, generation-linking customers, symbol, built-in thought leadership and a million different, emotionally compelling stories — competition among varying tiers of institutions is deadly fierce. This fact renders best-practice college and university marketing difficult because differentiation within university categories is nearly impossible (i.e., public research universities, small, private teaching universities, The Ivy League).

University Culture

In working to sustain revenue and attract, convert and win the market, you are also battling to evolve a traditional — even centuries-old — academic culture that moves at a wholly different pace. The clock-speed issue makes nimbly advancing new initiatives, innovations, approaches and strategies a glacial exercise. Partially due to bureaucracy and partly due to a calendar that runs on semester-meets-academic time, your attempts to meet ever-increasing market expectations of continual access in real time face a stiff headwind. Beware. Your cracking of the time barrier is one aspect of cultural evolution. You have another cultural challenge on your hands: a knowledgeable, accomplished and intelligent workforce.

Known as your faculty, this group of professionals is traditionally resistant to change that is pedagogical, technological or otherwise. Why? In oversimplified and even caricatured terms, faculties often hold philosophical differences around what a university should be and how it offers that raison d'etre to its customers. To be clear, this is evolving, but it's not yet at a pace or in step with society — let alone a once-in-a-lifetime pandemic. COVID-19 also severely compromised a core assumption of many faculty members: that "real teaching" can only happen in a physical classroom. (Before the pandemic, *Inside Higher Ed* found that just 39% of faculty fully supported an increase in the use of educational technologies.) This digital resistance did you no favors in convincing your customer base that they should move online for an entire year's worth of school.

Your faculty might also take offense at terming students "customers," upsetting the traditional balance of power in the classroom and lab. Worse, even though you successfully eliminated 75% of tenured faculty positions, that long-storied approach to no-questions-asked academic job security that originated in the 1940s, you have paid the price of trust. Now you have a group that requires a major rebuilding effort matched to clear pathways for professional development. You will be doing this among half of your faculty. The other half simply doesn't have as much skin in the game. They are adjunct, a term to describe part-time faculty members making a per-course wage. They may park and teach a 1:00 p.m. course on your campus and depart at 3:50 p.m. to teach another course across town at a competitor's institution.

Culturally, you stand upon a tightrope between your faculty on one side and your student body on the other. Your ability to succeed correlates to the depth and volume of interpersonal handholding you're able to maintain with both sets of constituents. In this way, the complexity of what you're leading distills into your role, and you must carry within you instant access to a host of avatars, including parent, politician, retailer, sports agent and ambassador, intellectual, visionary, torchbearer and fundraiser. Maintaining and cultivating a lean-forward culture is a balancing act of force of will, inclusion and emotional intelligence.

The University and Digitization

Further undercutting your business model, fundraising, marketing and building a strong culture is an era of digital transformation radically overhauling consumer expectations. A solid analogy for what's happening now throughout higher education is the year 1995, when the potential of online reality first dawned upon the corporate sector, giving way to the term "e-commerce," which began its slog to dominance. From there, take your pick of disruptive digital equivalents. Your institution could be like a traditional travel agency at the dawn of online travel agencies (OTAs), which will quickly and efficiently eliminate you. First, the likes of Expedia, Preview Travel and Travelocity automated research and transactions, and then novel variations like Priceline took low prices deeper by enabling you to "name your own price" for travel products and services.

Speed ahead a little more than ten years later when bandwidth and last-mile infrastructure transformed Netflix from an online video rental store to an over-the-top (OTT) media service that overtakes both your cable channel and your production operation. Just think: you could be Blockbuster.

So, you're mindful of the educational similarities to both OTAs and OTTs, and you have accessed some case studies from your business school. They're threats you're attempting to counteract through initial moves toward omnichannel, digital modes of recruitment, collaboration, learning and research. You know your progress is not keeping pace with what you can do in your own home as a consumer linked to the Internet of Things (IoT). As previously discussed, it's not easy for any university to entirely shift, adapt and integrate these changes with speed. Your attempt is no exception.

Digital innovation doesn't just mean a digitally connected institution. It's also creating a need for a new curriculum, one that can serve a student for 60+ years while pursuing a life of relentless, sometimes exciting and often trauma-inducing change thanks to automation.

This digital innovation is spawning another trend: the swift rise of a wholly new student population represented by working adults. Depending on how you respond to them, they pose a challenge or an opportunity. That's because they are different in almost every way from your traditional student population.

Working adults have different learning aspirations and needs. They are looking for professionally relevant education that helps them advance or remain relevant in their careers. They also hold a different definition of loyalty than your school colors, mascot or quad. Instead, they are choosy and seek education that serves them right now. That means they may come to you for a short-term certificate and then begin picking off credentials from multiple institutions. They have no time to come on campus for learning. You must deliver an exceptional, high-quality learning environment online.

Should you seek growth through this newest, largest and fastest-growing segment of learners, there is an unintended side effect: the matrix of competitors you face exponentially increases. You are now up against every private, public, for-profit and certificate-yielding educational entity in the market worldwide. Accordingly, this demands a wholly different go-to-market mindset and KPI trajectory. The rewards of pursuing these learners are incredible: it's an already large segment that will keep growing in direct proportion to the speed with which legacy skills in the workplace are rendered obsolete.

Recently, you were forwarded an article on this very topic —

something about a 60-year curriculum that is "tailored to the needs of the synergistic digital economy for non-traditional students across a spectrum of ages and career stages." It goes on to discuss the importance of a bona fide strategic response to this curricular and delivery-based need that leaves you reflective and somewhat confused. This nexus of digital and demographic change leaves you at a crossroads. You have a fiduciary obligation to bring the best of your university's capability to a new environment and a new, massive set of learners. Your existing institutional capabilities are necessary but not sufficient to address — let alone seize — this market opportunity. However, you are also painfully aware that someone else will if you don't handle it with speed. Nature abhors a vacuum.

CEO.com, CEO.edu Needs You

The American university is not dying or going away. As it makes the Herculean shift across colossal campuses (both physical and digital), these new learners demographically alluded to previously provide an opening. As you seek avenues for tapping the rich soil of higher education to solve for your workforce of the future, those working adults work for you. The university needs you to gain access. It needs your energy, urgency and creativity to make that happen in a win-win scenario. The question, then, is how? How do you engage to realize and fulfill the promise of workforce education with a college or university, when forging relationships with these unique and wholly different institutions isn't your focus? Before we answer that question with a comprehensive solution, we must first examine the existing means through which corporations and third parties pursue workforce education today. Most of these approaches are not working.

Chapter 4

Fax Machines Can't Zoom:
Workforce Education Today

"PC Load Letter?" says Michael Bolton. "What the <bleep> does that mean?"

This line sparks the climactic moment in the 1999 movie *Office Space*. Michael, Peter and Samir, three youngish employees trying to make sense of peak 20th-century cubicle culture, rage against the machine. The trio escorts what looks to be a constantly malfunctioning laser jet printer to a field. Baseball bats in hand, and to the backbeat of classic hip hop, they destroy the printer, one cathartic and deeply satisfying swing at a time.

According to the *BBC*, this was "the definitive film that skewers office banality," this precursor to *The Office* was a manifesto of dogged, righteous dissent. It connected. We've all been there. We've all had moments when a culture or a manager or a suboptimal technology sent us over the edge. Regarding the latter, those who worked during the era could contend with 30-minute paper jams that inflicted physical injury to resolve or multi-hour toner malfunctions that caused burns and ruined many a corporate wardrobe. Such was technology on the edge of the digital age, operating as co-conspirators in a plan to ravage an average day through the limitations of technology engineered from an amalgam of eras.

It was funny, of course, but *Office Space* also proved prophetic:

the cube, the management style and the work environment were about to transform. Tech's era of the solemn, silent and gray-cubicled world gave way to "corporate casual" cultures marked by on-campus scooters, foosball tables, free cafeterias offering organic-exclusive options and open floor plans. Within ten years, emblematic co-conspirators such as the fax machine, the printer and the copier would prove expensive relics of a bygone era. Despite best-effort innovations designed to keep them relevant (Fax on-demand services! Wireless printing! Fax, copier, scanner, printer all-in-ones!), their leading role in global business began to dim. Created for a different office universe, they presupposed paper would continue as the central, immovable currency and best-practice standard of communication. That assumption set their trajectory. By the time digital technology began consolidating nearly every piece of office hardware into the smartphone, their fate became sealed. Their tasks had vanished. Bill Lumbergh, the villain of *Office Space*, and his famous statement, "Yeeeeeahhhhh. You apparently didn't put one of the new coversheets on the TPS reports," went right along with them.

Similarly, in workforce education, the existing modalities corporations have long leaned on are proving vestiges of worlds that did not anticipate the speed of change nor the educational diversity of today's workplace. They come in four primary flavors: tuition reimbursement programs, corporate learning libraries, DIY corporate universities and direct corporate-to-university partnerships. Like paper-centric devices, the calculus of each modality makes it inadequate to the moment and off the mark. In other words, while initially useful and on-point, each modality is now moving away from the universe of present corporate reality and requirements. The modality's continued retrofitting intended to meet the occasion is not only impossibly expensive, but there is also no way for the modality to rise to it. Much like fax machines, printers and copiers, you will be hard-pressed to carry your workforce forward by continuing to hang on to them (no matter the amount of toner you've stockpiled).

Similarly, in today's workforce environment, there is no time for legacy workforce-education modalities. Jason Baumgarten, a Spencer Stuart consultant focused on CEO and senior leadership performance, describes this issue against the backdrop of a corporate landscape marked by a rising majority of private equity plays requiring diligent and formidable results. He suggests that offering legacy education modalities to employees is "the enemy of the urgent." In other words, if you're spending energy and money on investing in the fax machine, printer and copier of workforce education, it will negatively impact organization-wide return on investment in an era that demands faster impact. Exploring them amplifies this inadequacy.

Tuition Reimbursement: The Benefit Modality

Corporations introduced tuition reimbursement as a benefit designed to lure and retain ambitious, productive employees of quality. It's a mechanism introduced as part of a benefits package, allowing eligible workers to pursue their education proactively. The worker must front the cost and, if they complete a course, a certificate program or a degree program, they are reimbursed by the company. Corporations known for this "earn and learn" approach include UPS, which has distributed more than $200 million in reimbursements since 1999. AT&T's program is also well known. It offers union-represented employees and non-union employees reimbursement for approved degrees, capping assistance at $20,000 for undergraduate and $25,000 for graduate degrees, respectively. Some, like Wisconsin-based financial services and insurance provider Acuity, offer unlimited tuition assistance.

Tuition reimbursement administration most often resides in human resources, with budgets for reimbursement linked to individual business units throughout a company. Depending on the company, program structures vary, offering more or less freedom and more or less money to more or fewer workers. It is primarily run by managers who facilitate the program, much like a 401k or health insurance administrator. While it can be handled internally as a function of the company, it is most often outsourced to a third party. It can be handled by outsourced benefits providers such as WageWorks, which offers tuition reimbursement in a package along with health benefits, COBRA, commuter services and even smoking cessation programs. Others, like EdAssist, focus on tuition reimbursement as a specialty, providing a consulting layer that drills down to programmatic design, onboarding, launch and execution — offering both the company and learners a dashboard to track progress and submit expenses.

Outsourcing the function has enabled it to scale across the corporate landscape. It has also fueled change within higher education: a baby step toward leveraging the working adult market. Near the turn of the 21st century, certificate, degree-completion programs, full-scale associate programs, undergraduate programs and graduate programs developed, taking advantage of a tuition reimbursement program more attractive to working adults. Classes were offered in the evenings, on the weekends or online with periodic on-campus intensives. Higher education saw the opportunity and seized it.

The impact of tuition reimbursement is rarely known or fully understood across companies. After all, it's a benefit. Benefits are usually executed with high degrees of privacy. Therefore, just as a company doesn't know how many times a given worker has undergone a tooth cleaning or physical, they probably also don't have a handle on who, how and why an employee has access to tuition reimbursement. Benefits are also cost centers. In many companies, the HR organization benefits when the budget isn't fully used even as they derive a boost in public relations and recruiting from having the benefit included on their website.

Often reimbursement programs are the domain of knowledge workers, but that has changed in recent years, extending to junior skills workers. Access to the benefit varies. In most cases, it is accessed by white-collar workers, who use it to get an advanced degree such as an MBA.

Today, corporate America spends $28 billion on tuition reimbursement and assistance programs. It is one of its least-leveraged benefits. An InStride/Bain & Company study found that it accounts for roughly 15% of a corporation's learning and development budget. Still, as a rule, it is not aligned with the strategic priorities of the company nor formally baked into the corporate learning and development program.

Not even half of all workers — 40% — are aware of it. Fewer than 1 to 2% of workers leverage it. Many can't afford to front the money for their education, and only $5,250 of reimbursement is tax-free, meaning that any funds reimbursed become taxable after a few courses. Learner requirements can also prove onerous. Employees are tasked with finding the right university, executing all of the up-front admissions work, laying out tuition, and then fastidiously maintaining records necessary to collect reimbursement. Often, because the educational opportunity remains unaligned with the strategic needs of the corporation, there are few incentives for pursuing it. Because it's a benefit that costs corporate dollars, companies don't push it beyond their marketing materials. In this way, tuition reimbursement sits there, functioning mainly as a checkbox for recruiting, or a fancy statement on the corporate website, while remaining siloed from the guts of a corporation's strategic machinery.

Corporate Learning Libraries: The Compliance Modality

At the other end of the workforce education spectrum sits the corporate learning library. This easily accessed modality represents a company-owned or subscription-based way for workers to receive training in various predetermined disciplines. Corporate learning libraries began with books, videocassettes and DVDs focused on sexual harassment, anti-bias training and other compliance-based learning imperatives emerging from the *Office Space* generation. Then came training videos for specific job functions, such as sales or technical expertise. As companies sought ways to better leverage such libraries in the online era, they adopted third-party learning management system (LMS) platforms that would deliver the content and track progress and results.

Corporate learning libraries predominately carry regulatory — or skill-based — content. They don't offer the promise of a degree. However, the worker who completes a course will usually receive internal credit or certification. That is changing, and the evolution in this space will feature a move toward more robust academic rigor and, eventually, the granting of degrees. It's a crowded market. Skillsoft was an early player specializing in leadership development and other business skills, technology and developer skills and compliance-based skills. At the other end of this spectrum sits LinkedIn Learning, which launched its offering mainly through its acquisition of online course provider Lynda.com. It's focused on business, creative and technological categories of learning. Udemy touts itself as the world's largest LMS, offering more than 130,000 online courses with a heavy emphasis on technology-based disciplines. CrossKnowledge, a Wiley brand, offers the promise of digital learning solutions designed for skill acquisition.

More intentionally strategic than tuition reimbursement benefits, the learning library can prove more alignment-friendly to strategic objectives and professional development arcs. However, learning libraries don't offer the promise of a college degree, which in most companies is a prerequisite for acquiring or advancing to a higher-level position. While companies such as Apple, Google, Costco, Hilton and Starbucks don't require a college degree for employment, most enterprises still recognize academic degrees as the high-level proxy for whether a worker has accomplished something as a learner. The learning library industry has responded to this by offering third-party degrees of their own. This retrofit is less costly than the industry's higher education counterparts and is keen on disrupting this end of the workforce education market.

Learning libraries offer easy access to content that isn't very meaningful to the worker or the company at the end of the day. In some cases, whole libraries of direct-to-consumer learning content have been veneered with a business-to-business emphasis and built for the sake of monetization. Meanwhile, in the most recent LMS approach, a company pays whether the library is accessed or not. Similar to tuition reimbursement programs, learners must self-start, find the proper coursework in sometimes massive libraries and move through a process of initiating set-up on their own. Subject matter may or may not be aligned with an organization's strategic path. Corporate learning libraries are an expensive tool for companies attempting to externally demonstrate compliance or offer workers a road to advancement through learning opportunities.

Corporate Universities: The "DIY" Modality

Some companies commit to designing, building, staffing and launching their own learning journeys from scratch. Many of the best-known corporate universities and institutes were created to indoctrinate workers in a skill, or a way of being, that would directly map back to a brand promise and halo — be that entertainment based, food service based, customer service based or user experience based. In augmenting a traditional training department with a branded and expanded offering, the corporate university aspires to offer "real-world" education in business-aligned core disciplines. Some offer accredited degree programs. Lynne Doughtie, former chair and CEO, KPMG, discussed her company's questioning of its foray into DIY:

> KPMG's largest capital investment ever was in our training facility that we built in Lake Nona, Florida. We called it Lake House and it was really an investment in our people, our business and in professional services. It's all about how people

have to constantly be learning and innovating, but actually, there was quite a bit of debate about, you know, was that a smart investment?

Costing millions and even billions of dollars to build, corporate universities began before the democratized reality of online learning and online idea sharing and collaboration. In the past, disruptive companies who hit upon a wholly unique way to make a product or deliver a service or consumer experience designed corporate universities. They sought to advance consistent performance that led to those products, services and experiences to grow market share. Some even opened up their universities to the outside for training, team building and other types of learning experiences.

McDonald's Hamburger University is one of the oldest. Founded in 1961, its centerpiece is a week-long intensive focused on restaurant management and customer service. Bloomberg has reported that getting into it is more challenging than receiving an acceptance letter from Harvard. Its six-decade journey has spawned eight campuses around the world and boasts 275,000 graduates. Coursework can be applied toward a degree in "Hamburgerology" or activated as 23 credits toward an associate or bachelor's degree.

Disney University is a global training program for employees who work in the parks and experiences division of the Walt Disney Company. Known as Cast Members, these individuals take courses built and delivered by experienced professionals across relevant disciplines. Though non-accredited, enrollment at Disney University is contingent upon being enrolled at an accredited institution of higher learning. It often leads to internship credit at the source college or university.

Today, the launching of corporate universities continues, particularly in the technology sector. Some market leaders believe that their businesses are moving and transforming so quickly that their current training programs cannot stay on top of the growing knowledge gaps in their workforce. Some take that same university approach and then bundle it for companies in their sales ecosystem — buy the product and then sell the training as a staff development opportunity to become "insert favorite tech brand here" certified. Still, others recognize the workforce challenges they face, looking out on a vast, exponentially growing empire that begins with a low-level frontline worker and rises to knowledge workers, visionaries and futurists. They want to fully ensure that today's frontline worker is tomorrow's futurist for their brand and will spare no expense to take control of that learning process.

Building a corporate university proves a noble, if fraught, road. In addition to the issues of cost, hiring expertise, course development and factoring in market evolution, corporate universities must carefully do the math on success rates and/or "graduation." They must also be willing to part with a fundamental advantage of a university — someone at that institution has thought through, at scale, basics such as admission standards, sequencing of content/classes and graduation and evaluation standards. Accessing that in a DIY modality is not possible — creating and delivering education is not a core competency: it pulls from the corporate focus. It's also delivered with a corporate bias that may or may not anticipate and serve ever-shifting corporate objectives.

Can it be scaled? Can it account for the changing face of education with agility? Can it create an individualized journey for all workers and their learning styles and previous experience? Does it equate to any sort of loyalty or retention? As of now, the answer to all of these questions is no.

Direct Corporate-to-University Partnerships: The Uphill Modality

In unfolding workforce challenges facing corporations and the existential challenges facing universities, we have reviewed the foundational differences distinguishing each entity at the highest level. With that said, corporations and universities do form one-off collaborations. It's an arduous task. If their big picture differences prove stark, their on-the-ground differences grow in depth and intensity.

First movers in this effort included established for-profit institutions such as DeVry University and the University of Phoenix. Both entities sought to appeal directly to working adult students by tailoring programs to career-focused educational experiences. In both cases, these institutions proved attractive to large segments of the corporate community intent on educating and upskilling workers through direct-to-university partnerships.

Success came quickly. University of Phoenix enrollment peaked at nearly 500,000 students. Then, in 2019, NPR reported that the university settled a complaint with the Federal Trade Commission, paying $191 million after the FTC accused it of using deceptive ads to lure students with the promise of future job opportunities with large companies such as AT&T, Adobe, Twitter, Microsoft and Yahoo. DeVry traveled a similar path. In 2020, Crain's Chicago Business reported that its parent company, Adtalem, reached a $45 million settlement over a lawsuit alleging DeVry's deceptive manipulation of employment and future salary statistics used in student recruiting.

As we learned in CEO.edu, within nonprofit higher education, a corporation and university operate within significantly different cultural contexts that carry wholly disparate workflows and languages requiring precise translation. This translation must occur at a strategic level that flows to a mid-level effort to get the whole of a program to a starting line. Go deeper to the level of implementation, evaluation and measurement, and cultural differences amplify, impeding progress and utility.

We've discussed clock speeds. In a collaborative environment, both corporations and universities say they're working in real time. For corporations, that means minutes, days and weeks. For universities, that means months, semesters and years. The incentive for a university to move faster isn't there, which becomes a harsh reality of a direct partnership.

Additionally, there is the structure of leadership we touched on — in the corporate world, there is an agile style focused on vertical or horizontal solutions that maintain a semblance of personal accountability tied to corporate objectives. At universities, there are layers of colleges and departments that can impact a partnership and how quickly it is approved and activated within the university setting.

The KPI emphasis of corporations and universities also differs. For corporations, there is growth, impact and advancement. For universities, there is enrollment, fundraising and the diaspora of alumni who secure successful careers. The university KPI set, particularly with a hyperawareness of and emphasis on enrollment, hasn't yet led to successful outcomes for these partnerships.

As the differences mount, there is another outlying consideration when designing a direct-to-university partnership: one university may not be a single-source solution for all of the workforce education challenges a corporation faces today — let alone tomorrow. Having diligently and relentlessly built a collaborative program over months and years may still leave a corporation with severe gaps in addressing its unique set of challenges. For large employers with national or global footprints, a geographic challenge exists: even within online education, students want to study at universities that are geographically nearby. In 2019, the annual "Online College Students Survey" conducted by The Learning House, its parent Wiley Education and Aslanian Research, found that 70% of respondents attended virtual classes at institutions within 50 miles of their home. Those studying at schools at least 100 miles away dropped by more than half to 15%.

Of all the modalities we've explored, a university-corporate partnership foreshadows a great idea that requires next-level execution, choice and quality to work in ways that meet the current workforce crisis.

Empirically, we know from an InStride/Bain & Company study that the current workforce-education modalities are ineffective across industries. Worker awareness of the modalities is high — 80%. Learner participation is low — like tuition reimbursement, around 1 to 2%. At the same time, companies spend $180 billion annually to advance workforce education. It points to a fundamental flaw inherent in legacy workforce-education modalities: they are not built to meet the learning needs of the most educationally diverse workforce in history. They are fax machines attempting to Zoom and copiers attempting to Tweet. They are modalities ripe for parody à la *Office Space*. Chuck

Rubin, former chair and CEO, Michaels, supports this tough and yet true critique:

> Most of the conventional workforce education programs I have seen have been mediocre at best. I think CEOs have been confronted with how to build a program that's compelling and contributing to the ultimate objective, and I think historically a lot of these programs have been rather generic in form — like, here's a program to go back and get your bachelor's degree or an associate degree as opposed to specialized programs that may develop skills that are tailored to specific needs a given company has.

It's time for a new vision. We now sit at the threshold of establishing and dissecting C-Spark. Embedded within its thesis is a proposed rekindling of the partnership between corporate America and American higher education to set a genuinely strategic trajectory — one similar in texture to the collaborations that so effectively catalyzed the Atomic Age, Space Age and Information Age. In doing so, C-Spark offers both the high level *and* on-the-ground know-how for the "*And* shot" — the calling forth and seizing of the *Age of And*.

PART II

Eamybeg, Buck, Penrod, Waterboy and Bellgriffin. These five celebrated members of the American workforce paraded through Brooklyn on December 20, 1922. New Yorkers gathered in the streets, cheering. Their co-workers and managers were visibly shaken, emotional at this torch passing. The honorees arrived at the Brooklyn Borough Hall and were greeted by wreaths, cheers and excitement; the moment's backbeat contained certain levels of grief. Opposite sat a gleaming, new slice of automation that had captured the pulse of a city and an entire nation. It was an innovation that would alter life as most would know it.

This quintet of hardworking Americans, the last of New York's fire horses, were officially retired with speeches and proclamations. Sitting across from them was a freshly christened fire engine, the latest piece of automotive-related technology in a newly penetrated, vertical, business-to-business market.

In a comprehensive blog post about this disruptive event, Microsoft President Brad Smith noted:

By the start of the 20th century, Americans had grown weary of the "disorder" of society and called for better sanitation, order, safety and, above all, efficiency. The hard-working horse seemed antiquated and a wasteful, dangerous means of urban transportation. In 1908, New York's 120,000 horses produced a pungent 60,000 gallons of urine and 2.5 million pounds of manure every day on the city's streets. Auto enthusiasts dreamed of a horseless city with "streets, clean, dustless and odorless, with light, rubber-tired vehicles moving swiftly and noiselessly over their smooth expanse, would eliminate a greater part of the nervousness, distraction and strain of modern metropolitan life.

This tale is the analog of our moment. It's a moment that impacts legacy assumptions that have marked best-practice CEOs for a century. It's a moment that calls for reimagining the best-practice, universal set of strategic levers that you as CEO routinely pull to win the quarter, the year and the hearts and minds of your board and shareholders. It is a moment driven by a combination of digital technology, cultural evolution and political will. It's the moment of a new age — the *Age of And*.

Part II dissects what it takes to catapult into the *Age of And*. At its center sit people: employees, individuals, communities and the next generation. Keep in mind, this is not an exercise of maybe, what if or when. The moment transcends and includes the idea of "human capital," stewarding a new generation of humanity, period. It is not a hyperbolic consultant-flavored walk through a projected future. It is a chronicle of today that is speeding the changing nature of the corporation itself.

What of the fire horses? What do they represent? They represent the existing modalities of workforce education currently plied against this new age. Detailed in Part I, Chapter 4, they consist of tuition reimbursement programs, corporate learning libraries, corporate universities, direct corporate-to-university partnerships. "Antiquated, wasteful and dangerous," these fire horsemen of the past require a profoundly more robust and thorough way of delivering learning across your organization in the rhythm of its stride. That brand new and peerless engine — think of it as a McLaren, Hennessey or Bugatti that is the all-electric 600 horsepower supercar equivalent of your corporate dreams — on display across from the fire horses — is called Strategic Enterprise Education (SEE). In Part II, we explore SEE in detail, including its philosophy, approach, delivery mechanism and return on investment (ROI). It will propel your organization into the *Age of And*. What ignites it, though, is you, dear CEO.

If the *Age of And* is dependent on a workforce of the future, and SEE is the strategic engine that powers that workforce, you and only you can ignite that future. You *are* the C-Spark, and Part II concludes by providing a gut check, motivation and inspiration for why this is the case and why the quick success and ROI is solely in the hands of you, the CEO. We end by illustrating what corporate environments look and feel like once the C-Spark ignites. When Part II closes, you will be prepared to efficiently and powerfully integrate SEE into your strategic deck as a tool and resource that drives corporate growth and impact. Let's begin.

Chapter 5

When CEO Meets SEE: The Birth of a Flywheel

E arlier this century, Harvard Business School conducted in-depth research on how you, dear CEO, spend your day. It found that "where and how CEOs are involved determines what gets done. It signals priorities." It also found that one of six core dimensions characterizing the CEO role rests in the duality of power and legitimacy.

"CEOs hold a great deal of formal *power* and authority and exercise it in the many ways we have described," it said. "However, power, authority, competence and even results are insufficient to truly ensure their success. Effective CEOs combine formal power and authority with *legitimacy*."

The idea of legitimacy is tied to setting a cultural tone through fairness, lived values and a commitment to the company and its people. "Legitimacy gives rise to motivation that goes far beyond carrying out orders and can lead to extraordinary organizational performance."

Henry Ford understood this continuum. In 1926, Ford redefined time, creating what we now know as the 40-hour, five-day workweek. As a member of the inventor class of chief executives, he was continually looking outside the company and seeking ways to creatively bend the market his way even as he inspired his people. The tweak made an immediate difference for his people. Internally, it led to an energized, motivated and loyal assembly line. Externally, it set an industry standard that gave more Americans leisure time to shop for big-ticket items like cars. The move was seen as radical, but as *The New York Times* reported, "the announcement that the Ford Motor Company made … is the most recent of a long series of innovations in methods of manufacture as they apply to the workmen introduced by Henry Ford in the past dozen years."

You are moving through a daily struggle to triage, lead, inspire and activate new ideas that fulfill the promise of your strategic direction. In your effort to excite shareholders, reassure directors, drive revenue and move your firm forward, chances are workforce education has not emerged as a device of strategic utility. It's easy to see why. In both form and function, it has been conceived and implemented as an adjunct tactic designed for training and professional development or as a recruiting carrot — a benefit intended to excite high-potential and hungry employees. Yet, like hours in a day, it's an unexamined, untapped implement of power poised to become the strategic weapon that can do for you what the five-day workweek did for Ford: position you as an innovator, transform your culture and create new opportunities for growth, revenue, agility and brand leadership.

Barbara Desoer, former CEO, Citibank, N.A., and board director, Citigroup, Inc., reinforces the opportunity people at the intersection of education present you as you march forward:

> It is so much more valuable for a CEO to take into consideration the people that are within your organization when it comes to the changing future of your business. These are the people who share [and can live] your culture and brand.

David Hoverman, a partner at Bain & Company, asserts two core reasons why he believes companies have not yet committed to making a strategic investment in people:

> From a purely capitalist point of view, there is a group that has not yet felt enough market pressure to make these types of investments, and there is a second group that hasn't elevated it to the level of the CEO or as a leadership priority. In both of these cases, they share a commonality — they are laggards in their respective competitive landscapes.

Hoverman is encouraging you to access this newfound, strategically focused form of workforce education for competitive advantage. The question is, how?

How do you become strategic about addressing the roadblocks and seemingly irreconcilable differences within the workforce education paradigm? How do you move beyond well-intentioned and yet inadequate legacy methodologies, technologies and philosophies? How do you gracefully retire the last of the fire horses, knowing they can't be retrofitted or upgraded for the task ahead? How can you strategically shift to a boundary-spanning methodology designed to integrate your strategic priorities, your geographic footprint, the aspirations of your team and the promise of the future?

The answers lie in reorienting toward a CEO-focused vision of workforce education that delivers strategic clarity, simplicity, power and global savvy. It needs a systematic, linear approach that will upend and transcend any preconceptions and experiences you've had with learning, training and workforce preparation in the past. It must be capable of working up and down your organization, asserting, validating and road-mapping an approach to the workforce of the future that can easily integrate and make both a short- and long-term impact on your corporate direction. It doesn't stop there. As you'll discover, SEE can become the connective tissue of business units that ensures you're optimizing growth and impact across a universal array of strategic priorities. Importantly, announcing SEE to the world immediately imbues your brand with a new sense of commitment and improves perception. You begin to emerge as an employer of choice. In terms of hard dollars, it will start delivering ROI within the first year.

Once you ignite the C-Spark — that moment you commit to making learning the cornerstone of your organization's future — you are creating a "colinear flywheel of business growth and social impact." Within it, human capital priorities exert, generate and release energy that ensures maximum thrust across the organization. We will build to this moment throughout Part II, but before we dive into the details, let's discuss SEE.

The Anatomy of a Flywheel

A flywheel harmonizes and maximizes the raw power of an engine, supplying power in all directions. Flywheels are six-spoked disks that operate from a central core. Overlaying the analogy onto a corporation, SEE serves as the flywheel core. Solid, versatile and harmonizing, SEE comprehensively empowers you to seize opportunities and solve challenges across your array of corporate strategic priorities.

Through SEE, you assess skill gaps across your organization against strategic priorities. Then, you design a comprehensive program that equips employees with relevant education opportunities through partnerships with top-quality institutions that specialize in serving working adult learners. Along the way, a proven SEE-aligned strategy supports employees at every step of their learning lifecycle — from discovery to enrollment and through to graduation.

Because it is treated as a strategic investment in the company's future, not as another administrative cost center such as benefits, SEE creates new and elevated expectations for delivering the program and holding it accountable to drive results. Again, this investment in SEE is meaningful because it meets the strategic priorities you wrestle with quarterly.

If SEE is the crux of the flywheel, your strategic priorities are the spokes. Depending on your industry and corporate culture, they are unique and local in flavor. However, when distilled to their essence, they fall into the following six categories: revenue and profitability; corporate agility; talent recruitment and retention; diversity, equity and inclusion; corporate citizenship; and the brand. Each of these categories moves through multiple crucibles that include globalization, demographic change, digital transformation and the promise inherent in the *Age of And*.

Globalization and global connectivity have changed the way business and work are done. Globalization and global connectivity have also directly impacted the geographic and strategic footprint of most companies and created complexity operationally and in terms of regulatory compliance. They redefine competition. All of these considerations have seeped into approaches that companies take when going to market.

While you're encountering the most educationally diverse workforce in history, the "mosts" don't stop at education. They include the most socioeconomically diverse workforce, generationally diverse workforce, and the list goes on. They are challenges that more than likely have you reading this book even as you factor them into your overall corporate strategy.

Then comes the digital piece. Moore's Law, touched on earlier, states that computing power reaches a doubling or exponential increase in velocity every two years. At this stage in its trajectory, Moore's Law is delivering a tornado of digital and physical transformation, the effects of which are felt in every layer of an organization that is seeking to remain at the forefront of the markets it serves.

SEE is the basis of a flywheel that powers companies through these crucibles. That's because it focuses on a commonality across strategic priorities: your people. And it meets people by offering that direct and accessible portal to remaining current, pivoting, learning and advancing within the fury of change, which was made even more acute by a global pandemic. Coinciding with the crucibles are the sociological accessories of technological change referenced in our examination of the horse and the automobile: cultural and political dynamics have created terrain ripe for ever-accelerating change. When SEE enters an organization, it evaluates, analyzes and gears itself to grow, solve problems and catch the flow of change while accounting for its complementary social and political forces — the flywheel activates.

Revenue and Profitability

These standard bearers are still the royal metrics for CEO performance. As you may have already experienced, quarter-by-quarter growth is increasingly dependent upon a nimble workforce locked into a constant state of learning that drives the intelligent machinery powering your strategy. It has become evident in moving through and past the COVID-19 pandemic, with companies seeking a way to open up low-risk opportunities to diversify revenue streams. However, can SEE move the needle on growth? A global leader in veterinary science believes so.

This leader has put learning at the center of revenue and growth strategy and uses the principles of SEE to bring education to the masses within his or her business. Recruiting individuals who have a desire to become veterinarians, this leader is educating them and churning out doctors of veterinary medicine. Why? The more of its workforce that it can educate and board certify, the more hospitals it can build. It is ambitiously attempting to disrupt the veterinary medicine model by scaling from within and increasing its share of a $19 billion industry. En route to market leadership, it is also addressing a major issue plaguing companies across industries: 68% of corporate leaders acknowledge that skills gaps in their current workforce are limiting growth.

Importantly, this global leader is also deriving deeper benefits across the revenue and profitability continuum. Knowledge acquisition increases productivity, engagement, creativity and strategic acumen. With SEE, this acquisition can be targeted, and SEE can be deployed in direct service to a revenue and profitability strategy.

In the future, digital transformation will diversify wholly new avenues and channels for growth through precision-based approaches to sales, customer experiences and ever-diversifying channels through which customer relationships are built. People who are educationally leaning in will be the ones creating and churning out these new revenue opportunities, and SEE ensures the lean.

Corporate Agility

We know that the speed of business adaptation, reinvention and disruption is accelerating. You undoubtedly feel it on the ground every single day. Alongside this acceleration, there must be an equal level of human capital adaptability, reinvention and innovation. Without it, market leadership will prove elusive. This is especially true in industries where the rate of technological change is currently outstripping the rate of skill development.

Software is one such industry. Within it are software developers, a workforce that has grown exponentially over the last four years to nearly 18 million. Here's the issue: the rise of artificial intelligence over that same period has leapfrogged the developers, and today, the software is literally writing software.

In 2017, Microsoft and the University of Cambridge "created a system [called DeepCoder] that could allow non-coders to simply describe an idea for a program and let the system build it [by] piecing together lines of code taken from existing software — just like a programmer might." That same year, *WIRED* reported that Google had developed a tool, AutoML, to build machine learning software. It could identify and mark the location of many objects in an image at once. This autogenerated system scored 43%. The best human-built system scored 39%.

In 2019, two MIT professors, Armando Solar-Lezama and Josh Tenenbaum, developed SketchAdapt, which can learn to "compose short, high-level programs while letting the second set of algorithms find the right subprograms to fill in the details." What makes it intriguing is that "it knows when to switch from statistical pattern-matching to a less efficient, but more versatile, symbolic reasoning mode to fill in the gaps." It has already outperformed DeepCoder.

Notably, within the SketchAdapt example, its developers have positioned it to "complement human programmers." It enables people to tell SketchAdapt what they want, and SketchAdapt takes it from there. This highlights how the role of the developer will change from a step-by-step, from-scratch, rules-oriented engineer to an agile maestro.

Accordingly, these events have created a sudden and real need for the almost 25 million developers worldwide to quickly build minimal expertise in data science and stay continually current on where these innovations are headed (see "agile maestro" on the web) in accordance with where the business itself is heading. The software industry simply can't recruit its way out of this challenge, and retooling the workforce isn't optional: it's mandatory.

SEE creates workforce learning pathways that can fast-track skill acquisition and continue to top it off over time. If you don't, you'll join more than half of today's corporate leaders who responded to a Capgemini LinkedIn survey by saying a widening digital skills gap is hampering them. Specifically, a digital talent shortage is eroding their competitive advantage because, in an era of digital transformation, they can't apply digital technologies to all aspects of their business fast enough.

Importantly, though, this digital piece extends to other industries and other employee functions. Hoverman contends that it can likely impact any job, anywhere:

> You used to be able to train a food service employee on how to work the register, and that was adequate, but how do you now integrate that with a lean team that includes drive-through and

web ordering. Or what about call center employees who now, instead of just working a phone, must become fluent in a full VR system to at once handle calls and do customer service? With the call center, there's a real revenue imperative around it because all the simple things now take place on the web, so you need employees to undertake value-added, web-based activities.

SEE closes this gap by creating workers who are able to meet a future that demands them to be in a state of constant curiosity, creative productivity and knowledge acquisition.

Attracting and Retaining Talent

A SEE framework model for strategic talent acquisition and retention resides firmly in the professional services arena, particularly among management consultants. The core tenet of management consulting recruitment rests in education. McKinsey, Bain and BCG, for example, offer their associates, analysts and consultants paths to a cost-free MBA. This is an enormous investment. This largess shows how, within that industry, luring the best, brightest young minds and then unlocking a next-level education work.

In doing this, management consultancies have always been ahead of their time when thinking about the workforce, particularly one that Doug Haynes, former senior partner, McKinsey & Company, and president, The Council, refers to as the "giant free agency system." He believes that because people live longer, with a career arc topping 60 years that is supported by multiple employers, loyalty isn't always in their best interest:

If I'm managing my career in the workforce, I should constantly be monitoring the market to determine my worth. However, if you begin investing more in your people, you can begin to reverse the engines on this. You can attract better people if you have built a reputation for investing in your people, and you can give them that compelling reason to stay. You can outpace the market.

SEE offers a similar opportunity to invest in, secure, nurture and maximize the potential of your workforce's talent. However, this level of investment might prompt a question in the mind of every CFO: "What happens if we train these people, and they leave?" Your answer should be in the form of another question: "What if we don't train them and they stay?" What matters most is what happens to those who stay and how they ultimately help your company.

What can you do about those who do leave? Let's revisit SEE-oriented management consultancies. Their workforce often leaves for greener pastures, and they have a solution for that. Each firm maintains a thorough alumni program that accomplishes a few things. The program enables the consultancy to claim the employee for life. It also creates a rich network of business development opportunities for the firm over the long haul. Although many of the consultants may leave, they will become very loyal alumni, which is also a payoff.

This has proven true in my own personal experience as well. Like all consultants at McKinsey & Company, I have my own "My McKinsey"— a rich network of personal connections built over eight years with consultant colleagues on multiple project teams, with client team members, and with mentors and role models in the Singapore and Chicago offices. This network has endured and, in a very real way, was also instrumental in the founding of InStride. Jonathan Lau, InStride Chief Operating Officer and Co-founder, was a "day one" McKinsey associate on one of my project teams nearly 14 years ago.

Finally, in the strategic context of attracting and retaining talent, SEE vests recruits with a vision and can align your objectives with their careers even prior to their employment. With education linked to the corporate trajectory in a way that makes sense, it vests a prospective hire that you have a game plan for them as individuals. It is front and center in the hiring process and can be discussed as a part of the professional development and skills development roadmap from day one. Importantly, it is consistently communicated between HR, you, core members of your executive team and the prospect's direct report. This reflects an environment of lifelong learning and skills development that can solidify and fast-track hiring as the vision and culture prove contagious.

On day two, your new talent can engage immediately on their educational journey. This is also strategically powerful. A day-one learner on day two of their journey with your company is already investing in themselves. The tone is set, and because their learning is operating against the backdrop of their role and the corporate trajectory, the seeds of retention have been planted, and the cultural DNA is imprinted.

Diversity, Equity & Inclusion

In its 2020 annual board index, Spencer Stuart found that women and minority men composed the majority of the new S&P 500 director class. Of the incoming class of more than 400 directors, 59% of new directors are classified as diverse. Women made up 47% of the new class. Minority men, which Spencer Stuart defines as Black/African American, Asian and Hispanic/Latinx, composed 12%. It pointed to shareholder and key stakeholder pressure over the last decade as a driver of this change. This pressure is making a dent. Slowly but surely. However, when you are talking about the entire workforce, solving DE&I by appointment — or recruiting — is simply unrealistic. Yet, according to a Glassdoor CEO survey, diversity, equity and inclusion are figuring heavily into your strategic approach.

It's the right thing to do, but it also pays off. McKinsey has found that 35% of companies that identified as more diverse and inclusive are more likely to outperform the competition. Deloitte noted that nearly 75% of millennials believe their organization is more innovative when it has a culture of inclusion, and nearly 50% look for diversity and inclusion when sizing up potential employers.

SEE is a strategic tool for DE&I because the educational opportunity is the missing link for ensuring a diverse workforce. Employees of color, particularly Black and Hispanic individuals, statistically possess less education, lost more jobs and wages through the pandemic and yet are hungrier to learn. In fact, they are more likely to enroll in an education or training program in the coming months. More than likely, you have a real need to address this issue with haste, and if you're at the forefront of this trend, you might have set up a special department dedicated to DE&I.

In the post COVID-19 era, SEE will be a critical way to regain DE&I footing. Job losses have been 4.1 times higher for women than men and more than 1.3 times higher for Hispanics and African

Americans than whites. These categories of workers are among the 100 million who have switched jobs during the pandemic. They are also frontline workers who will never have a chance to climb your corporate ladder. Still, you are undoubtedly and aggressively pursuing DE&I. Amy Miles, former chair of the board and CEO at Regal Entertainment Group, believes all companies are.

"Every corporation I'm affiliated with today would put DE&I at the top of the list. Everyone is trying to figure out how to be successful in that path, and you know all are on the journey," she said.

Miles suspects more progress has been made on the diversity side of the equation. It's on the inclusion and equity side where the largest gap exists. She points to her own tenure at Regal. According to Miles, from the entry-level to the next two promotion cycles, there was a bona fide, diverse workforce. The second layer up to top management was a different story. This created recruiting problems. Those at the bottom saw the lack of diversity. It sent a message. Miles believes workforce education strategically plied toward DE&I is a real answer — one that holds the promise of retention and if linked to a career pathway, promotion.

A global dairy leader in the upper Midwest moved in the direction Miles suggested. They could not recruit their way toward a meaningfully diverse workforce. Furthermore, those employees who fit the DE&I category often came to the company qualified for a factory job, but, due to traumas, lack of access and other disadvantages linked to their education, held no shot of advancing in their careers. The company made a strategic decision to leverage SEE-focused principles and develop education pathways for their employees. For those at the bottom, a high school opportunity could offer a way into a shift supervisor position. From there, and using SEE, they will be able to create a more diverse and equitable environment that equips them to accelerate their corporate priority around DE&I.

Transcending these data is the notion of authenticity. DE&I can no longer prove a checkbox. Nike is a prime and ironic example. Even as it was set to launch a major ad campaign around diversity and equity featuring soccer star Megan Rapinoe and tennis star Serena Williams themed "You Can't Stop Us," Black employees within the company spoke up to voice disapproval around the campaign's release until Nike had solved for its own issues around DE&I internally. As a result, its first chief diversity officer left, and its CEO John Donahoe announced a "structural shift" to allow for "more meaningful change" while acknowledging double standards at play between its internal culture and external brand.

At the other end sits Apple, which has gone all-in on a SEE-aligned approach. Apple asserts that a more diverse future rests in more opportunities and, consistent with its brand, it has "always believed education is the great equalizer." Apple focuses on community college partners, historically Black colleges and universities (HBCUs) and minority-serving institutions while "developing partnerships to reach even more diverse talent across all ages and career stages."

Apple's move foregrounds its focus on a DE&I roadmap meant to be systemically operationalized. In solidifying a systemic approach, it further distances itself competitively. As the battle for talent in this arena intensifies, authentic and systemic DE&I will rest on the ability of every company to offer access to learning, skill development, training, upskilling and educational opportunities that communicate meaningfulness and durability.

Corporate Citizenship

In American business, the power of corporate citizenship has its roots dating back to the early- and mid-20th century. The IBM of the 1950s and '60s was a great example. Living out a value of "respect for the individual," the firm set up career pathways as "cradle to grave" and created a loyal and devoted workforce through the 1970s.

Additionally, corporate headquarter towns have always proven a driving force for localized impact. An HQ provides jobs, grows cottage industries, creates corporate and individual taxable income, stimulates economic activity and even drives increased charitable giving. It's why politicians spend so much time and energy attempting to attract one. When Henry Ford engaged in innovating the workweek and making the car accessible to the middle class, he intentionally and methodically improved the lives and city of his corporate headquarters: Detroit. In 1914, he made another bold stroke and nearly doubled his workforce's salary to $5 a day. It gave him access to the best talent for scaling Ford Motor Company. In one fell swoop, he lifted his team from working class to the middle class. Prior to the conception of Ford Motor Company, Detroit was America's 13th largest city with a population of just under 300,000. By 1930 and largely thanks to Ford, it was a burgeoning metropolis of more than one million.

You're thinking, "It was a different time and a different place. Just not possible today." You'd be wrong. According to Tsun-yan Hsieh, former senior partner, McKinsey & Company and chairman, LinHart Group, authenticity and opportunity for real impact still exist.

"The telltale sign is when there is strategic integration between the business and social impact," said Hsieh.

He believes that if the approach proves segregated, varies between good and bad performing years and doesn't connect the company's trajectory to the heartbeat of the community in which it operates, it will ring hollow. SEE solves this by creating a cohesive story and delivering a cohesive impact.

To that end, envision a massive company leveraging millions of automobiles and with a presence in every town across America. It's a company offering a free college degree to 300,000 workers. The company, incredibly thoughtful in its approach, knew many of its top employees were working multiple jobs at once and decided to extend the program to all families connected with its 300,000 workers. In fact, 40% of participants in the program are family members. They have their pick of more than 100 degree programs. Tuition is 100% covered. The social impact this move is having is nothing short of staggering. Families and their circle of friends are transformed. In communities, it raises the standard of living and, over the long haul, yields economic benefits. Generations to whom the torch is passed will stand on the shoulders of the graduates, and the impact will exponentially grow.

This is not just vision. This is Uber, and they are bringing to life the truism within education circles that gets attributed to many luminaries of the past, including Plutarch and W. B. Yeats. It states, "Education is not the filling of a cup but the lighting of a fire."

Uber used strategic workforce education as the strategic centerpiece of a corporate citizenship and driver recruitment approach for their top drivers, whom they call "platinum drivers." It is by far one of the strongest levers of social impact at scale. It calls forth another truism offered by Nelson Mandela, who said, "education is the most powerful weapon which you can use to change the world."

Mandela's words proved true for InStride Chief Customer Officer Sean Flynn. Flynn's mother immigrated to the United States from Guatemala. She took time off to raise three children before returning to work as a paralegal during Flynn's youth. She quickly recognized that she was often smarter and more qualified than her attorney counterparts. When Flynn was in high school, his mom decided to attend law school. She became an attorney and went on to have an accomplished career. Witnessing this changed Flynn and set his own trajectory. He had his parents sign a waiver so he could attend West Point as a minor. After six years of active duty, he moved into civilian life. Through a well of military contacts, he ended up at IBM. Hungry and taking big bites out of his career, he worked hard, and soon he found himself in his mom's position, noting that most senior leadership at the company had an advanced degree. IBM sponsored Sean's MBA at the University of Virginia. It changed him:

> Much of my education up to grad school was about task excellence. It was focused on delivering a specific mission to time and standard. Grad school was about understanding the five levels of "why." The one common thread: education. It's one of the truest, most authentic, most impactful drivers of corporate citizenship.

Part I detailed how millennials, boards and CEOs are forming a movement, advancing corporate citizenship — first movers in the *Age of And.* Just like Uber's approach, corporate citizenship strategies must presuppose the corporation of tomorrow will either competitively seize or be mainstreamed into expanding its role in society for good. The double entendre is purposeful. A corporate citizenship posture that seeks strong impact must be embedded in your business strategy, relevant to local geographies where you do business and be doing actual good over the long haul. It must be sustainable, and it is increasingly being held to account. When it fulfills these requisites, it becomes an asset that can weave its way through your internal culture and external brand.

The Brand

Your brand is encompassed by two sides of the same coin. One side is the external brand — the face of the company to customers and outside stakeholders. The other side is culture — how the brand's promise is actually lived by those engaged in the enterprise. SEE meets the coin and is equally effective at equipping both sides of the coin by supercharging engagement in ways that transform an internal culture that is felt externally. Tom Staggs, former COO, The Walt Disney Company, discusses the implications of leveraging strategic workforce education in this way:

> The nice thing is that the brand is a rallying point to talk about what you stand for — including your investment in people and why that investment is important. But you have to carefully and clearly connect the dots between the brand and the education initiative, demonstrating how the initiative is an investment in the long-term health and "leveragability" of the brand itself.

Starbucks is the prime example of this truth. When Starbucks partnered with Arizona State University to launch SCAP, the brand was a core priority. By 2020, SCAP enrolled more than 16,000 Starbucks partners. It meant that three out of every four U.S. stores had SCAP-engaged partners. Nearly 7,000 have completed their bachelor's degree. Since implementing SCAP, Starbucks has enjoyed the highest employee retention rate in retail while continually raising the bar on customer connection.

SCAP participants register a three-times faster internal promotion rate than nonparticipating Starbucks partners. However, anyone who completes the program is free to leave Starbucks. In doing so, they remain loyal alumni of the company. The program also impacts recruiting, with more than 20% of applicants pointing to SCAP as a motivating factor in pursuing jobs at the company.

Phil Regier, university dean for educational initiatives and CEO EdPlus, Arizona State University, emphasized the deeper implications of this SCAP-catalyzed energy:

> Howard Schultz always knew, and he always said, look, people don't buy this coffee because of me. They buy the coffee because of the people we have in the stores. And we have to keep those people happy because they will keep our customers happy. And that is true. It's one of the only companies like that. And keeping those people happy and connected with customers is at the front of everything they do.

For Starbucks, the SEE framework best demonstrates the colinear flywheel because it is powering an array of strategic initiatives from the core brand. It touches internal culture, talent retention and brand communications. It touches external recruitment, social impact, revenue growth, customer relationship management (CRM), marketing, sales, trust and brand loyalty. It creates a scenario whereby Starbucks lives its brand, increases its differentiation and extends quality and leadership to its customers, stakeholders, investors, influencers, employees and the market. Starbucks underscores how this brand discussion began. It supercharges engagement externally and internally, thereby supercharging the brand. SEE, they have found, is integral to great brand strategies and, when packaged in brand-consistent ways, can also become its own tool for marketing.

It's called Strategic Enterprise Education for a reason, and now that you understand that fact, you have a superb weapon to deepen your power and legitimacy as a leader inside and outside your company. This comes with a catch that will be reinforced throughout the process. It has to be you. As Harvard's study made clear, "Where and how CEOs are involved determines what gets done. It signals priorities." With this fact in mind, it's time to lead your organization in calibrating it to your unique trajectory.

Chapter 6

Corporate Strategy + SEE: Kindling the C-Spark

Imagine a countertop of dark wood grain that forms a squared-off, u-shaped bar seating no more than 12 people. On one wall hangs a mid-century clock with a swinging, golden pendulum. The other wall displays a single-item menu written in sharpie — pork miso soup combo — augmented with beverages such as beer, sake and shochu. A dingy railway map hangs nearby, and a colorful, '70s-era white thermos flourished with a thick, orange stripe dispenses hot water at one end of the counter. Periodic islands of sauces and tightly-stored jars of chopsticks further dot its surface. The entrance — a sliding door — offers a portal to the "yokocho," a tiny alleyway that leads from a main street. Patrons must duck under a banner hung like a short shower curtain across the front entrance. A "chochin" — the familiar, oblong collapsible lantern — lights up the night. The establishment's name is Meshiya, an "izakaya" — or cantina — that serves alcohol and snacks between the hours of 12:00 a.m. and 7:00 a.m. and is situated, unassumingly, in the thick of Shinjuku City, Tokyo's bustling nightlife district.

This ingenious and intimate setting serves as the backdrop for Yaro Abe's manga (Japanese graphic novel) titled *Midnight Diner* that was produced into a Japanese anthology television series since acquired and extended by Netflix. Tokyo's largest is distilled to a single focal point, and inside the diner, an array of characters from all walks of life — businesspeople, outcasts, partiers, creatives, burlesque performers and gang members — gather in common to share food. And the food is amazing. The man who runs the diner is simply called "The Master."

Each episode focuses on a set of characters who arrive with a specific craving that is satisfied through the apparent top-chef status of The Master. The life of the diner orbits around his pragmatic, philosophical, mystical presence that brings calm to the center. From the fulcrum of his kitchen, he sparks memories through flavor, listens, stares into the distance, smoking, and through subtle or sweeping actions, impacts the lives of his patrons.

This show, in all of its thoroughly Japanese beauty, patience and elegance, unfolds narratives that are sometimes poignant, sometimes triumphant, sometimes tragic or hilarious and sit at the edge of magical realism. And in the middle stands The Master. In his tiny work space and in a haven that arrests time amid the neon blast of the world's largest city, he affects change. It is The Master who is the catalyst.

So it is with the C-Spark. As CEO, you are the one in your organization who can effectively set the course for your entire workforce. You are the one who holds the future of the business in your hands and leads through your unique blend of skill, wisdom, charisma and political savvy.

You hold the workforce of the future and the community that stands behind those employees in your hands. And with them rests the destiny of your venture.

Therefore, your commitment to SEE means everything and must be visible and tangible from the start. Just as the story arc revolves around The Master in *Midnight Diner*, your company orbits around you, and you must be willing to be the standard-bearer and driver if workforce education is to fundamentally serve as the colinear flywheel that accelerates your company's growth and impact.

Mark Fields, former CEO, Ford Motor Company, extends this thinking when he reflects on how CEOs should assess and design a SEE approach within their organization:

> First, the problem you're solving for has to be thoroughly defined. Second, how's that income statement doing, particularly when the general and administrative side is flyspecked to death? Third, what's my time and resource allocation look like, and how do I justify using my workforce and time in ways that aren't directly related to products, services and sales? Fourth, can what I'm investing in truly be co-owned by business units?

When the pathway to answering these and many more questions moves through a linear approach, you can advance the critical work-streams for your company that lead to C-Spark ignition. Having established that SEE is a strategic tool that meaningfully impacts revenue and profitability, evolution and relevance, talent attraction and retention, social impact, DE&I and the brand, it's time to drill down and align your priorities and SEE. It's time to clearly articulate how workforce learning will advance each priority.

Importantly, there are expectations on you if the process is to be successful. To do it well, there has to be leadership, presence, interactivity and engagement from you, dear CEO. You hold the strategic priorities and are The Master of your business at scale. You understand your workforce and its context. Now, through SEE, you will take a once amorphous concept of workforce education and up-level it to tangibly advance your company and solve its problems.

This begins with aligning the strategic priorities and strategic workforce education by translating those components into SEE objectives. From the outset, it is important to note that this translation must not be governed by an outside context. It's your context, and you must always stick to your language, your vernacular and your workforce and render the whole of SEE into your environment — not the other way around, which has proven a pitfall with legacy work-force-learning modalities.

Next, taking those objectives, you analyze and develop SEE's scope, including its learning pathways linked to career pathways and ultimately tied to a budget. Finally, your approach to SEE is mapped to ROI. That ROI correlates to your corporate priorities, and as you'll witness, companies leveraging SEE begin accessing its benefits quickly. With this process in mind, let's unfold the process in action with some companies that have taken this approach.

Translating Strategic Priorities into SEE Objectives

This phase is best initiated through a CEO-led conversation with senior leadership and critical stakeholders companywide. Here, strategic priorities are identified and articulated, and then a SEE objective set is rendered in a co-creative process. It's a process best reflected through real-world examples across industries. It's worth mentioning, here, that this is driven by you, dear CEO.

With this in mind, let's dip our toe into some of your industries and examine a few strategic priorities tied to larger opportunities and concerns you face in the immediate future. This exercise will enable you to appreciate the extent to which SEE can serve as the core of your flywheel even as you begin to understand the common workforce issues plaguing a host of vertical markets across the board.

If you're a telecommunications CEO, you know that as you attempt to recruit and retain talent for frontline opportunities, there is a perception hampering the industry: these types of jobs don't lead to careers. This fact directly affects the number and quality of candidates you're able to attract, thereby inhibiting growth, widening the skills gap, leading to seasonal hires for skilled positions and rendering a lean talent pool for high-liability positions. This issue is magnified by a lack of standardization in skills, pay and credentialing across the industry (read: AT&T, Comcast, T-Mobile, Verizon and other major players) at a time when upskilling is necessary. COVID-19 created a massive and thorough demand for more broadband connectivity even as 5G's rollout was initiated. That means you also need qualified 5G broadband technicians. They don't really exist at scale. If you engage in SEE, you can cut through these challenges, offering pathways to differentiation in recruiting and a tool for retention. You can also stack necessary training programs for upskilling and, in the case of 5G, quickly anticipate the educational requirements for hiring unskilled technicians and training them up efficiently and effectively.

For those of you helming a retail operation, you need a frontline workforce that can drive revenue growth and customer loyalty through top-flight customer service. You know first hand what the data bear out: only 34% of frontline retail employees are engaged.

If you cross borders into the global marketplace, that number decreases to 15%. So, while your frontline is very literally the brand's front line, it's more important than ever to make sure your workforce is locked in, living the brand and remaining enthusiastic on the job. That's because if they are, you're more likely to wow and cultivate repeat customers while reducing customer defections. PwC illuminated this fact, finding that 80% of customers see friendly services as a key element in a positive shopping experience. As you're aware, repeat customers have up to three times higher conversion rates in-store. And if you can decrease defections by just 5%, you can increase profitability by more than 25%. Vying for a tie with engagement is attrition among your frontline management. All would be well if you could develop a skilled pipeline of erosion-proof frontline leadership. They're struggling, though, and 80% of them cite high employee turnover and understaffed stores as critical issues as they seek to reach sales goals. On top of the front line sits your supply chain and reshoring. If you can get them in order, then you stand to increase market share at a time when 90% of growth will come from directly engaging with customers and meeting their needs on demand. In this quest, your warehouse workers are of priority: they account for 1.25 million employees nationally, which is not only higher than levels before the pandemic began — it's the highest level ever recorded. Your immersion in SEE has the ability to transform employee engagement, create leadership career pathways and enable nimbleness and knowledge growth throughout the supply chain to stem the tide and ride it.

Food production and consumer packaged goods CEOs, you are feeling retail's frontline pain. One out of every six Americans has a food production and distribution job, and 90% of those positions are considered frontline. Competition is now as fierce as in the early part of 2021 alone, and there is a 55% increase in frontline job openings. It's a recruiting challenge you're balancing alongside a newfound reliance on technology to meet customer demands. Importantly, though, these can't be "automated away." This recruiting challenge and reliance on technology create an agility challenge: by 2026, one in three of your frontline job roles will require upskilling, and humans in these automated contexts will need a basic understanding of technology and supply chain management. Foodprocessing.org found that nearly all frontline jobs will require upskilling to meet industry demands by 2026. And while frontline posts have not historically required college degrees, increasingly, they will require a more robust skill set. Workers and consumers expect you to hold high integrity in the arena of corporate citizenship, including wages, environmental sustainability, DE&I and boosting the rural communities that form the backbone of your operation. Your use of SEE as a strategic tool forms the core of a flywheel to ensure progress, growth and meeting customers at their point of pain and desire in complex ways.

If you're a tech CEO, you know you are dealing with a demand for talent that is outstripping supply. You also know that it costs six times more to hire externally than nurture and promote from within. It's a challenge amplified by vertical industries hiring out of tech to lead and manage digital transformation efforts. As you bleed talent, upskilling is the predominant phrase across the board in tech, and retaining employees will be cheaper and more effective than hiring new ones. Depending on your firm's age, brand and talent issues, it will mean different challenges. If you're a Silicon Valley leader such as Apple, Google or Microsoft, it's a matter of retaining your most valuable employees across the board. Developers, yes, and also customer service operations and the like. For technology's old guard such as IBM, HP and Honeywell, it means finding the opening to once again be relevant to a developer or designer who has the choice between you or Google. Also? You have a real diversity problem. Only 26% of your workforce is made up of women, and only 17% by people of color. By owning SEE, you can attack these issues across your priority set with speed and deep impact.

Industrial CEOs, you may have heard about the three Ds: dark, dirty and dangerous. They compose an erroneous perception about your industry inhibiting recruiting efforts among Generation Y and Z, and in fact, 70% of you are finding recruiting from these generations a painful, uphill battle. It's one you're waging even as you're experiencing on-site "brain drain." Among your skilled talent, 30% are near retirement age and 100% of them are inside the tornado of digital transformation, all of which is creating a skills gap. On top of these issues sit Industry 4.0 technologies and digital fluencies, and three in five of you will be investing in at least one 4.0 innovation, ranging from additive manufacturing and 3D printing to robotics and AI, within the next few years. Current technology skills will be obsolete within four years. A third of you say this is making top talent hard to find. Stunningly, while 70% of your workforce say their leadership skills are not being developed, 90% of you believe that developing those skills while undertaking succession planning are keys to your future. In the meantime, on the business impact side, 20% of quality losses can be attributed to lack of employee skills. In your case, leveraging SEE can transform your workforce and how it will operate for years to come throughout your priorities of value.

Among healthcare CEOs, the nursing crisis has only become worse through COVID-19. Turnover rates are 17%, and each departing nurse costs you between $40,000 and nearly $65,000. More than 200,000 nurses are needed annually, nationwide, and that need will increase by 28% by 2028. It's chaos complicated by a need for upskilling across emergent digital technologies. During COVID-19, telehealth usage rose by 42%, and training for this and other digital capabilities is a top priority for nearly 30% of you. Upwards of 80% of you are feeling the supply chain and reshoring shift, too. Leading your company on a SEE-focused journey is ideal in the effort to ensure you can hire, keep and advance your nursing and supply chain professionals in ways that move beyond a triage. It can heal this gaping workforce wound.

Financial services CEOs? You're undergoing a fintech renaissance that is disrupting your entire industry, to the tune of more than 25,000 startups as of the first quarter of 2021 and coming off a year that totaled more than $105 billion in investments throughout the sector. This renaissance is forcing more than 75% of you to invest in your IT roles, rethink your "frontline" roles and equip your customer-facing staff to match evolving business and customer expectations. For example, there has been a 120% growth in digital banking and a 50% growth in retail banking digital sales, which is creating a new focus at branches and financial centers: offering hyper-personalized services with customer's financial well-being as the foundation of customer experience, value and loyalty. All the while, robo-advisors are growing at a tick rate of more than 20% per year, and that's driving an upskilling renaissance among human wealth managers who are doubling down on their skill, agility, attentiveness and the return they deliver using an array of physical access and digital technologies. You can use SEE as a critical harmonizer between automation and human talent that can ensure you get the best of both worlds.

Notice the common thread of talent that runs through each industry snapshot. Jason Baumgarten, partner, CEO and board practice at Spencer Stuart, believes that talent crosses a company's strategic priorities and that you must have a thoroughgoing talent strategy around which strategic workforce education is wrapped:

> [SEE] needs to be part of your holistic talent strategy. And if you don't have a talent strategy, it's a good motivator to create one. And so, I think it's critical for CEOs to think about what is their talent strategy and how does workforce education play a central role and in what way does it play? Again, is the main lever to create an incredible employer brand? Is it to drive engagement? Is it to drive retention, or do you have a long-term performance orientation where you're going to invest over a long period in people so that they do become the very best employees through education? In every case, don't do it indiscriminately. Don't have a poster and program strategy when it comes to talent. Have a real strategy.

With this in mind, let's follow two Fortune 500 companies as they leverage SEE to unleash their respective, colinear flywheels.

A centuries-old multinational financial services company identified two critical strategic priorities: recruitment and retention, and DE&I. The company had tried and failed to leverage legacy workforce-education modalities (the fire horses) in an attempt to expand recruitment, retention and growth of top talent across very specific business units, including customer care, risk and governance, and data science. They were also aggressively working to accelerate diversity, equity and inclusion and had even formed a relationship with a regional jobs council to help make that happen. It was not enough. In this case, objective translation was swift. First, SEE would address recruitment, retention and employee growth. Second, it would forge the company's first real, systemic approach to fulfilling the company's DE&I objectives.

A major retail grocery chain operating in most states sought to leverage SEE as a major force in strengthening both sides of its brand coin: externally, it wanted its in-store employees to match its brand promise that was centered on vibrance, hospitality and food quality. Internally, it was set on building an opportunity culture where people recognized, understood and pursued both a career and innovation within their roles at the company. In both cases, it sought to scale this across its thousands of stores. The retailer's objectives proved more complex. SEE would enable the scaling of workforce education opportunities throughout the enterprise. It would establish a brand-consistent learner experience that would reinforce the external brand and internal culture. Finally, it would gear learning opportunities for retention, advancement and entrepreneurial risk-taking.

In both of these instances, CEOs and senior leadership were able to recognize and articulate specific strategic priorities through which a SEE-oriented approach could prove powerful. SEE alignment was then ferreted out and articulated with CEO oversight. Both of these discussions lead to the next stage of strategic energy: establishing the approach for fast-tracking ROI across the objective sets.

Workforce Targeting: Who Learns What, When

Once strategic alignment is secured, you then evaluate who within your workforce should access SEE. It's an exercise marked by several precision-based assessments. It begins by targeting SEE within your enterprise and initiates several questions. Based on the required capabilities and skill sets, what type of learning landscape do you need to activate to most efficiently meet your SEE objectives? How about learners? Who among your business units needs SEE? What's the total number of learners who need to be served to fulfill the objectives? This inventory will directly impact how and how quickly you are able to ramp up the opportunity.

Concurrent with the breakdown of learners is the integration of SEE with career pathways. Through this step, learning will be directly linked to career growth, and an *Age of And* micro-threshold has been crossed — the destiny of the worker *And* the destiny of the company are now allied. Corporate growth and social impact are uniting. Let's revisit our two cases to see how this played out.

With the financial services multinational, a detailed breakdown of key functions within the organization in need of recruitment, retention, job growth and DE&I was identified. The functions included business development, customer engagement, leadership and engineering/IT. Specific skills were matched to each function in detail. For example, business development's skill sets included business analytics, corporate finance and negotiation. Customer engagement emphasized skills such as interpersonal communications, personal finance planning, building teams that work and reskilling in analytics and tech. Leadership focused on principles of leadership, modern leadership and organizational culture and diversity. Engineering/IT requirements included Lean Six Sigma Black Belt certification, Python fluency and leadership for digital transformation.

Once identified, skills were directly linked back to career pathways for the individuals involved. Career pathways were then matched to learning pathways tailored to specific learners with specific needs. Some learners required short courses in the form of certificates and continuing education. Others required bachelor's and master's degrees.

In the case of the grocer, the same process played out. This time, the functions included store managers, skilling up in logistics management, data analysis, retail and customer service, emotional intelligence, operations management and written and verbal communication. Retail clerks focused on merchandising, sales, customer service, product expertise, interpersonal communications and attention to detail. Distribution center supervisors centered development around logistics, people and process management, organizational skills and problem-solving. Distribution center handlers concentrated on quality assurance, mechanical tools, inventory management, logistics and operations basics and key concepts tied to measurement and math. Learning pathways for the grocery's workforce matched these career pathway skills to bachelor's and master's degree programs.

In both cases, determinations were also made in terms of learning pathway sequencing. It included decisions around nonlinear and linear sequencing of courses. With a scope and budget in hand, it's time to intentionally discuss and establish what ROI looks and feels like once you ignite the C-Spark.

Setting the Baseline ROI

In case you've skipped ahead to this chapter prior to reading any of Part I, workforce education's problematic legacy rests on its notoriously low return on investment. To review, corporations spend $180 billion per year on learning programs while less than 2% of the workforce actually accesses the tuition assistance offered. Abysmal. That's largely the result of a lack of oversight or accountability at the intersection of outcomes. As an aside, InStride once facilitated a dialogue with an executive leading a major cellular network provider's tuition assistance program. The person waxed eloquent about the company's tuition assistance program, which included proclamations around transformation, industry disruption and impact. In the end, an InStride executive asked about ROI. The person said, "That's not my job. You'd have to talk to someone else about that." Accountability and outcomes are critical to measuring SEE ROI, and it's the lifeblood of InStride, where it is clear, comprehensive and tangible. As with InStride, you should use a simple formula that both of the companies we've been following have put in play — the annual cost per learner measured against the estimated value per learner. The cost per learner is straightforward — it factors the cost of the degree, the course set and tuition while factoring in deductible expenses along the way. The estimated value per learner is a set of dollar amounts that illustrates the value of the educated worker against the strategic priority SEE is fulfilling.

For the financial services multinational, the learning pathways included short courses in the form of certificate and professional development learning opportunities. The pathways also featured undergraduate and graduate degree programs. The total weighted average per learner cost across the selected functions of the enterprise averaged between $5,000 and $7,000.

On the learner value side, retention and DE&I were broken into separate strategic value centers that included the value of keeping an employee, the value of employing a culturally- and career-engaged employee and the value of skill-building across the board. Let's break these down.

With regard to the value of retaining the employee, the multinational established an equation based on average worker salary. In this case, $100,000. It costs approximately 40 to 50% of the average annual salary to replace an employee or $40,000 to $50,000. The company multiplied the cost to replace an employee by the company's 20% annual turnover rate. For this subsegment of the strategic priority, the per learner value of retaining an employee was $8,000 to $10,000. The same exercise was repeated for values tied to culturally engaged and career-engaged employees and the value of skill building. Totaled, the average value per learner sat between $12,000 and $17,000. The estimated time for realizing ROI was within one year.

The grocer measured its external and internal brand-focused outcomes into retention and cultural engagement value. Again, the cost per employee in that context was roughly $4,000 to $6,000 per employee. Per employee, value rested between $9,750 and more than $10,750. Payback was set to begin within the same year of implementation.

SEE was able to deliver two times ROI within a year at this level. And it's just the start. It does not factor in new opportunities opened up by your workforce or the value of partnering with institutions of learning that truly grasp SEE and tailor their work to your needs and trajectory for a long-haul relationship.

The rigor applied through this SEE alignment process also pays off immediately. By leading this process, you are vested in the case you need to make to your board members, engaging them in necessary and fruitful dialogue. To reiterate, it is you who must sell this to and mobilize your board members. If you are the bridge between your public and internal corporate face, they are your gatekeepers in both directions. And it should go well, offering you a TED Talk moment wherein you succinctly lay out the workforce challenge and then back it with your plan of attack: lighting the C-Spark and ushering in the *Age of And*.

Yet that's not the only sell. Revisiting the Mark Fields question set, you also need to signal your drive and commitment to your business units in a way consistent with your organizational culture. Your business units need to understand that workforce education has risen to become, and will now be embedded as, a tool for organizational growth and impact in the hands of the future CEO that you will pass on to them.

In doing so, Chuck Rubin, former chair and CEO, Michaels, believes you, dear CEO, should plan the rollout of a strategic workforce education program to create winning momentum within the organization:

> CEOs have to submit to the discipline of thinking through which part of the organization will most benefit from this so they can get a couple of wins. Then, when they want to go broader, they can hold those wins up as success stories for the rest of the organization, because not everybody in the organization will believe that this is a good investment. To do this well, they have to be personally engaged from the start.

Greenlighted, funded, supported and empowered, you are ready to take the next step toward C-Spark ignition: becoming conversant in why a dynamic core of high-quality institutions is critical to realizing the potency derived from the groundwork you've laid here. Unsurprisingly, you must drive that selection process, too. For, like The Master of *Midnight Diner*, the magic and change he makes is only as effective as the quality of the ingredients he selects.

Chapter 7

Academic Partnerships:
Fuel for the *Age of And*

In America, tangible rites of passage are few. There may be religious milestones in a community of faith. There is the driver's license in the mid-teen years. At 18, voting is a threshold. At 21, many celebrate legal adulthood. For most reading this book, you were privileged to have most of these events occur while on a traditional college campus. It is here where an unspoken four- to five-year rite unfolded — where you extracted yourself from your family and your village, hurdling into a wilderness of near or total autonomy. Time was suddenly your own. You learned to live with people. Your destiny was never more in your hands.

If it was a great experience, you might be reminded of its place in your life every late summer. The sky turns a Kodachrome amber. Football season kicks off against a backdrop of autumn leaves. You summon an image of that joyous first week of class. There were friends you may not have seen since spring and activities in every direction. You can call forth the scents and sounds wafting from your residence hall. Maybe you have a seminal moment of joining a fraternity, sorority or honor society. Perhaps you played intercollegiate athletics, a full-time job all its own. Your college or university campus was a nexus of life present and life in the future, wrapped in possibility, excitement, romance, unpredictability and, if you took the academic side seriously, a tinge of pressure and fear. You probably mined rich veins of mentorship and networking that sparked something inside you and led to a career path — or gave you entry to a gap year in Europe, two years of waiting tables, a couple of false starts here and then a career path.

The question is, do you remember how you got there? Do you remember the reams of paper that hit your family mailbox or the digital "lookbooks" that inundated your email inbox? Discussions with your guidance counselors and maybe even teachers about the right move? The conversations and travels embarked upon with your parents to find the school of choice? Then when you gained acceptance at an institution either for its academics or its loyal spot in your heart, do you remember wearing your school colors with pride and a newfound sense of identity? Or you went to a "Plan B" school that ended up being just right for your journey?

Fast-forward 20 or 30 years, and many of you have moved through this same experience with your offspring. You have diligently stewarded your children through their pre-K-12 education. You've driven them everywhere. You've coaxed them and encouraged them through service organizations, academic preparation, athletic programs, clubs, a labyrinth of standardized tests, and all of it to ensure they have the GPA, the AP class credits, the essay writing ability and the intangibles to punch their own ticket.

You've sought that unique destination for them based on your battery of prerequisites. Quality is usually queen. Alongside it rest the number and diversity of majors. Outcomes play into the decision-making, too: will your children have the gateway to internships, cooperatives and graduate institutions of their choice once they've secured a bachelor's degree? Can they study abroad and gain the experiences they want and need? What about the vibe of the school: is it a right fit for your son or daughter?

Then you visit the schools. Are they safe? Does the feel of the campus match your kid's personality? How do the culture and the student population feel in relationship to your child's direction? Will it cultivate a sense of possibility and kindle their scholarship? Bring out the best in them? Help them blossom and set them on their way to a life and career path that will bring them joy, fulfillment and prosperity?

If college can stir such a felt sense of nostalgia, richness and passion in you, and if you were so incredibly persistent and diligent in ensuring your children had a shot at seizing that same experience for themselves, what of your workforce and the generations that follow them?

> *Why wouldn't you, as a CEO, exact this same level of due diligence for the people who drive your organization forward and ensure you hit your strategic objectives all year, every year?*

It can be a vision-altering aha moment when you see the power you hold in the lives of the people in your workforce. With your strategy, budget and scope in hand, you are ready to understand how you go about setting up partnerships with leading global academic institutions to establish the right learning and career pathways for your workforce. You must explore this topic through the lens of your company and think about approaching this vital process with care, diligence and the same sense of possibility, excitement and anticipation that you had as a budding undergraduate and possibly as a parent of an undergraduate.

As a prelude, let's acknowledge that your workforce will require a different framework than you or your children. College football, study abroad opportunities, a vibrant campus vibe and learning how to live as an autonomous adult may be important to some of your workforce learners but are probably not essential for most. The majority are at a different stage in their lives. They have partners, families and an entire life functioning in cooperation with and outside of their careers. They have different needs.

InStride's Chief University Officer Michelle Westfort was among that majority when she pursued an employer-sponsored global management program for executives at a well-known and respected business school in Asia. Highly motivated in her career and the learning opportunity extended to her, she, in retrospect, identified three key elements that highlight the different needs of workforce learners and how, through that experience, those needs went unmet. During her course of study, Michelle found that while she could do as much learning herself through textbooks, online and in engagement with a cohort of individuals, she realized that her learning needed to more thoroughly connect to what her employer sought from her. It did not. That same learning path required a more direct link to the new skills she needed. It did not. Finally, she needed her employer to be more in touch with her learning experience at the intersection of her career, offering her an opportunity to practice on the job. They were not. At work, she was on a team involved in mergers and acquisitions and wanted to flex her newfound financial knowledge base, plying it toward valuating corporations — something which at that time in her career she had not done — and it never happened.

Adding to Michelle's trio of needs was an on-campus requirement, meaning she had to leave the States and head to Asia for a block of time. Perhaps many of you reading this can empathize with Michelle, a parent, putting long hours on the job and in the classroom and then, due to the on-site requirement, missing her daughter's kindergarten graduation and instead, joining her through Facetime halfway around the world. In Michelle's case, even with the most well-intentioned and resourced company partnering with a leading institution to facilitate substantive learning, there were significant gaps in her experience that left her wanting and frustrated. As you embark upon this stage of the C-Spark build, accounting for needs like Michelle's is make-or-break as you select and form a relationship with partner institutions. They must meet you in your bespoke quest and collaborate to carefully match their dynamic core of knowledge to a learning path seamlessly linked to a career path.

With that in mind, you must evaluate, vet and assemble your network of academic partners across four imperatives. You should deploy this same set of criteria as you build alliances en route to igniting the C-Spark. First, ensure that your partners have the depth and breadth of high-quality programs to meet the learner where he or she is. Without this level of diversity and excellence, you will fail before you begin. Next, match the academic footprint with the geographic footprint of your corporation. There are myriad reasons why this ultimately proves so essential. Furthermore, validate that your network of academic partners carries proven credentials in, and demonstrates a mindset and orientation around, life-changing outcomes for your learners and flywheel-activating results for your company. The C-Spark is not about enrollment. It is about graduation and a meaningful new skill set. It's about career advancement. Finally, pursue partners with the strategic potential to grow beyond the initial relationship, flourish and offer a dynamic, two-way connection that enables both of you to bring a range of value-added services to one another. It equips you to unlock the *Age of And* in ways that impact how you shape strategy for the long haul and establishes the C-Spark as a flame that continually intensifies as it matures.

Ensuring Depth and Breadth of High-Quality Online Programs

In the trenches, you must size up education partners beyond their reputation by paying close attention to breadth, depth and true quality of their online programs. Do the online experience and the quality of learner engagement match the institution's well-regarded in-person offering? In other words, can a student interact with content, peers and instructors through a thoughtfully built ecosystem that delivers an environment as rich or richer than in-person learning? Does the online experience balance self-paced learning with the right live interactions at the right time? Does it marry an elegance of look and feel accounting for both cinematography and crystalline audio? Does it harmonize listening and engagement in ways that avoid simply spewing content at a learner? If these elements are in play, the experience will engineer a synergy among students, the faculty and the individual learner, which is fundamentally different — yet equal in quality to — in-person instruction. If these elements augment learning with student services such as success coaching and tutoring, the online experience will ensure a workforce transformed.

Building on learner experience, your prospective partner should also be able to clearly and effortlessly articulate how its offerings will match the outcomes you seek. Specifically, that partner must be able to demonstrate how its offerings meet the workforce learning and career pathways you've developed within your strategic alignment exercise. It should also present use cases that show high completion rates and how those rates translate to higher career success levels. Such comprehensive vetting ensures your workforce will receive a life-changing opportunity that will concurrently drive flywheel velocity.

At InStride, these first-level essentials lead to another consideration: quality. Quality starts with reputation. Accordingly, you should seek institutions that are proven world leaders in discovery and innovation while balancing programming designed with intentionality and sophistication for learners to pursue their intellectual curiosities. The institutions' offerings should consist of online programs and degrees developed for adult learners by learning scientists, instructional designers and media specialists. Quality can also be measured by a much simpler yardstick. As you evaluate a partner, do you believe your workforce will want to log on and go to class? It's instinctual, and it should feel aligned with your brand values. If you can say yes when correlating the offering to your own corporate culture and strategic focus, you are on the right track.

Examples of partnerships from InStride's network include Arizona State University, ranked first in innovation for six years in a row and sixth in online learning by *U.S. News & World Report*, the City University of New York School of Professional Studies (ranked eighth in online), the University of Wisconsin-Madison (ranked 13th among public universities) and the University of Virginia (ranked second on *Money's* Best Value Public University rankings). InStride has also added the University of Memphis, ranked in the top tier for U.S. public universities by *U.S. News & World Report*, with their online bachelor's degree programs and four graduate programs ranked among the best in the nation.

Depth and breadth also translate to geography, and therefore InStride's network also includes Top 100 global institutions such as the Dublin City University (Ireland) and Universidad Tecmilenio (Mexico). These schools are committed to and recognized for their research, interest in the public good, excellence and impact and exponential returns linked to employability and outcomes.

As you develop your partnership network, emphasize diversity of programming at every turn. InStride has put a premium on breadth and diversity through its partnership strategy. It pairs 250+ degree programs (high school, undergraduate, masters and doctoral) with shorter and equally well-designed certificates and credentials. It has amassed more than 1,700 learning options that meet learners where they are in their career journey. Why? To reiterate, you're dealing with the most educationally diverse workforce in history. At InStride, this is accounted for by designating a path to every workforce member, no matter where they are in their learning journey or how easily matched to their career journey, while giving learners at any level the resources they need to complete their education.

With quality assured, depth and breadth are imperative for successful outcomes. Harken back to your own experience in selecting a college for yourself or your child. You attuned your ear to the number of program options and the support structures to match those options that could give you the best chance at success. Depth and breadth lead to the second imperative.

Matching the Geographic Footprint of Your Academic Network to Your Corporate Footprint

Even though an institutional partner is 100% online, its geography still matters because it matters to your workforce. A chief learning officer at a large and influential financial services company put it this way in an InStride/Bain & Company proprietary workforce education survey:

> Geographic proximity, when it comes to [institutional partner] selection, is more about community relationships and local affinity more than anything else. [We have a] call center in Columbus, Ohio, so it would've felt great for those employees to go get a degree at Ohio State University. We also made sure to reach out to the University of Illinois in order to show deference to the local public university in the area where our headquarters was located, partly for relationship reasons.

In this single quote, read the strategic priorities between the lines. The company strives to ensure access to education from a local school. Buckeyes want to be Buckeyes. Illini want to be Illini. In Big 10 country, it's not trivial, and it maps directly to social impact and brand-focused cultural priorities driving the company's decisions. Additionally, there are revenue and profit sub-motivations at work, too, as the chief learning officer describes the relationship implications of selecting a partner.

Match that statement to a public one made by FedEx as it launched its strategic workforce education program called Learning Inspired by FedEx (LiFE). When it launched, Barbara Wallander, FedEx senior vice president of human resources, discussed how:

> FedEx is excited to be working with the University of Memphis to offer our team members at the Memphis World Hub the opportunity to earn a tuition-free degree. We expect the program to make a difference in the lives of our team members, and we remain deeply committed to supporting our community here in our hometown of Memphis.

Here, social impact once more rises to the fore, backed by the internal strategic motivations that led FedEx to offer degrees in the first place: employee retention.

A Wiley/Learning House survey further validates these assertions, finding that among working adults, "two-thirds of learners stay close to home" — choosing a college or university within 50 miles of where they live. In fact, 44% selected a school within 25 miles of their homes. And the share of students enrolling in a school more than 100 miles from home fell from 37% in 2014 to 15% in 2019. When correlated to a *Chronicle of Higher Education* study that found more than 30% of traditional freshmen stayed within 50 miles of home to attend school, a larger point emerges. No matter when they begin school, U.S. learners tend to prefer local institutions, and it should figure into how you map institutional partnerships to your geographic footprint.

When your business crosses borders the opposite is true. Geography matters here because workers abroad often seek educational opportunities at U.S. universities. A major diagnostic corporation's CEO framed it this way:

> [We] believe that accessible education is incredibly important to our employees. Especially for international employees, the ability to pursue and receive degrees from U.S.-based universities makes us an employer of choice in some of the countries where we do business. Most of our international employees are in the drug development and diagnostics fields, which already require a degree. When a company invests in helping their employees achieve additional education, it separates them from other employers in the market.

As you remember this fact, also remain sensitive to the region in question. A country-by-country or region-focused (read: EU, Asia/Pacific) approach to partnerships is needed. In doing so, realize that your learning network will need to be positioned thoughtfully with an eye toward different cultures, languages, national requirements and skill sets.

Ensuring Partners Drive Transformative Outcomes

Amazingly, traditional workforce-education modalities see enrollment as a critical metric of success. In SEE, only results count. Therefore, SEE's impact on your workforce and on your strategic priorities is the true measure. You need partners who share that same sensibility and have proven they can deliver on that front.

Among InStride's array of partners, Arizona State University offers a prime example of this orientation. ASU's enrollment is at nearly

100,000 and represents a globally diverse, multigenerational student body. The quality of its research is recognized worldwide even as it has modeled innovation and agility. Much of this is by design. ASU President Michael Crow tested eight interrelated yet independent design aspirations to find which ones most inspired creativity, sparked innovation and fostered institutional individuation. These aspirations "represent ideals for institutional culture as well as strategic approaches to accomplishing [the university's] goals and objectives."

The aspirations call for a different kind of academic community — one that is agile and proactive enough to respond to the whole of the communities it inhabits. One that seeks to be invested in knowledge entrepreneurship for the sake of societal transformation. One that can demonstrate tangible difference-making at the intersection of corporate America, while advancing global engagement. One that can be a true a partner in the *Age of And*.

Phil Regier, university dean for educational initiatives and CEO EdPlus, ASU, offers the rationale for this level of specificity when it comes to pursuing educational partners:

> There is an advantage of a great university. [There, your work-force learners are] going to encounter and be exposed to and begin to understand what a learning exploration journey is. And they'll understand what it means to learn and how to learn. This isn't about absorbing content and taking a test and moving on to the next class. This is about living in the 21st century and becoming a flexible and adaptable learner. Researchers model this, and great universities place them at the core. In turn, they are constantly expanding knowledge

and exploring new dimensions, whether it is at the sub-microscopic level or whether it's on Mars or whether it is under the ocean or whether it is in the human psyche.

When ASU engages with the corporate world, it looks at human capital as an asset that should be cultivated and improved as much as financial capital. In turn, ASU offers what Crow describes as the "empowerment of a learner," not the "training of the worker." Crow says that training a worker provides a narrow window — addressing a small aspect — of that worker's performance. Crow said:

> This is true if you're running a chain of convenience stores, a restaurant, a railroad or a healthcare company. Take healthcare. If you have a company wherein you could get everyone to understand biology up to a certain level in a healthcare organization, you could alter the performance and innovative nature of that organization because you wouldn't just have doctors and a few key nurses innovating, and you would no longer have to buy innovators at top dollar from some other company. You'd be producing your own innovations because you would have a more thoroughly innovative workforce.

Your next question might be, can we take visionary thinking such as Crow's and match our strategic priorities and outcomes on a timeline consistent with our need for transformation? In its work with Starbucks, Adidas, the United States Air Force and others, ASU has done just that and copiously recorded the outcomes matched to third-party data. Learners experience between a 12% and 21% lifetime rate of return on the degrees they earn from ASU. A Gallup Poll found that nearly half of employed ASU graduates are engaged at work versus 39% of college graduates nationally. Regardless of graduation cohort, they are also more likely to be engaged in their work than graduates of other large public universities. Alongside worker transformation sit the companies themselves, meeting and exceeding goals set through their strategic priorities in alignment with a SEE approach.

ASU is just one example of an InStride institutional partner who carries a vision for how the university can deliver real value and offer outcomes to the exacting standards you should have for your company.

Pursuing Partners with the Strategic Potential to Grow Beyond an Initial Relationship

Your partnerships aren't one-and-done or tactically focused engagements. Strategic workforce education at its best is not a transaction tied to simple inputs and outputs. Instead, it's focused on leveraging workforce education as a strategic tool of enduring value. Likewise, you must seek out partners that will serve as strategic collaborators for the long haul and with whom you can mutually build a value-added relationship. In essence, it's no different than other strategic partnerships and alliances you develop across your go-to-market strategy. It ultimately takes the C-Spark's intent and develops a powerful, smooth-running engine reliably built for long-haul innovation that can benefit you across your evolving priorities within the *Age of And*.

It can begin simply. A strategic partnership might grow through simple program expansion. The City University of New York School of Professional Studies and JetBlue expanded an initial partnership dubbed the JetBlue Scholars program, wherein the airline offered crew members an undergraduate education. In its next-level partnership, JetBlue and CUNY partnered on a master's degree program offering. The new program under JetBlue Scholars, known as Master's Pathways, followed a direct request from employees for the option of graduate study.

Similarly, and within the government sector, the University of Virginia has continually expanded its partnership with the U.S. Navy. It most recently developed a course set giving Navy personnel, most of whom come at their work from a military-based context, a window into the culture, motivations and best practices of private industry. In particular, the Navy sought to develop fluency among its force in "cash flow, profit, risk and contribution margin in industry decisions, and to predict how the industry will react to government proposals allowing them to structure proposals for favorable outcomes to government."

The University of Pennsylvania (Penn) has also formed innovation-based partnerships with Pfizer and Intel. With Pfizer, the collaboration centers on areas of scientific research, clinical development and clinical care and policy. Martin Mackay, president, Pfizer Global Research and Development, said:

[This gives us an] opportunity to build and implement a new model for interactions between industry and academic medical centers. We are pleased to have such a distinguished partner in this venture, which could provide a powerful example for how we will work together to improve outcomes in research and clinical development and, most importantly, in the lives of the patients we all serve.

With Intel Labs, Penn's Perelman School of Medicine is co-developing technology to enable a federation of 29 international healthcare and research institutions led by Penn Medicine to train AI models that identify brain tumors using a privacy-preserving technique called federated learning.

"AI shows great promise for the early detection of brain tumors, but it will require more data than any single medical center holds to reach its full potential," said Jason Martin, principal engineer, Intel Labs.

Aldevron, a biotech company that supplies the raw materials for breakthrough therapies, expanded an initial partnership by establishing a physical lab facility on the University of Wisconsin-Madison campus. It gained access to the real estate and research personnel it needed to expand its capabilities in gene editing and specific enzyme development, both of which are integral to expanding its profitability and revenue. The University of Wisconsin is also working in partnership with clothing and gear retailers Lands' End and Oshkosh, both of which opened up offices in Madison, to collaborate on digital change throughout their industry. Additionally, UW–Madison students worked with JARP, the forestry, mining and defense hydraulics manufacturer, to boost output.

At its pinnacle, SEE literally becomes a way of seeing. Starbucks, once it realized that ASU could deliver on the SCAP program, began looking to ASU as "its" university and a core strategic partner — a $4 billion knowledge enterprise that could deliver a host of cost-effective solutions tied to corporate strategy.

The two entities collaborated on developing the Starbucks Technology Center in Scottsdale, Arizona, which gives university technology students the chance to intern at the intersection of the company's technology roadmap disciplines such as information security, application development and business intelligence. ASU also trained 30,000 Starbucks partners in sustainability.

Most important, when Starbucks was in crisis, ASU immediately explored how it could offer a time-critical solution. In 2018, a Starbucks location in Philadelphia refused two Black men entry to one of its bathrooms and called the police to intervene. It turns out, both men were waiting at the Starbucks for a friend. Nonetheless, the men were arrested. The video went viral. The backlash was swift, and negative media coverage and public outrage ensued. Starbucks acted quickly. It opened its restrooms to all, reversing a policy that required individuals to make an in-store purchase. It closed its stores for initial anti-bias training. Then, it turned to ASU. Activating its renowned President's Professor of Indigenous Education and Justice Brian Brayboy, the university set about to fast-track an anti-bias training program. Brayboy gathered other leading-edge scholars grounded in systemic bias to develop a 30-part, 15-module curricula titled "To Be Welcoming." Because it had a university partner, Starbucks was able to execute on this in a matter of months — not years — and trained all of its partners through the program. When the social unrest of 2020 reached its most intense points, Starbucks offered that training, free of charge, to the general public.

"When this happened, they didn't even have to think about where they would go next," said ASU's Regier. "They just turned to us."

The two entities have also launched their most ambitious project yet — the ASU-Starbucks Center for the Future of People and the Planet — a research and rapid innovation facility combined with an on-campus, nine-store Starbucks ecosystem geared toward finding new ways to design, build and operate Starbucks stores. It will serve much like Starbuck's Tryer Center, the company's incubation lab where partners quickly test, learn and adapt ideas for more rapid decision-making. Michael Crow, president, ASU, said:

> ASU and Starbucks are aligned in our missions to be of complete service to the communities we serve and build a better future for both people and the planet. Through this new center, ASU will provide unique value in terms of research and trans-disciplinary expertise in order to collaborate with Starbucks to develop, test and validate strategies that can ultimately be scaled to stores and communities globally.

Once you've ignited the C-Spark, partnership is the engine that powers the *Age of And*. It sets the tone for how SEE is integrated into your organization as a strategic tool. Vetting partners is serious business requiring that you — and this means you, dear CEO, as the surrogate parent for those workers whom you seek to activate your colinear flywheel — find a collaborator set who can take what you've developed strategically and deliver high-quality learning experiences that produce change and impact.

Your head might be spinning at the thought of taking this on. Steve Ellis, managing partner at TPG, understands your potential feelings of being overwhelmed and feels your pain. In the wake of the Great Recession and while a managing partner at Bain & Company, he sought a global partner in Bain's quest to do well by doing good, that *Age of And* cornerstone. For Ellis, the key was finding a partnership of fit, ease and growth:

First, we had to make this initiative a cornerstone and not an adjunct exercise. Second, we looked for a partner who spoke our language, who shared fluency in the day-to-day. Third, we looked for a partner who could seamlessly appeal to our global audience and whom we could sponsor in any market around the world. Fourth, I grabbed the best people from the organization to vet and then lead the initiatives that sprung out of the partnership — the busiest people in the entire company with the biggest jobs.

This task wasn't easy. Ellis and his team found themselves vetting organizations that were operating in less familiar or totally unfamiliar domains. The effort began feeling risky. Finally, the team found Bain's match in Endeavor, a global, nonprofit social enterprise that seeks to catalyze long-term economic growth by supporting high-impact entrepreneurs around the world. Bain has worked with Endeavor to develop and implement its global growth strategy. Through the partnership, Endeavor has doubled Bain's country expansion rate and has demonstrated clear improvement in high-impact metrics — including a three times increase in average annual revenue growth. According to Ellis:

Because of the fit and because Endeavor sat right at the center of what we were trying to do from a strategic standpoint, a relationship that began in 2011 endures and thrives to this day. Here's why. They have a central organization, that coordinates and synchronizes all this programming, and I felt like we could plug in. It was instant. It felt more like an institution that mitigated some of the risks that you otherwise would be feeling.

Similarly, as CEO, you sit at the intersection of risk mitigation, propagation, efficiency and speed to revenue. Here, your strategic lexicon engages a global operation fluent in multiple time zones, multiple languages and the rigors of cross-border business. Your partner in developing a companywide learning initiative must share this scope of understanding and fluency, slotting into your organization seamlessly.

Building on this notion of fit and throwing another variable into the mix is Charles H. Fine. In his 1998 bestseller, *Clockspeed*, Fine argues that the faster the clock speed of an industry, the more temporary the competitive advantage:

> History provides one absolute. All competitive advantage is temporary. This is true whether your business is large or small, diversified or focused, publicly or privately owned, high-tech, low-tech or no tech at all. The faster the industry clock speed, the shorter the half-life of competitive advantage … In a fast clock-speed industry, [true] advantage arises from a concurrent design of products, processes and capabilities.

Think of it this way: in your case, as you search for education partners, the notion of concurrent design requires understanding and chemistry that enables working closely and consultatively in partnership. Then having the right capabilities would correlate to a given institution's education programs being relevant to your workplace.

Once your network of academic partners is selected and in play, you can move on to the next, most important run-up event of the C-Spark — one shared by The Master of *Midnight Diner*. With his quality ingredients at his fingertips, he can develop the ambiance that will deliver a customer experience filled with emotion that cultivates attraction, engagement and more customers. So too will you develop a learner and corporate experience that seals the deal on participation, implementation and ROI.

Chapter 8

The X-Factor:
A C-Spark Infrastructure for All

In returning one last time to the quietly charismatic Master of *Midnight Diner*, there is a ninja-like reverence and meticulous nature tied to the environment in which his customers receive their food. In the warmth of his little diner, an evident discipline emerges in the way he wipes down a counter and sets it for service. For him, the simple practice of cutting a daikon radish showcases an artistic flow and economy of effort. The plating of food is effortless — beauty mingling with comfort and a sense of arriving safely home. When dishes are delivered, porcelain strikes the tabletop's wooden surface with a single and distinct tone, percussive and singing. There is a sense of quality and simplicity. If given brand attributes, the *Midnight Diner* might embody unassuming elegance, hole-in-the-wall charm, simplicity, hospitality and flavor richness. The thing that keeps patrons coming back is its total experience.

Most of this work coalesces in a tiny kitchen — a largely unseen and unspectacular realm of The Master's establishment. Here, his operation's infrastructure takes over, making what appears on the plate, on the table and within the diner beautiful, warm, inviting. In the hyper-competitive world of food, where all five senses are enlivened by what's to come, what is and, ultimately, what was, the experience must be spot-on. If something is off — the aroma, the taste, the ambiance — the establishment will perish.

Predictably, as we have demonstrated, the same goes for how online workforce education should be delivered, administered and paid for. The encounters backing all three are equally essential to the presentation of the learning — the learner's experience, the experience of your team facilitating the learning and the financial experience that enables the scalability of your program.

In *From Dawn to Decadence, 1500 to the Present: 500 Years of Western Cultural Life*, Jacques Barzun points out:

> the designers of [technological] domestic products often lack imagination … or consult economy in manufacturing and for these reasons neglect points of discomfort in [a] device. This is such a general drawback to living among machines that the term "user-friendly" had to be coined to lure the purchaser, who frequently finds the reassurance in the printed leaflet rather than [in] the object itself.

Barzun was writing in 1995. User experience (UX) has come a long way, and it extends beyond technology. Whether in-store or online, brand-based, consistent, memorable and smooth interactions between a corporation and its stakeholders have become the centerpiece of sales, marketing and CRM. You meet those stakeholders in every conceivable way, wherever they live their lives. You know and demand this already. You strive to design seamless touchpoints between your company's and customers' offline and online worlds. You use this consistency to accelerate community building and commerce while offering attentive and responsive customer care. Consumers have learned to pay attention to how this plays out. Store aisles matter, smartphones matter and consumers recognize and are either impressed or off-put by inconsistencies in experience between a physical encounter, a web-based encounter and a smartphone-based encounter with a brand. The fluidity of the experience across contexts are basic rules of entry in most markets. It's expected.

Within online strategic workforce education, the X-Factor facilitates an infrastructure vital to the success of the C-Spark. All of the attention paid to strategy and partnerships means nothing if the end product doesn't convey a sense of brand-consistent grandeur and an attractive opportunity to learners — that "it" factor that lights a fire and fuels learning for the long haul.

A mastermind behind the X-Factor's philosophical and experience design role in the run-up to the C-Spark is Jonathan Lau, Chief Operating Officer and Co-founder, InStride. A firm believer in lifelong learning and professional growth, Jonathan strategically built his career at employers that were willing to invest in him.

After graduating from MIT, Lau joined Microsoft when it had created a new marketing leadership-recruiting program, and new high-potential training program in partnership with Northwestern Kellogg School of Management. After four years at Microsoft, he had a choice between an MBA at Harvard Business School or joining McKinsey & Company as a consultant. He joined the latter because it offered him an in-house mini-MBA program from McKinsey Alpine University in Kitzbühel, Austria.

At his most recent role at Cengage, he expected that providing learning opportunities to Cengage center's own employees would be straightforward. However, it turned out that it was incredibly hard to figure out the right education to provide key skills, how to get employees to then pursue that education and how to track all the information. There were also all sorts of disparate resources — some subscriptions to learning libraries, a relatively unknown tuition reimbursement program and a bunch of in-house developed courses — none of which was curated or easy to use, and it was not clear to any employee why they would take the extra time to learn.

These experiences as a professional learner fundamentally shaped Lau's thinking about the X-Factor — a "high potential" learning experience for every employee. Per Lau, what was needed was a consumer-grade, enterprise-class workforce education platform. For an employee used to interacting with modern online shopping or information sites, the experience needed to be mobile, personalized, supportive and simple. As an employer, the solution needed to be turnkey, flexible, secure and reliable — everything you would expect to meet the demands of today's corporations. And the amazing experience had to include a breadth of learning options needed for any corporate workforce that demonstrates outcomes for working adults. That is the appeal of the X-Factor. Its conceptual architecture carries the simplicity, elegance, depth and ruggedness of a Volvo interior. Its under-the-hood thinking offers the reliability of a Toyota, and to drive it? Think of a Porsche or Tesla — or a Falcon 9 rocket. It redefines what the workforce education experience should look and feel like — from marketing to budgeting.

You should be considering the full X-Factor up to and through the C-Spark. It's the UX as expressed through three additional and powerful micro "Xs" — together, they form the backbone of SEE and represent an X-Factor that inspires, motivates and serves as the critical infrastructure for the C-Spark. It starts with the learner experience (LX) and how every interface with the program along a learner's decisioning cycle and learning journey matters. It includes how the platform looks and feels as it moves through an engagement cycle that attracts, markets, enrolls, engages and stewards learners to completion.

In his recent bestseller *Rethinking Competitive Advantage*, author Ram Charan talks about the critical importance of customer experience and how digital platforms (which, for our purposes, we label learner experience (LX) and corporate experience (CX)) enable it. He talks about the importance of mapping the customer journey. In this case and for added relevance, we've shifted his terminology to a "learner journey":

> [It] is emerging as a distinct expertise. It involves breaking apart all the interactions and decision steps a [learner] goes through from first exposure to an idea or recognition of a need through to what happens after the person makes a [commitment].

Applying his concepts to the LX, power emerges once the focus is placed on the learner's journey in light of the power and sophistication of that LX. Charan writes:

> It is now possible to ... serve M = 1, where M is a market segment, and there's only one person in it. You will not be able to create a superior end-to-end experience that is personalized for each [learner] *and* at scale unless ... you have an [LX] that fuses an ecosystem together ... which customizes the end-to-end [learner] experience.

In addition to LX, SEE-aligned objectives and partnerships can't be activated, implemented, measured or marketed if they don't provide a corporate experience (CX) notable for its ease of administration and access to real-time information on your workforce-learner set. A streamlined CX creates a reliable tool for facilitating and extracting strategic insight, increasing efficiencies, measuring and reporting ROI and equipping you to embody and exploit the *Age of And.*

The financial experience (FX) that facilitates the learning opportunity must prove equally empathetic to the learners' situation and, hence, be designed to maximize learner participation and ROI. When it comes to money, a critical shift in your mindset around SEE's financial side and a modernization of billing for workforce education is in order, and these will cement loyalty with your workforce and ensure prospective learners among them take the opportunity you give them and pursue it. This shift and modernization also create a centralized model that makes economic sense and clarifies ROI.

It is a heavy lift that delivers a flow of oxygen that ignites and brings the C-Spark to life. When it's effectively designed, the C-Spark will give you an infinite and agile source of fuel that creates the promised evergreen strategic tool that propels a colinear flywheel for maximum thrust.

LX: Accelerating C-Spark Adoption to Win Hearts, Engage Minds

A middle manager at a telecommunications firm started but didn't finish college and saw a career ceiling looming. His company offered him a learning opportunity for an undergraduate degree. He seized it and will be the first in his family to graduate from college. He discusses this life event in terms of changing the shape of his family tree.

A bank executive raised kids while doing her job full time. Education was a priority for her, but her circumstances prevented her from going back. It's something she's wanted her whole life. Her employer extended her a similar learning opportunity, which she frames in terms of loyalty to her company and her commitment to her family.

Another financial-services employee had his sights on college right out of high school. After having a child, his girlfriend left both of them — father and child — unannounced. His life plans were upended overnight, and his new role of single father was suddenly and intensely focused on making ends meet for himself and his child. College was unthinkable. Getting the chance to attend college through his company-funded SEE program understandably leaves him in tears. He never thought he would get the chance, let alone have it fully subsidized.

These could be members of your workforce. Busy. Caring for those they love. Trying to advance with you. In their digital lives, they are afforded experiential unity across multiple digital devices. Their smartphone, laptop, and smartwatch aggregate and facilitate text, email, calendaring, productivity, collaboration, fitness, personal finances, and work and life administration. Personalization is everywhere, and the ability of individual websites and social media to harmonize your habits into big data-driven algorithms of tailored content and offers runs a continuum from convenient to creepy. Over time, their brand experiences across devices and platforms give a sense of cohesion, accessibility and ease of use. They are among the most discriminating, sophisticated consumers of information and automation.

That level of "haute digital life" makes LX a massively critical component of your strategic workforce education initiative. Sophistication must be figured into the SEE-grounded learner experience to attract, engage and convert your workforce into an enrolled squad of committed and progressing learners. Now is the time, dear CEO, to build the digital-enabled learning platform that will match your strategy and your institutional partnerships with an alluring and engaging LX.

At its best, your LX will reflect a natural, easily trusted extension of your brand. It must look, feel and sound like what you're taking to market and the culture you're building internally. It should reinforce your vision, mission and values. It should also anticipate and meet learners within your organization where they are. It should leverage your positioning and messaging and integrate your imagery and brand identity. It should be available anytime and anywhere on any device. Diversity of access is everything.

With this basic sensibility in mind, LX must serve as a flexible digital tool capable of triggering engagement. An InStride/Bain & Company proprietary survey of Fortune 500 companies noted that 80% of employees wanted to attend school while on the job. Less than half knew their company offered a program to do just that, and less than 2% actually participated. These numbers reflect a lack of C-level attention to workforce education. Still, they also illustrate the importance of program awareness building up to and through its launch. Do so, and you can truly unleash the colinear flywheel an engaged and learning workforce can provide. As you will soon understand, the C-Spark moment is only your first step. You must forcefully and maniacally leverage a digital platform that can deliver a scaled, multichannel approach to reinforcing awareness with every eligible employee. They must know they are just a single click away from a life- and career-changing learning opportunity via email, text or what they see through your single sign-on intranet. Like any other brand campaign, it is a promise to the user. In this case, the awareness part of the engagement build must prove ubiquitous and top to bottom: an effort throughout the organization to promote and reach the *Age of And*. It must come from managers in reporting relationships and among mentors with mentees. It must be reinforced on the factory floor walls, near the water cooler, in the cafeteria and at entrances and exits.

With awareness established, there is the need to meet learners across the organization with the resources they need to evaluate, grasp and embrace your SEE-empowered vision and initiative. A Wiley study found that more than 80% of workers offered fire-horse legacy modalities of workforce education immediately began researching educational opportunities online. InStride has gleaned insights as these learners move beyond this initial stage of awareness. Through its surveying and in-depth qualitative research, InStride knows learners are usually concerned with how the educational opportunity maps to their career aspirations. Then, the thinking shifts to time: How much time will it take? Will it be overwhelming and disruptive to their already overburdened lives of families, kids and competing priorities? After that, a serious evaluation begins. Will this opportunity truly make the difference they dare hope it will?

Authenticity, transparency and clarity should be your tone at this stage. Here, story is a faithful ally. It should begin with yours, and it should be front and center within your LX, discussing the why of your C-Spark moment, unfolding your commitment and offering an intimate look at your own journey with learning. Next, creating a community where shared stories, support, questions, challenges and victories among your set of learners is critical to building trust and momentum. Within it, your C-Spark extends: Your employees catch the vision and the flame and embody a safe space for future learners. Fortifying story and community should be consumer-grade touchpoints offering avenues that address the step-by-step process learners can take to begin their journey.

Once they begin, a new phase of LX kicks in. Onboarding should be easy, enabling learners to identify their goals and learning interests and to connect them to learning opportunities. It should shuttle them to a personalized dashboard. Here, careful and precise curation of learning paths offering coherent routes of success should appear. At this critical stage, it must account for a nonlinear process and accommodate for the unique psychology of decision-making that your diverse team of working adults brings to bear. Nurturing this online process is offline support: Your managers need to be equipped and prepared to give learners the requisite help they need when they embark on this journey. It should be envisioned as a series of thoughtfully planned in-person touchpoints blended with manager-originated, micro digital campaigns.

When a worker initiates a program, the LX serves as the portal to the learning itself. The portal is cocooned in the tutoring and success coaching that workers might need along the way and maintains the link to the learner community. It also begins a systematic process of reinforcing your SEE visibility, awareness and education arsenal: Developing success stories that can inspire your next-generation learners will make the whole of your LX more effective and efficient.

CX: Reclaiming and Simplifying Corporate Experience for the *Age of And*

Often, the sheer magnitude required to serve, deliver, monitor and administer a strategic workforce education program has proven, at best, radically expensive and formidable. At worst, it's been a catalyst for opting out of workforce education altogether. In an InStride/Bain & Company proprietary study, several senior executives weighed in on fire-horse legacy modalities and the experience for those inside the company who have to implement the program. A vice president of HR and labor relations said:

> Lack of awareness within the company is the biggest barrier to increased participation. We need a [workforce education experience] that can market a program internally and help communicate a program externally to increase enrollment. [We] need to [be able to] do a good job engaging employees by laying out the potential career development originating from the program.

For one chief human resources officer (CHRO), it all came down to an ROI dashboard:

> It was exceedingly difficult to measure ROI for the learner and for the organization. We looked at some basic metrics, but it's very hard to be holistic — doubtful people can do it well.

This fact really underscores a below-radar challenge among the fire horses. The onus is placed upon CHROs for the ROI of a workforce education program. This marginalizes the program and dooms it as a low-level benefit — and not a strategic investment — that dies on its own or is easily cuttable. Additionally, in larger organizations, there is a demand for real-time ROI that current modalities can't deliver on through a CX. Workforce education programs in these contexts have a hard time with stickiness.

This fact has birthed providers from three of the fire-horse legacy modalities that bundle services for outsourcing this function. In the tuition reimbursement modality, one provider charges $92 million to do so.

By embracing SEE, you simply reject this approach. A SEE-based initiative presupposes a single digital platform that powerfully implements a program with multiple educational partners, while consistently monitoring enrollment, tracking progress, serving the learner and the managerial stakeholders in that learner's career path and measuring ROI across the enterprise. Along the way, it equips the appropriate collaborators behind SEE — the C-Suite, senior management, HR and learning and development — with what they need to execute their part of the game plan.

There are several baseline standards for consideration as the CX portion of your digital platform is built. It should be able to house, stack and make accessible all the learning pathways in aligning corporate objectives to your strategic workforce education initiative: the training programs, certificate programs and brand–recognized university programming.

The CX should also automate critical tasks, including decision-making for program selection, confirming eligibility, driving and tracking participation, troubleshooting learner issues and tracking ROI. This last critical task links to reporting. Today, as with many data exercises within organizations, there is a lack of data purity and consistency.

In InStride's research connected to CX needs and wants, InStride found that most companies surveyed are using manual processes (read: spreadsheets) sometimes put together by a single person across an entire enterprise. Not only does this prevent multi-validation of those data in real time, but it might also mean those data aren't centralized and secure.

In the CX vision, the digital platform consolidates, makes accessible and reports on learner data sliced and diced in customized ways in real time. It also should be equipped to interface with performance management and other crucial HR-related systems to immediately link learner success to impact a promotion, a raise, a better career. Ideally, it should track your bespoke strategic priorities, enabling SEE to evolve, accelerate or hold steady in relation to on-the-ground performance. It should also break down learning by business unit, constantly auditing financials against budgets while gauging participation and repeat participation by the learner.

FX: Standardizing a Financial Model for Accuracy and Loyalty

If the modernization of workforce education begins with linking it to a corporation's strategic priorities, it might very well continue to evolve in powerful ways by establishing a financial model that makes sense. Tuition reimbursement is the incumbent model. It's antiquated. It's based on little to no trust in the learner. It can't scale.

Most in your workforce can't begin to access it because of their own financial constraints. If they had a glimmer of hope before the

COVID-19 pandemic, for many, that light vanished. According to the U.S. Census Bureau, since the pandemic began, nearly 60% of American households that make less than $35,000 a year struggle to pay household expenses. Almost 75 million people lost their jobs during 2020, most of whom were in industries that paid below-average wages. Those unemployed folks are struggling to find work, let alone earn a degree or certificate. How will these individuals, many living paycheck-to-paycheck, be able to front the cost of their education while awaiting repayment from their employers?

In its most effective implementations, SEE takes a sensible step to recalibrate the financial experience for everyone involved. It takes a direct-bill approach, where the employer takes care of the education expenses directly, without any cash-flow risk to the learner. It takes the repayment risk off the table for your workforce even as it grows gratitude, loyalty and productivity. It also makes workforce education a scalable proposition. This approach has a valuable byproduct. It demands a centralized budget for workforce education at a corporate level. The strategic priorities link to learning and career pathways tied to a budget that can be precisely managed. It makes an immediate difference in participation. If this was the only thing you did in relation to your workforce education effort, it would yield a 10% bump in participation.

When it comes to finances, leaving your workforce without student debt is the final and ultimate function of FX. Completely underwriting the program guarantees participation and builds instant loyalty to both your strategic education initiative and the corporate direction that serves as that initiative's impetus. Kevin Johnson, CEO, Starbucks, shared how Starbucks learned this as it moved more deeply into its SCAP program:

When we began SCAP, we offered it for the last two years of an undergraduate program, and we would help fund the junior and senior year, and we made it too complicated. We adapted very quickly, and now we pay for the entire [4-year] program in partnership with ASU, grants and other things — Starbucks will fund the balance and get a student all the way through their undergraduate degree. So, by simplifying the program, we were able to increase enrollment dramatically.

The X-Factor — the experience — of SEE serves as the basic infrastructure of the C-Spark. Without it, you cannot achieve the outcomes you set forth in developing objectives for your initiative. Through LX, you give your employees something log-on worthy and supportive, setting them up for learning success. Through CX, you offer an easy-to-implement yet highly sophisticated approach for HR, learning and development, and business unit leadership for executing the program, while maintaining control, oversight and monitoring of it. Through FX, you seal the deal by baking a direct-bill model into your budget and freeing your employees to learn without regard to paperwork or a financial burden. If you pay attention to all three, you do The Master of *Midnight Diner* proud. Bidding him a fond farewell and with the whole of the internal components of your strategic workforce education initiative, it's time. Come. Let's experience what it's like to definitively light the C-Spark and fully power up a colinear flywheel across your business.

Chapter 9

Igniting the C-Spark:
Entering the *Age of And*

What if the C-Spark was all you had? What if hiring from the outside wasn't an option? If recruiting meant everything? If, in most cases, your success was dependent upon a senior executive team that would serve alongside you for more than 30 years? What if your frontline workers and middle management were reevaluating their positions every two to six years?

There is a parallel universe where this reality has played out every day for more than 200 years. It's the U.S. military. It's an enterprise wherein failure is not an option and where there is no ability to sign a free agent from outside the organization. They are an all-volunteer force — volunteers get recruited on front-end promises focused on their individual lives. Perhaps you're familiar with the slogans. The Few, The Proud, The Marines. Army Strong. Be All that You Can Be. It's Not Just a Job, It's an Adventure. Aim High. Whether it's the Army, Navy, Air Force, Marines or the Coast Guard, there is a need to recruit between 20,000 to 80,000 new people per branch every year. Diversity across demographic data points is radical. Turnover is great. At the top, there is also a need to recruit more than 2,000 officers per year. What is the very public and front-and-center promise of the military? Career advancement with education and training as its cornerstone — not simply messaging on a recruiting poster. Ray Mabus,

149

the 75th Secretary of the Navy and former governor, Mississippi, says the C-Spark is the prime strategic tool within this personnel quest:

> The military prizes education and training more than any other place that I've ever seen, ever. From when you bring people in whether through boot camp or through officer training school, ROTC or the military academies, you spend an enormous amount of time — before they ever do anything in the military — training and educating them. And then it never ends.

Mabus is credited with advancing several transformations to modernize the Navy and Marine Corps during his tenure, and one of those arenas was education. He made graduate school more accessible to officers. For the enlisted, he made learning on the job concurrent with duties. Previously, boot camp graduates would head to specialized training for logistics, IT or cryptology specialties. Putting them in the fleet or on a mission and linking the career path with the career created a continuous learning scenario. Accountability and advancement became dependent upon reaching dual benchmarks on the job and in the learning environment:

> Before this shift, sailors were in school for a long time prior to engaging with the larger mission of the organization. We were able to fast-track their learning while equipping them to be current on what they needed to do for their organization from day one. We also created a culture of curiosity, creativity and learning.

Training, education, certification — it's a way of life across the military, and while it's not a requirement for entering into service, it's a threshold for senior leadership. According to Mabus:

> Boards select admirals and generals. A board is convened and, in the Navy, that board will review up to 1,000 records of captains in the Navy. Out of that pool, the board will pick between 20 and 25 admirals. In the Marines, a board will evaluate 500 colonels to select 10 to 15 generals. It's way tougher than Harvard. And so, one of the key elements examined is who has a graduate education. For example, John Allen, who retired as a Marine four star and was the commander of troops in Afghanistan, has three master's degrees. Jim Stavridis, who was an Admiral and NATO commander, earned a Ph.D. in law and diplomacy.

Allen serves as president of the Brookings Institution. Stavridis is currently an operating executive with the Carlyle Group. Military veterans dot the C-level and senior leadership of the Fortune 500. They bring with them a deep understanding of strategic and tactical know-how blended with an embrace of lifelong learning. They have breathed the C-Spark. However, this isn't limited to the highest levels of the military. In Mabus' opinion:

> In the future, if the military had every enlisted person up to the level of an associate degree, the military would be able to take on more and more complex issues and problems without having to train and retrain and train and retrain because you'd have more capable adaptive learners.

The Army and Navy are considering that exact move and are exploring ways to offer every soldier and sailor the opportunity to pursue an associate degree. It reinforces how the armed forces culture is composed of a million C-Sparks, where a very public commitment to education is a way of life. It has also proved a beacon in the work I do as a board director at JetBlue Airways, where General Stanley McChrystal preceded me. Here's someone who seamlessly walks the halls of leadership — be it the armed forces or corporate America. Like so many others who have come out of the military to serve in the private sector, he has business experience, but he is shaped by the ongoing and exquisite education and training he received from the armed forces.

This shift into military life is designed to assert one thing, dear CEO: for the workforce of the future, the C-Spark is not the only thing you have, but it's one of the most important things you have. Ray Mabus backs this up.

With the strategic groundwork laid, the partnerships set and the infrastructure solidified, it's time to ignite it and make the story of this book your own. As we've learned above, ignition is not a metaphor. It is an act. It is not an unspoken beginning or a back-office power switch; it is an intentional proclamation among your key stakeholders, core management, workforce and public. It's not a recorded message with a lobby soundtrack. It is a live, bold stroke that formally visions your SEE initiative to all of your audiences and ushers in the *Age of And*. Importantly, it is not an isolated, siloed or sequestered initiative. It is a vibrant path forward that directly ties an employee's career — a career that can last up to 60 years — with a concurrent and evolving learning path that directly impacts that career's advancement and direction.

Igniting the C-Spark by your public fiat will ensure three things. The entire enterprise understands that the buzz around strategic workforce education is true: it fully aligns with your organization's corporate objectives. Then, because of your involvement and the link between you and managers across the company who champion SEE, engagement and adoption rates among your workforce skyrocket. Finally, your support makes it a high-level priority that ensures a culture of learning for the long haul.

If you have followed the game plan laid out to this point, you're poised for this critical next step. It's time to invest your energy and resources to officially and successfully launch your program, igniting the C-Spark. It's a process that happens in a three-stage launch. At the bottom is your investment — both in strategic program creation and this moment of gravitas — that gets it off the ground. Next is a rollout approach that will maximize ignition and increase differentiation, enabling you to grasp a competitive advantage. The final stage is grounded in the clear and refreshing link between the program you launch and the careers of your people, a link that fully engages the colinear flywheel and offers maximum thrust. This launch, a single stroke, ushers in the *Age of And* for your company, your people and your community.

Commit to and Ignite the C-Spark

Ron Sugar, former chairman of the board and CEO, Northrop Grumman, offers this story about how a C-Spark–oriented CEO commitment happens in a flash and must be authentic:

You build trust by telling [everyone] how it's going to be and then walking the walk. You say, "I'm going to tell it to you like it is, and you're going to see me as I am, and there's no hidden agenda. And I want that behavior for every one of you dealing with me and with each of the others of you." But know this. If you're a leader — a CEO who gets up and stands behind a podium and lectures by script — you'll see a lot of heads peering down to a smartphone. But if you get up there, you tell a campfire story with bravery and honesty; you tell them about your personal history. A couple of things you screwed up. And you end by making sure you tell all of them out there that they're going to be successful and that you're committed to making them successful. That is the pivotal moment.

That is a prime example of a C-Spark ignition. A moment where you publicly unveil your strategic workforce education initiative with honesty, sincerity and personal history and draw that direct line to the company's future. A moment that, if done right and done well, will resonate with immediate impact and buzz — inside and outside your firm.

Sugar's moment came when he was consolidating more than 27 companies and 100,000 workers into a single Northrop Grumman. He decided to leverage the Phoenix Symphony Orchestra and commissioned a classical arrangement titled the "Northrop Grumman Overture." Within the orchestra seating, there were empty chairs. Employees from the various newly acquired companies were called up to sit in the chairs. They experienced firsthand the vantage point and sonics of a performing orchestra — the players playing harmoniously, powerfully and tenderly. Some were called upon to take a stab at conducting. The point was simple. Unity and trajectory were mandatory, and the conductor's role was absolutely critical for Northrop Grumman to move forward powerfully.

Sugar underscores something that transcends a blessing, a nod or a seal of approval. The C-Spark is deeply personal. It needs to be your baby. Steve Ellis says that any CEO who seeks to engage in workforce education will be best served if they're not afraid to put their name on it.

"It's going to require leadership. Your leadership," said Ellis. "It doesn't mean you have to do all of the work, but it does mean that [publicly] you've made clear to the entire organization that it is [your] priority."

Then, says Ellis, you bake it into the organization and, by involving the right people, it's an initiative of priority. It is important. Right now.

At this point, I know what some of you are thinking. You're taking Ellis's words and seriously reflecting on empowering your CHRO with all the rights and privileges of leading your C-Spark. Wrong, dear CEO. Your leadership is at the heart of how the C-Spark works. Delegating it is dooming it.

Teri McClure, former general counsel, CHRO and vice president of labor relations and communications, UPS, agrees:

> Getting greater buy-in for [strategic workforce education] by the existing leadership team and having the CEO drive that and [align it] to their development and their compensation, and, quite frankly, their success matrix, is key. That is where a CEO's ownership, buy in and help [make] a big difference.

In the wake of McClure's words, it's time to conjure a Jack Welch moment. To paraphrase in gentler terms GE's iconic chief executive:

"Anyone can lead a company through a quarter. Anyone can lead a company for three years. The key to a real CEO is doing both."

Dear CEO, this is the moment to seize strategic education, embrace it, live by it and wield it as the true scepter that shows you have the "right stuff" for the *Age of And*:

The Age of Business *And* Social Impact.
The Age of the Employee *And* the Learner.
The Age of the Customer *And* the Community.
The Age of the Shareholder *And* the Society.
The Age of the Good Fiduciary *And* the Good Citizen.
The Age of Doing Well *And* Doing Good.

When it comes to igniting the C-Spark, it comes down to you going big or going home. Truly. It's nonnegotiable.

Back C-Spark Ignition with an Awareness Powerhouse

Launching the C-Spark is just like launching a product. Start by considering it as a part of your brand architecture and name it. Starbucks landed on the Starbucks College Achievement Plan (SCAP). Car retailer Carvana went with KEYS (Keeping Education in Your Sight). LabCorp branded its program Education Advantage. Desert Financial Credit Union dubbed its program InvestED. Adidas chose Here to Educate; NewsCorp calls its program NewsCorp NEXT; and Prime Communications, the largest AT&T retailer, dubbed its program Prime Scholars. Accolade (Accolade Education Program), Aramark (Frontline Education Program), Banfield Pet Hospital (Banfield Educational Pathways) and WinCo Foods (WinCo Foods

Education Program) chose more traditional, education-focused nomenclature.

Naming something demonstrates commitment and builds buzz. The workforce will feel it, recognizing a movement sweeping up the company — not a training taking place in a vacant conference room like a dirty secret. Then, as you take it externally, it will also deliver a more significant impact and become sound bite- and hashtag-friendly in the media and across your social channels.

From this starting point, position it using the core strategic priorities you initially identified with careful attention to your target audiences: your senior leadership and rank-and-file workforce, your board, your shareholders, your customers, key influencers — both industry- and customer-facing, your prospects, the media. In the case of Starbucks, the company rallied around the notion that SCAP was a first-of-its-kind program, but the program quickly became more sophisticated, and the company focused on the notion that "future leaders start here." It has since built internal- and external-facing positioning to match that idea. This offers an aspirational quality internally. Externally, it offers an immediate way into conversation with customers, media, investors and other key stakeholders. It also offers a powerful hub for developing both internal and external content — Starbucks ingeniously owns the future, and nothing prepares you for your future like a grande double-shot triple mocha whip latte.

Once positioned, develop the go-to-market strategy for your initiative: that core set of marketing assets to be deployed across your marketing channels. Launch the digital wing of your infrastructure that enables two-way communication for your learner set within a vibrant community — it's that all-important component of your learner experience. Along the way and ideally, your go-to-market will reflect a multichannel approach that consistently and loudly hails the new program and its achievements — internally and externally. Through Starbucks' C-Spark moment, it created a unique mix of national and local events that maximized visibility. Heartfelt and real, Starbucks told the stories of partners and unveiled the program. Starbucks was the poster child of audacious. The company unleashed its SCAP stories, and content began coursing through its multichannel empire: social feeds, thought leadership efforts, digital and traditional advertising, in-store environments and media relations rhythms. Starbucks also didn't forget its academic partnerships, coordinating its launch in lock-step to maximize the program across SCAP's audience sets.

With your go-to-market set, make sure your senior leadership gets on board in the pre-ignition phase to ensure consistency and frequency of messaging that cascades to managers and targeted employee populations. Set a goal for participation and meet it. It could be 100 learners in 100 days or 10,000 learners in 10 quarters. Additionally, as you consider managers in this process, make them your greatest champions. Develop a manager toolkit, furnishing managers with everything they need to convincingly evangelize the program with sincerity, answer their critical questions, communicate the details and discuss how you will manage the program and drive participation.

As it launched SCAP, Starbucks took a very intentional approach to its messaging that fused Starbucks' partner dreams with the American dream, giving the company an instant platform and high ground from which to tell its story.

"In the last few years, we have seen the fracturing of the American Dream," said Schultz to reporters. There is no doubt, the inequality within the country has created a situation where many Americans are being left behind.

"The question for all of us is, should we accept that, or should we try and do something about it? Supporting our partners' ambitions is the very best investment Starbucks can make. Everyone who works as hard as our partners do should have the opportunity to complete college while balancing work, school and their personal lives."

He also pointed to having a conscience — making SCAP a moral issue — and he cited internal research on the matter. These are key data for taking the C-Spark public. In the case of Starbucks, "Seven percent of Starbucks employees do not have a degree but want to earn one; some have never gone to college, some have gone but dropped out, and others are in school but have found it slow going."

The *Atlantic* pointed out:

> Critics often bring up the point that with degrees in hand, workers may then leave for better-paying jobs. Schultz responded that "it would be accredited to our brand, our reputation and our business." Shultz believes that it will "lower attrition, it'll increase performance, it'll attract and retain better people."

Embedded in this marketing phase rests the thoughtful and intentional plan for the C-Spark event itself. Establish creative concepting behind it. House it in a dramatic location. Deliver on a grand gesture and a righteous photo opportunity that considers your brand, your workers and the communities you call home. Cocoon it in hashtags and prompts for user-generated content at the event that extends visibility and power of the spark. Declare it a new day — day one of the *Age of And* — and ground the event in demonstrating how this initiative will deliver corporate growth and impact to the entirety of your audience set.

Back the C-Spark prelaunch and ignition with full integration into your year-round internal marketing, external marketing, public relations and investor-relations mix as relevant. Doing so ensures a drumbeat of morale-boosting inspiration, visibility and thought leadership that considers intimate success stories, community-wide stories, award programs for the initiatives and traditional and social campaigns, investor days, recruiting efforts and social-impact awareness. Celebrate your learners at every turn. Illustrate progress and milestones. Announce new growth in the partnership. Starbucks SCAP is a fully integrated component of the corporate brand, and its flywheel status across its strategic priorities makes it a major touchstone for ongoing efforts — from newsworthy announcements and breakthroughs to ongoing progress updates and poignant Starbucks partner stories. Likewise, be poised with data and anecdotes that paint the picture of the *Age of And* from your vantage point. The extent to which you can exploit the C-Spark is the extent to which your marketing machine will be able to activate learners internally and build more profound differentiation and competitive advantage externally.

Fuse Corporate and Career Destiny, and Engage the Flywheel

As you launch the C-Spark, tell its stories and celebrate its success and as you implement it, make sure that at every turn, there is a direct line between your corporate, strategic priorities and the career destiny of the learner. Explicitly and consistently communicate this fact. Expressly integrate it into your management function and manage to it. Ensure every employee who is eligible for learning within your company understands what participation and completion will mean for their careers. It will paint a picture of the future and offer them more than pure aspiration: Learning and getting the job done is doable and will be duly rewarded.

As you articulate this, you can discuss how you've developed a master blend of curated learning opportunities that will open thousands of doors across your workforce for advancement and a better life. You can illustrate how you have multiple on-ramps through partners who deliver certificates, varying levels of high school, college and graduate degrees and specific trainings that will contribute to advancing the employee. If you're already deploying a corporate "culture as strategy" approach, this set of facts will only enhance its effectiveness. It begins to address what 68% of business leaders see as skills gaps limiting their corporation's growth. Significantly, this fusion accelerates your strategic workforce education initiative's success and fully engages the colinear flywheel that will offer your company maximum thrust.

To witness it is world-rocking. When a nursing assistant understands that he can progress through a career path complemented by a learning path that directly accelerates his ability, and, ultimately, to advance to a role in nursing or healthcare leadership, it lights a fire. When a part-timer in a warehouse gets that she can leverage a mosaic of degree programs, industry certifications and supply-chain knowledge alongside leadership and management skill–building into a supervisory role and, ultimately, a leadership role, it lights a fire. When a team of software developers sees the mix of educational opportunities that can take them from a software developer role to a manager role, it lights a fire.

The powerful byproduct of this fusion of corporate and career destiny is that workforce education makes strategic sense for the first time — to everyone. It reinvigorates a sense that the American dream is alive and well in the American corporation in a big way.

Congratulations! With ignition completed and the flywheel activated, you can begin to seize the rewards of your personal commitment to the C-Spark, firmly grasping the baton that ignites it. Now, we actually will pass go. At this stage, I will venture into mind reading once more: You think it can't be this good, this impactful, this effective for your company. It sounds too idealistic and carries an undertone of sentimentality and aspiration. It's okay. There's room for that. However, a quick request: Make room for imagining what it's like to start with your own people and to truly invest in them in a way that has personal, professional and community-wide impact that will last for generations. Imagine what it's like to do so in full alignment with your corporate direction and in full synchrony with your brand. You will be shocked at the profound awakening that results within your company. You will begin to reap the benefits of leading from your head And your heart. You will become a CEO who is at once worthy *And* for real. With that in mind, let's take a peek beyond the C-Spark afterglow and take a maiden voyage into the *Age of And*.

Chapter 10

One More Thing:
Previewing the *Age of And*

When you, dear CEO, step to the fore and publicly ignite the C-Spark and when you speak into existence the *Age of And*, everything changes. The culture shifts. The mindset shifts. Maximum thrust. You will not seek a return to the fire horses — the legacy modalities of workforce education — ever again. You will experience firsthand the strategic power of SEE.

The C-Spark does for people what Steve Jobs used to do for products. He was The Master of the product-focused C-Spark — simple ingredients, careful attention to detail, thoughtful experiences. Jobs laid the foundation for the first several decades of Silicon Valley chic, eventually distilling his wardrobe to a black, long-sleeved mock turtleneck, thoughtfully curated wire-rimmed glasses, jeans, a pair of New Balances and a way of being that seemed to consistently say "bring it" behind the veil of a mischievous smile. He had the corner on personal technology's "it" factor. He would appear in his low-key getup on stage in front of a big screen and change everything at least once a year. He'd roll out a bunch of new products, and then, in 1999, he began to offer that magical phrase, "Wait a minute, there's one more thing." That statement would be reserved for the "big one." PowerMac, iMac, iPod, Pro, Magic Mouse and, oh yes, that iPhone. Imagine being the leader in flip phones when the iPhone hit the market (and who knows? Maybe you were the leader). The iPhone shifted the entire mobile industry overnight!

Remember the anticipation and the results of moments in the lives of people everywhere? Maybe you were the one at the Mac store, camping out all night just to be one of the first to have the newest Apple product. Maybe you invested in the full lineup of hardware that would identify you as a Mac and not a PC person. Jobs, The Master, held the corner on making personal technology exciting because Jobs was the CEO out in front of his entire product line building the buzz and reveling in taking a saber to the champagne bottle to once more proclaim that he held the competitive advantage. The C-Spark tied to strategic workforce education is your "one more thing" moment. It's your chance to change everything. And as it grows and shifts throughout your tenure, you will call it forth again and again.

Tom Staggs, former COO, The Walt Disney Company, portrays it as multidimensional, carrying the power to motivate and inspire:

> What you're doing is laying out to people an opportunity for them to take advantage of. If you [do this in a] well-articulated, well laid-out, well-communicated way, you've created an invitation for people to invest in themselves with you footing the bill. By doing so, you tap into the potential of your organization in a fundamentally different way ... and you send a strong signal to the organization that you care about your people and their development, and that leads to powerful, positive word of mouth.

To Staggs, this initiates a chain reaction that ripples instantly as the flywheel begins its first rotation. It creates a momentum of perception.

"The opinions, the word of mouth and what your folks say about you and your organization has a bigger impact than it's had before," he said. "Which means [that by your] investing in those people, their sense of loyalty, their sense of being cared for by an organization — it becomes more important than ever before."

Lynne Doughtie, former chair and CEO of KPMG, said that not until she was actually sitting in the CEO hot seat did she realize the great responsibility she had and how an investment like SEE would offer significant ROI:

> You realize that it will pay tremendous dividends. The things that make people loyal and connected and wanting to do their best for an organization — that comes when they feel that the leaders of their business care for them. When you get that person that's going to be committed to your organization for the long term, that will go the extra mile [and] that will have the kind of work ethic that you're looking for — I think the CEOs that get that will have the most successful companies.

This is certainly reflected in Starbucks SCAP. At the 2019 ASU-GSV summit, CEO Kevin Johnson reflected on it this way:

> You ask yourself, what does the ROI look like for this thing. For us, it starts with retention. Our retention is higher than almost everyone else's in retail. Because of that, our Starbucks partners are better able to better connect with customers. Our customer connection scores are at an all-time high, and that is driving the growth that you're seeing in our business.

At the end of the day, my view is that every company has to be thoughtful about their purpose. And if that purpose is only for the pursuit of profit, then that will not be an enduring company that lasts centuries. And so, what we aspire to at Starbucks is to build an enduring company, a company that moves far beyond the pursuit of profit. And this program is one example of that.

Johnson doesn't stop there. He also paints the profoundly personal side of the equation. Johnson recently hosted a Starbucks SCAP–partner roundtable at one of his stores. Twelve of the Starbucks partners were leveraging the company's strategic workforce education initiative to get their education. A young woman who had been a Starbucks partner for 16 years shared her story. She has a seven-year-old daughter, and she is the first in her family to get a college education. She was about to graduate, and she began crying because she is so proud of what she has achieved and so grateful for that opportunity. Johnson said:

She shared with me that her seven-year-old daughter is now thinking about what she wants to do with her life. And her husband, also a Starbucks partner, is enrolled in the program. So, to sit across the table from her and hear firsthand how this has changed her life, changed her family's life and given her daughter inspiration beyond what she'd imagined she'd be capable of doing — it has an impact on the individual, it has an impact on the communities that we all live in, and it has an impact on our company and its businesses, and it has an impact on society. I'm a believer. I believe great things happen when you do this.

So many *Ands*. So much lift and thrust to the entire organization. And it begins upon ignition. Hearkening back to the military, you can see why its version of the C-Spark — its investment in people — is so valuable. The services are convincing young men and women to be ready to lay down their lives for their country, to believe in the mission and to advance that mission wherever in the world that might take them, no matter the risk. However, and importantly, the C-Spark also extends outward to external audiences.

The C-Spark drives immediate brand visibility. Hundreds of employees viewed a short film created for the Starbucks SCAP program and centered on young adults as a part of the New York City ignition. It was attended by the U.S. Secretary of Education. Then it was released to the press, where it attracted more than two billion media impressions.

Global hospitality leader Aramark's C-Spark resulted in 300 employees lining up within the first day, showing interest in its Frontline Education Program, and that was based on a single, circulating press release. It was also covered by *The New York Times*, *The Wall Street Journal*, *CNN*, *FOX News* and critical trade publications such as *Food Management* and *Nation's Restaurant News*, on its way to driving nearly 167 same-day stories and 155,000 unique visitors to its program's landing page.

Impact doesn't stop there. Culturally, change is now palpable. On the front line, the members of your workforce see beyond a workday or the next paycheck. They see in a blink that something new, something big, is possible for them and for their children: that opening they needed to become their best, most authentic selves. That's what Aramark discovered. It employs nearly 150,000 people. The relative and immediate speed and momentum of its program proved decisive. Within the first 90 days of its C-Spark, nearly 6,000 within its workforce began examining the program. More than a third of those were eligible and began enrolling. Within four months, classes began.

At a managerial level, nagging questions about meritocracy and personal growth give way to a clarion call around corporate and individual advancement. Curiosity, proactivity, learning and risk-taking pave the way for managers. SEE also equips them with a playbook to oversee, inspire and motivate the people underneath them.

At a senior level, the colinear flywheel unifies and accelerates the company's direction at a strategic level. Strategic priorities touched by the C-Spark begin to shift in positive and tangible ways. Auto-buying disruptor Carvana, the company that delivers premium used cars, not unlike pizza, experienced the C-Spark difference across the board. Its strategic priorities included recruiting, retention, DE&I and the ability to promote from within for some of its most technically challenging jobs. Mobile retailer Prime Communications was able to link its program to the front line and impact revenue growth and brand awareness in a crowded market. Similarly, Desert Financial Credit Union's C-Spark sent ripples of possibility and unity across its culture in a market that requires unrivaled customer experience to win new deposits and organically grow client relationships.

And for you, dear CEO, your day one experience gives you a boost in the immediate moment and into the short term. It also sets the stage for your legacy while adding a proven leadership methodology that will serve you well across your career, at your next company or on your next board. That ripple extends to your board, a team that now looks like champions and sages, even as it reenergizes both existing and prospective investors and elevates you across your industry. When you make this real for your people, you can claim your "one more thing" that changes everything in the blink of an eye.

The *Age of And* begins at that moment.

What's next?

Turn the page. Immerse yourself in the first movers within this new age. Experience the C-Spark through the eyes of your colleagues' learners. See the link between the employees who are shocked and amazed by their learning and new career pathways and how respective corporations fulfill their unique take on universal strategic priorities. Witness doing well by doing good. In the learning journeys of actual companies, you will find case after case of the C-Spark creating market leaders and disruptors who are wielding strategic workforce education for maximum thrust — that golden colinear flywheel of corporate growth and social impact.

PART III

The *Age of And* will now unfold before you. Dive into the following samples of how innovative and disruptive companies across industries nationwide are interpreting, leveraging and igniting the C-Spark. First, feel the impact on the learners within those companies — the names of whom have been changed to protect their privacy. Then reflect on how that learner experience directly feeds into the unique, yet universal, strategic priorities of each corporation. Trace how the CEO seized the C-Spark and elevated strategic workforce education in ways that drive corporate growth and social impact. Ask yourself, "Which of my business priorities can be accelerated through strategic workforce education, increasing my revenue, market share and competitive advantage?" As you do so, notice the colinear flywheel that engages at the point of ignition. Then act, dear CEO, with haste.

Chapter 11

Banfield Pet Hospital: Educational Pathways

Alayna owns five pets: a German shepherd named Shep, three Chihuahuas named Nugget, Harlow, and Nash and a cat named Mr. Ginger. She has always loved animals. As a teenager, she began working at a local pet retailer in her hometown just southeast of Raleigh, North Carolina, and loved it. It combined two of her passions — animals and talking. She trained as a bather in the grooming department. Then she helped out in customer service, as a cashier and in the pet care section of the store. One day, Banfield Pet Hospital opened up a clinic within her store, and she became curious about the career path to veterinarian.

Ask almost any veterinary professional when they knew they wanted to go into a career working with animals and their story likely starts at a young age like Alayna. For most, veterinary medicine is a true calling. This is something Banfield Pet Hospital hears over and over from the thousands of veterinarians and certified technicians that work at their hospitals nationwide.

Banfield was founded in 1955. Having started in Portland, Oregon, it grew to more than 1,000 clinics across North America and Washington D.C., Puerto Rico and Mexico. Subsequently purchased by Mars, Inc., it employs more than 19,000 people, including more than 3,600 Banfield veterinarians who are committed to providing high-quality veterinary care to over three million pets annually. Banfield is an industry leader, hosting the annual Pet Healthcare Industry Summit which brings together leaders from all facets of the profession, including academia, national associations, nonprofits, suppliers, media and more. Together, they discuss opportunities and collaborate on solutions to elevate the veterinary profession.

Alayna's journey with Banfield started when she struck up conversations with the new team that opened the clinic within her store. She knew she needed to start making more money. She also felt a call to work with animals more seriously.

"When the vet assistants would come out of the clinic or buy supplies for their animals in the store, I'd ask them, 'How'd you get into that [line of work]. How easy is it? What kind of training do you need?'" said Alayna.

The assistants told Alayna the assistant position she was interested in didn't need much prior training and that she'd learn a lot on the job. She worked up the courage to apply and was hired. Over the next seven years, Alayna realized she had found a job and company that she loved, describing it as one big family.

As Alayna's career progressed at Banfield, she thought to herself about possibly heading back to medical school to become a veterinarian. It was a goal that seemed far away. She had gone to college for a while but did not finish. Then, Banfield ignited its C-Spark: the Banfield Educational Pathways Program. Alayna was a part of an associate survey to see if there would be interest in joining it.

"I was actually really thrilled. I was one of the first ones who responded, and I was like, yes, yes, yes!" she said. "I had been to college before, but I couldn't really afford it and never felt like I found my place. So, I never thought I'd have an opportunity to go back. When I thought there was a real possibility, that's when I started to dig into it."

After expressing interest in the program and meeting eligibility criteria, Alayna was pre-selected to move through the application process. If accepted, she would get access to a tuition-free, four-year bachelor's degree — no strings attached.

"When I got the email, I just remember crying at the news," said Alayna. "I was like, I have to pray about this because it's a huge deal. I never thought I would have a second opportunity to go to college. And I so love this company and that made participating in the program easy."

Banfield prides itself on not only listening to the needs of its associates, but also making changes and investments to meet those needs. Banfield president Brian Garish says it's this people-first culture that enables the practice to really understand the key challenges its associates — and the larger profession — are facing. This puts Banfield in the unique position to not only make a difference in the lives of pets and the people who care for them, but society as a whole.

Alayna's story aligns with the incredibly creative use of the C-Spark by Garish in his quest to leverage the company's Educational Pathways Program to accelerate business growth and social impact. The program provides meaningful career growth and pathing by offering a select group of paraprofessionals Banfield-paid tuition to complete an online STEM-related undergraduate degree. As part of the program, selected Banfield associates have the opportunity to pursue a bachelor's degree from their choice of more than a dozen science- and health-focused programs.

"We are focused on the intersection of pet health, human health and societal well-being," says Garish. It is a concept not lost on Banfield's associates like Alayna who expressed how much she loves working for Banfield because she feels that Garish gives everyone a voice.

Passionate about fostering a learning culture, Garish collaborated with InStride to conceive and launch the Educational Pathways Program in ways that will help Banfield creatively combat the veterinary workforce crisis and increase its standing as a recognized leader at the forefront of the veterinary industry. Even after C-Spark ignition, Garish has repeatedly foregrounded the program. He hosted an Instagram Live conversation around why it's so pivotal for the future of the company. His post that accompanied the dialogue discusses how:

> Banfield's Educational Pathways Program is an exciting venture that will provide meaningful career growth opportunities through practice-paid tuition for our paraprofessionals to complete a [science, technology, engineering and mathematics-] STEM-related undergraduate degree. I believe that providing ongoing opportunities for growth is critical to the associate experience.

Within eight years, it's estimated there will be a critical shortage of veterinary professionals in the United States, a recent Banfield study found. That means an estimated 75 million pets may not have access to the veterinary care they need. Because of the passion veterinary professionals have for helping pets and the lengths they go to do so, they are faced with rewarding opportunities but also are exposed to significant challenges — from compassion fatigue to high amounts of student debt to meeting the needs of the growing number of pets in the U.S.

Banfield understood that simply adding more doctors of veterinary medicine (DVMs) to their roster wouldn't fix the situation — there aren't enough of them to make that a viable option. A strong pipeline of paraprofessionals is needed to be able to better support the growing needs of the industry. Moreover, the pipeline from student to DVM can be an arduous, costly eight-year climb for most individuals. This program could open doors to growth and opportunity to the numerous "Alaynas" throughout the industry: passionate vet assistants with a major obstacle between them and a difference-making advancement.

Banfield's C-Spark is a classic illustration of how the program activates on the elements of the colinear flywheel: revenue and profitability, corporate agility, recruitment and retention, corporate citizenship and the brand. In working through the program as a tool for growth and agility, the company also equipped itself for long-haul leadership in the recruitment and retention facet of its industry.

"It's our responsibility to leverage our size and scale to do our part to bridge the veterinary talent shortage gap and establish a strong pipeline of paraprofessionals to better support the growing needs of our industry," said Dan Aja, chief veterinary and transformation officer, Banfield.

The Educational Pathways Program is creating new and increased interest in veterinary medicine as a career while inviting more prospective employees into the fold. The program was created with the goal of keeping finances out of the equation so people can focus on career development and long-term goals. Since starting the program, three out of four participants report that enrollment alone has increased their desire to grow in the field of veterinary medicine.

Additionally, 100% of participants say that the Educational Pathways Program increased their belief that Banfield is committed to their growth and success, and 81% are more likely to continue working at Banfield because of the program.

Through the program, Banfield is demonstrating its commitment to corporate citizenship. Through its purpose — A Better World for Pets — Banfield seeks to "put our principles in action and serve those who need us most; inspire current and future generations of veterinary professionals and support and scale the work being done by shelters and rescues with love, compassion and with an emphasis on quality, responsibility and mutuality." Banfield's C-Spark ladders up to these ideals.

"By having a strong focus on societal well-being, we want to be a beacon for how other companies ought to behave, not just in the veterinary industry, but across all sectors," said Garish.

This commitment is felt directly through Banfield's focus on caring for people, pets and communities. The Educational Pathways Program offers a rallying point and underscores both the internal culture and external brand of the company.

Aja puts it this way, "When veterinary professionals get to practice at the top of their license, hospitals get the best results: engaged clients and a unified team that delivers superior care."

In working with InStride, the Banfield Educational Pathways Program launched within four weeks. It included a complete internal and external awareness building program. It began with communicating internally to key stakeholders to share details about the program, inviting their questions and demonstrating how each of them could foster participation among eligible team members. Once the program officially launched, feedback among participating associates was overwhelmingly positive. Garish also used his personal LinkedIn and Instagram feeds to reach an even broader audience.

Garish believes business leaders should consider ways to not only promote the benefits of higher education, but also create actionable paths to affording college:

> I was very lucky to have someone who saw my potential and encouraged me to finish my education. This led me to understand the importance of rounding out real-world work experience with a college education. Throughout my career I've strived to give back and help people because I saw firsthand how that hand up can be such a transformative experience. If you take care of your people, everything else will follow. Over the past few years, we have built programs based on associate input. These changes have had a big impact on our business, resulting in a significant reduction in turnover — the lowest in our history.

Alayna describes her life of work and learning at Banfield as "one of those jobs where you go in and it's easy to be there and to love your job." Even with some serious challenges and complications in her life, she is on target to finish her bachelor's degree, courtesy of Banfield. Eventually she wants to advance to veterinary medical school to become a doctor. She's honored to be in the program.

"Every month, I see the bill, and I see what the school costs and what Banfield is covering. It makes me feel valuable and like someone out there cares about my education and is willing to help me," said Alayna. "There are not a lot of companies that offer this sort of thing, and it's been huge and life changing for me. I believe it will be for other people too — one hundred percent."

Banfield's use of the C-Spark and workforce education as a strategic tool is exemplary. Through Garish's leadership, it illustrates how a firm can meaningfully and decisively move the needle on strategic priorities. Banfield's Educational Pathways Program aims to positively impact its people while helping to create a more sustainable future for the veterinary industry. Through it all, it personifies any early pacesetter in the *Age of And*.

Chapter 12

Carvana:
The KEYS Program

It wasn't long ago that researching information online about car buying was revolutionary. Consumer Reports and Edmunds.com led that charge. Then came online car listings. Price comparisons ensued between dealers and private party offerings; eBay Motors, CarGurus and CarMax made that a possibility for new and used vehicles. Even so, you still had to drive somewhere to pick up the car or pay to arrange for its delivery.

Carvana set out to make car buying easier and more enjoyable, disrupting and transforming this industry with an entirely online car shopping experience. Through it, you can research, finance and buy a car without leaving your couch, then have it delivered to your driveway. No dealership. Founded in 2012, the company has reinvented the car buying and selling experience by taking the process 100% online, offering a great selection of cars, at great prices, with great customer service.

By 2019, it had posted triple-digit growth over 23 straight quarters. In 2020 through 2021, it rode a wave of online consumerism arising from the COVID-19 pandemic. Over a three-month stretch in mid-2020, it posted revenue of $1.12 billion. It has accomplished all of this in an auto retailing industry that is difficult to break into (let alone become successful). It was the first auto retailer to launch a series of coin-operated, fully automated Car Vending Machines, making purchase pick up at the vending machine locations free for customers, along with a 7-day return policy. In 2021, it debuted on the Fortune 500, one of the youngest tech companies to reach the prestigious milestone.

Even with over 10,000 team members and more than $5.5 billion in revenue, it is on a mission to change the way people buy and sell cars. Carvana's brand maintains its mission of "putting people first and selling cars second." Its core values include: "Your next customer may be your mom. We're all in this together. Be brave. There are no sidelines. Zag forward. Don't be a Richard. Stay scrappy."

Eric is 35 and works in the inspection center for Carvana, where he loves his job and everyone with whom he works. He and his wife have two boys who are 12 and 13, and Eric primarily supports the household because his wife has a heart condition that only allows her to work part time.

Like any parent, Eric sometimes watches his sons play together and feels as if he's watching his life flash before his eyes. He thinks about how they will soon be in high school and maybe even college after that. It's a little triggering. He begins to worry that his high school diploma and few college credits have taken him as far as he can go financially. If one of his sons gets into a college, he wants to be able to afford to send them there and be the most supportive parent he can be.

Every Monday, when Eric hears about job openings at Carvana, he gets interested in new technical roles at the inspection center that could open more doorways for his career. This also reminds him of his dream of going back to school to get his degree, but reality sets in. Family comes first. Worry gives way to hope when, one morning,

Eric finds out that Carvana has started a new career upskilling program called the Keeping Education in Your Sight (KEYS) Program. KEYS will allow team members to earn a four-year degree. In addition, each degree is relevant and useful for several full-time jobs at Carvana; so now Eric can get the education he wants and stay with the company and culture he loves. After reading more about it online, he reaches out to his manager, who shows him all the steps to inquire and apply. Within a few weeks, Eric is accepted and enrolled.

Today, Eric can't believe he's back in school and working toward a job at a company he truly loves. It makes a significant impact on his life because Carvana is investing in him. He could see himself staying at Carvana for a long time. Eric's wife is so proud to see him studying because she knows he's finally working toward his dream. And when his kids come home to share the "As" on their report cards, he knows they're proudly sharing in a learning journey together. What's more, those kids are on their way and optimistic about their future.

Eric's experience is all a part of Carvana's plan. Their Founder and CEO Ernie Garcia and his team are future-proofing the business and continuing to transform the auto retailing industry by igniting a C-Spark. In collaboration with InStride, Carvana focused KEYS on three universal strategic priorities: corporate agility, recruitment and retention, and the brand.

At Carvana, there was an increasing demand for specific technical roles at its inspection centers, but a small talent pool existed for filling them. Carvana recognized these roles were outstripping qualifications today and would only increase in the future. Carvana led the creation of KEYS to ensure corporate agility by upskilling the Carvana teams in-house, enabling its people to evolve with the business. Carvana now has an approach for employee growth that sets them apart from the competition and keeps it agile. They can evolve as the nascent industry of digital car sales shifts.

Furthermore, already built upon a strong culture and boasting a fantastic work atmosphere, Carvana easily attracted employees, giving them a leg up on recruiting. But to retain its people over the long haul, Garcia and the Carvana talent team knew they needed something more. After all, remember that while Eric loved his job, he also worried whether he had reached the end of his career line. To Eric and many team members like him, KEYS offered an unparalleled way to stay at a company they loved.

"We're proud to support the diverse backgrounds, experience and talents of our teammates who have yet to complete, or pursue, a college degree with Carvana KEYS," said Garcia upon the ignition of KEYS.

Carvana KEYS enables the company to express this internally and externally, fortifying its brand promise and manifesto. Crucial to Garcia and Carvana's approach alongside InStride was a need for depth and breadth among educational institution partners, creating a need for ultimate customization for learning paths that would bring new opportunities to their workforce and help their business goals excel.

"As a vertically integrated company, we have a myriad of jobs across industries and recognize that there are numerous paths that lead to Carvana," Garcia said.

After naming the program KEYS for its easy recallability and auto industry relevance, Carvana launched the program with ambitious speed. Its accelerated rollout began at the end of 2020, with its business shifting into high gear through increased demand because of COVID-19. Of particular importance was its goal of hiring more than

300 new associates per week. Carvana's People Operations team knew that KEYS would be integral to this recruiting effort and requested that its pace to launch be swift.

To ensure success, Carvana girded its C-Spark with an aggressive internal and external awareness program, leading to national and automotive trade media coverage. The company used every internal channel at its disposal, including consistent content through its internal "social" media channel and video screens and a communiqué from the Vice President of People Operations. Its 10-day internal email series enjoyed a massive 50% open rate. People Operations teams and new hire learners received webinars. Through messaging and tactics like an "eligibility countdown," they could keep their talent informed, retain new hires and show future learners that Carvana KEYS was more than just a typical benefit, and Carvana was more than just a typical company. Externally, Carvana embarked upon a media relations blitz that included coverage from global business press and auto industry trade outlets.

In a 2020 ad campaign, Carvana spoofs a dealer professional development meetup. Comedian Rob Corddry fronts a two-person team designed to be quasi-motivational coaches to car salespeople. In one spot, Corddry's character focuses on the fact that Carvana provides 100% online car buying.

"How does someone find a car on the site without someone like us checking in?" he says.

In another ad focused on car delivery, Corddry's character wonders how a buyer can truly receive a car without first exploring a dealership. It's the stuff of disruptive technology companies, having to evangelize and educate on its differentiators to fast-track adoption.

The campaign also highlights why digital workforce education through KEYS is a natural fit for Carvana. The company and its future-focused CEO get it. They get that just like changing the car buying experience by making it 100% digital, the delivery of a 100% free digital education to its workforce can change its company, its brand and its workforce for good.

Chapter 13

Desert Financial Credit Union: InvestED

Growing up, James always assumed that he'd take a traditional education path. This meant graduating from high school and immediately going to college. But when he unexpectedly became a single parent at 20, James saw his life change rapidly. He put going to college and earning a degree on the back burner, while balancing 12-hour workdays with raising his young son.

He adores his son and being a father, but James admitted, "It was a struggle for quite a while," expressing that he often saw going back to school while working full time as impossible. On the other hand, James has a natural drive to move forward and evolve. He was determined to go back to school, support his family and make ends meet.

James is a full-time, hourly sales and service quality analyst at Desert Financial Credit Union. Desert Financial is nearly a century old and among the largest credit unions in the United States. Based in Phoenix, it blankets Arizona with banking and financial services matched with a commitment to give back to the communities it serves. Like all credit unions, it is a nonprofit that is designed to create economic vitality in its branch cities by offering easy access to banking, financing and financial planning.

James came to Desert Financial after working at another firm where he felt secure and maintained a solid rapport with management.

However, after he moved to Desert Financial, the credit union began offering a game-changing initiative, InvestED, a program that promised a 100% company-sponsored college education. Integrated into its management structure, InvestED would allow James to begin working on a degree right away.

"Desert Financial is a place that values its people and values learning. Going back to school enabled me to move forward at a time when I really needed to get moving. You need to keep learning," said James.

One evening after work, James's family threw him a party to celebrate this new scholastic chapter of his life. They surprised him with a video that featured more than a dozen congratulations from close friends and family. This tribute, he says, is something he'll remember for the rest of his life.

InvestED was the C-Spark brainchild of Desert Financial CEO Jeff Meshey who sought to fortify and amplify the firm's twofold mission — a "commitment to fostering a positive experience to ensure credit union member needs are fulfilled, and to provide an enjoyable place for staff to work that fosters team spirit, enjoyment and satisfaction." Through it, full-time employees could access undergraduate and certificate programs tuition-free. Those seeking graduate degrees received a $10,500 annual stipend. With InStride, Meshey focused InvestED on three strategic priorities: recruiting and retention, corporate citizenship and the brand.

Among credit unions, retention of frontline tellers is difficult, with up to 30% turnover in a given year. Through InvestED, Desert Financial was able to solidify a long-term "Best Places to Work" ranking. It has also earned Meshey a nearly 75% approval rating on Glassdoor, which is top tier among financial institutions. Since igniting the C-Spark,

Desert Financial has also created a new depth of loyalty among its team that has led to greater unity. It is also cultivating an ethos Meshey calls "big thinking." He defines it as an insatiable curiosity and a desire for continuous growth. InvestED is a big part of stoking both facets.

Big thinking also applies to Desert Financial's approach to corporate citizenship. Every credit union delivers on a promise of citizenship because by their very nature, they are set up to serve the community. With InvestED, Meshey sought a way to elevate and differentiate Desert Financial's difference-making capabilities within the communities it serves. InvestED did just that.

Finally, Desert Financial's brand promise and brand values tie to education. In doing so, the credit union sought to establish the most educated workforce in Arizona. InvestED is helping Desert Financial realize that objective. It is also serving as the bedrock of Desert Financial's culture, where questions are asked and opportunities are probed through the lens of curiosity. Additionally, Meshey noted that the organization's brand has remained strong through the pandemic, serving as a resource for COVID-19 relief while maintaining service to its membership.

> I truly believe our InvestED program is one of the strategies that, from a cultural standpoint, got us through the pandemic. Employees wanted to stay with us and work towards our goal because of initiatives like InvestED.

While many other companies scaled back, Desert Financial forged ahead with a new program that reinforced its learning culture and the belief that all employees should lean on big thinking, for which education is a catalyst. At its C-Spark moment, Meshey said:

> Desert Financial Credit Union has full-time employees who invest their time and talent into our company, and we believe in returning the favor by investing in their education and development.

Leading up to and through its C-Spark, Desert Financial undertook a massive visibility campaign, which included a virtual launch event, one-on-one enrollment center appointments and branded InvestED merchandise, such as backpacks and gift cards for early participants. The webinar received a huge response, with more than one-third of the company in attendance.

InvestED's branding for the program was also leveraged for visibility externally across its marketing channels and brick-and-mortar branches. Through custom-designed desktop backgrounds, CEO announcements and even Desert Financial's company app, the entirety of the effort carried the look, feel and company ethos throughout the campaign.

Momentum quickly picked up speed, and Desert Financial beat its ambitious goal of enrolling more than 10% of its workforce within 90 days of launch. More recently, InvestED expanded with more than 100 new skill-building courses. As Desert Financial continues its big thinking trajectory, Meshey, its CEO, is all about learning:

As a lifelong learner myself, I appreciate the value higher education brings to our company growth, employee morale and ability to meaningfully impact our employees' lives and futures.

Chapter 14

Intermountain Healthcare: PEAK

Camila's appreciation for nursing began at home, tending to her 78-year-old grandmother Rosa. Rosa had long been a ray of the most vibrant sunshine in Camila's life. Rosa took a tumble and broke her hip. Camila decided to move in with Rosa to provide full-time care and ensure healing. Camila became Rosa's primary caregiver. It was exhausting, but fulfilling, and it unexpectedly led her into the medical field as a career.

On one of her many trips to the hospital with her grandmother, Camila learned of several openings for a medical assistant. Having already pursued medical assistant certification to better equip her in caring for her grandmother, she landed a position at Intermountain Healthcare with Rosa's endocrinologist and mastered the basics of her role in short order.

Intermountain Healthcare is a non-profit healthcare system so named for its intermountain regional footprint that touches Utah, Idaho and Nevada. It sets a new standard for medical care, operating 24 hospitals and about 225 clinics and urgent care facilities. In 2021, four of its hospitals ranked in the prestigious Top 100 Hospitals by IBM Watson Health and *Fortune*. In total, Intermountain employs 41,000 caregivers, delivering daily on its mission to help people live the healthiest lives possible.

Camila is one of those difference makers. Whether sanitizing a room between patients or filing Current Procedural Terminology (CPT) paperwork when billing needed an extra hand, Camila did so happily and with an attention to detail required in a medical setting. The desire to make a difference in the quality of care for patients pushed her to be the best that she could be. "How would I want my grandmother treated?" was her North Star standard for care.

Camila was recognized for her work. She'd received regular raises and had been named employee of the month after streamlining their patient intake process. From the managing physician to the charge nurse, everyone knew Camila was bright and ambitious, with a passion for caregiving and the chops to get things done.

Her dream was simple: Become a nurse and provide her patients with the best care possible. But the roadblocks were feeling bigger than the dream. The year before, she became aware of capping out her hourly wage as a medical assistant. A reliable car and some much-needed dental work she'd been putting off would have to wait. If she pursued a registered nurse position, though, her salary would double. It would give her the ability to save money and make her much-needed purchases while doing a job she loved. However, RNs need to pass a certification exam called the NCLEX, which requires nursing school.

While she possessed the drive and passion to take that step, Camila's financial situation did not support it. Her family had no money to contribute, and she was in no position to pursue a loan. The idea of financing and pursuing a bachelor's degree in nursing was totally out of reach.

Many Intermountain team members faced this same hurdle. Across the board, many of its employees wanted opportunities for education and growth, but finances and logistics stopped many before they even started. Intermountain acted quickly. In 2021, led by CEO Marc Harrison, who was moved by the Starbucks program (SCAP) and saw its potential for application at Intermountain, the healthcare company designed a strategic education program for its workforce known as PEAK (Path to Education, Advancement, and Knowledge).

When Intermountain's C-Spark ignited, Camila's supervisor had the pleasure of sharing the details with her facility's entire practice. In between patients, she pulled Camila aside. "Apply STAT. You got this." Intermountain was not only going to help finance Camila's degree, but give her the flexibility she needed to manage both work and school.

Camila finished the application process quickly and recently received news of her acceptance to a nursing program. The real work is about to begin. She has decided to keep her course load reasonable for this first semester while she learns to navigate her new path. The whole experience makes Camila feel a combination of excitement and anxiety to pursue her dream. She also reflects on how grateful she is to her grandmother — still her North Star — and this opportunity to pursue her dream.

Recognized nationally as a model health system for high-quality, lower-cost care, Intermountain has received accolades from Congress as a blueprint for other hospital systems. For Harrison, the C-Spark represents a series of CEO-championed initiatives that will take his company's already standard-setting approach to care to the next level. Harrison was among *Fortune's* 2019 list of Top 50 World's Greatest Leaders. He made Intermountain a part of OneTen, a nonprofit membership group of large companies committed to creating one million careers for Black talent within ten years. He has joined healthcare's CEO Coalition, a group of CEOs from "leading hospitals and health systems across the U.S. convened virtually to examine standards of safety and trust for healthcare team members at every level of their organizations." Harrison saw the C-Spark as integral to Intermountain's trajectory:

> As a value-based healthcare system, we are on a mission to help people live the healthiest lives possible, backed by a commitment to providing extraordinary care and exceptional service at an affordable cost.

However, this is no small feat. Intermountain understands that wholly engaged caregivers are the foundation upon which its future will be built. To deliver on this promise to patients, the company is starting first with the core of its organization — the caregivers themselves — and directing substantial efforts toward an unparalleled caregiver experience driven by educational training and career advancement. Harrison is plying the C-Spark toward maximizing business agility, recruitment and retention, organizational citizenship and the Intermountain brand.

In healthcare, agility matters. Among new therapies, new research and digital transformation that accelerated through the COVID-19 pandemic, Intermountain saw the C-Spark as a prudent way to invest in keeping its professionals at the top of their license at a time when more than a quarter of all healthcare CEOs are saying that digital upskilling is critically important. To remain nimble and to adapt in the Intermountain context requires constant innovation while finding ways to keep costs low. The C-Spark enables this commitment to agility throughout the organization.

It also delivers competitive advantage when recruiting and retaining employees. Healthcare talent is in short supply. There is a need in the U.S. for more than 204,000 new nurses and projected job growth of 12% through 2028. These realities make turnover costly, ranging nationally from $40,000 to $65,000 in replacement cost. Intermountain is getting ahead of both data points by using the C-Spark as a key component of recruitment and retention and doing so in a way that positively impacts diversity, equity and inclusion.

Intermountain was intentional and thoughtful about leveraging its C-Spark against what is already a profoundly strategic community citizenship approach. By equalizing access to transformative education through PEAK, Intermountain is able to improve the careers and lives of its workforce throughout its three-state region. In turn, transformative education results in caregivers who can deliver more positive patient outcomes, directly impacting the community both socially and financially. It's an approach that plays directly into the Intermountain brand.

Intermountain recognizes that the quality, capabilities and engagement of its workforce directly improve patient outcomes, increase the strength of its culture and differentiate it as an industry beacon and disruptor. Its emphasis on education creates an environment of inquiry and energy. It also gives patients peace of mind in the quality of their care. Kevan Mabbutt, chief consumer officer, Intermountain, said of the C-Spark:

The experience patients have with their caregivers, whether orderlies, surgeons or nurses, informs their opinion of the entire Intermountain system. Ongoing training of a caregiver can ensure continuously improving service to and outcomes for patients. Our PEAK program aims to elevate the healthcare experience as employees learn, grow, and deliver world-class care.

As it pursued its C-Spark, Intermountain has developed an infrastructure for career pathways that sets the tone for what nursing education will look like over the next half century. The program was designed to be expansive enough to accommodate Intermountain's thousands of eligible employees, yet flexible enough to fit the varied educational needs of caregivers across medical disciplines — from surgical technicians and physicians to nurses' aides and high-level managers. No employee would be left behind.

For the initial phase, Intermountain developed attainable learning paths with multiple on-ramps for its vast workforce. Accordingly, the company is implementing both degree and nondegree options and providing caregivers personalized guidance to help chart the best path for their goals. This access to education benefits both the caregiver and, ultimately, the patients of Intermountain Healthcare, while underscoring Intermountain as a national provider of choice. Of this approach, Heather Brace, chief people officer, Intermountain, said:

People are the life blood of what Intermountain promises and delivers to everyone we serve. This program acknowledges that fact and shows our commitment to setting our people up for success in ways that impact lives for good. Specifically, in providing educational opportunities for all our caregivers, we are opening the door for their advancement while improving patient care. It will also directly equip us to continue attracting and retaining the highest quality workforce at Intermountain.

Intermountain's ambition to change healthcare comes back to a single pediatric doctor with a burning vision — Marc Harrison, CEO, is also Marc Harrison, M.D., and he believes affordable healthcare is a moral imperative. The C-Spark is one of his most valued strategic tools in making that happen. When *Forbes* named him among the 10 CEOs Transforming Healthcare in America in 2021, Harrison described his workforce as a team of "41,000 of the best human beings in the world." Harrison has put the C-Spark to work in service of Intermountain's caregivers' mission to help people live the healthiest lives possible.

Chapter 15

Magna:
EPIC

When you think of the learners in companies throughout the automotive industry, it's hard not to picture a workforce in motion across an assembly line. A rivet. A cog. A tire upon an axle. A body of a Model T lowering gracefully to a chassis. Those who could learn on the job and perform with precision would be rewarded over time. That was the promise of Henry Ford.

Ford was rigorously looking for a competitive edge throughout the manufacturing process. This included his supply chain. According to the Henry Ford Museum, beyond creating the assembly line, Ford's main manufacturing objective pointed toward "total self-sufficiency by owning, operating and coordinating all the resources needed to produce complete automobiles." He owned forests, mines, quarries and briefly set up a small city in Brazil in an attempt to extract rubber. He was never able to fulfill this vision of total verticality, but he came close and, in doing so, created one of the most vertically integrated industries in the world. Magna International has different, yet no less audacious, priorities in the automotive space. If Ford recognized the automobile as a vehicle for mass mobility, Magna recognized it as the ultimate mobile device for the digital age.

Magna is a mobility technology company and one of the largest automotive manufacturers in the world. As the fourth-largest manufacturing provider in the world, Magna has more than 158,000 employees and nearly 350 manufacturing facilities worldwide. As a $40-billion company, it's firmly positioned to capitalize on the rise of the car of the future. The powerhouse company supports big-name automakers like (yes) Ford, BMW and Nissan specializing in everything from electrification to autonomy. Innovation is the heartbeat of Magna, and their technology is changing the way drivers stay mobile today.

Keeping pace for Magna requires navigating and maneuvering through the many sea changes in the auto manufacturing industry. New technology, knowledge and skills are in constant demand. There is immense pressure to keep up with a rapidly changing environment.

That's one of the reasons Magna has launched a pilot program called Magna EPIC (Educational Pathways for Innovative Careers). It offers 100% tuition coverage toward a choice of curated undergraduate degrees, graduate certificates, professional skills certificates, high school diplomas or language courses from seven different academic partners.

Magna's CEO, Swamy Kotagiri, is a futurist who sees the automobile as a technology platform. His support of EPIC is a natural extension of his belief in technology and learning — he came to the United States from a small town in India (a childhood experience to which this author also relates) to pursue his engineering studies. He quickly understood that education delivered digitally could scale across his massive workforce. Magna collaborated with InStride to develop a pilot program that pulls the C-Spark through three universal priorities: business agility, recruiting and retention, and diversity, equity and inclusion.

Kotagiri is also known for his emphasis on business agility, and Magna's mantra is about staying ahead of a rapidly changing industry, requiring an understanding of where it's going.

"How do you develop your strategy so you have the ability to pivot as necessary but stay at the table?" he told audience members at the *Automotive News* "Congress Conversations":

> I think it's a balance of those two themes that we have to constantly keep in front of us. Working in an ecosystem and keeping your differentiation, I would say, is the most important part to be successful in the industry now. If you're waiting for the customer to come and ask you something, I think it's already late.

This continuum of agility meets relevance must be the mindset of Kotagiri's entire, massive team. That's because the auto industry is a rare sector where three major transformations are occurring simultaneously. It's transitioning from the internal combustion to the electric engine. It's navigating the transition of all different modes of mobility. It's also transitioning into the status of an autonomous, also known as self-driving, vehicle. The learner is not on the line as in Ford's day. The worker is everywhere, physically and digitally.

Kotagiri is uniquely adept at all three of these shifts. He knows firsthand that everyone must possess the capability to integrate industry trends and be skilled at constant upskilling — a never-ending virtuous dynamic between learning and career pathways. Every piece of nimble mindsharing counts. The C-Spark delivers the knowledge required for employees who can shift on demand while remaining deeply skilled in their existing roles.

To that end, Magna is focusing on ensuring maximum retention enterprise-wide. Within the automotive industry, people are precious — losing a single employee can cost nearly 60% of that employee's salary. With its various learning programs including the piloting of EPIC, Magna can retain its workforce and elevate people into leadership and specialized roles from within. It can also reduce Magna's hiring costs.

Magna's EPIC pilot program strives to deliver strategic learner paths and on-ramps to open up the program to Magna's diverse population of adult learners. The C-Spark is helping bridge the gap and making more education accessible. It brings more opportunities to thousands of hard-working adults who previously didn't have the resources to earn an education, learn advanced technical skills and earn promotion from within.

In working with InStride, Magna tailored EPIC to essential skills and roles aligned to the next era of the auto manufacturing workforce. It will lead to targeted learning paths that prep teams in anticipation of more significant roles in leadership and management, project management, industrial technology and supply chain management.

Magna is also intentional about making EPIC accessible for a vast set of individual employee education levels. Hence, nearly anyone eligible has a program "on-ramp" relevant to their needs, whether it is a degree, undergraduate courses or earned admission for those who don't meet the academic requirements.

"Our industry is increasingly high-tech, complex and changing. How we look at and address the future of mobility will have far-reaching consequences," said Kotagiri.

Magna is changing lives for the better every day, thanks to the power of education. With Magna's vision and reputation already solidified in many current and future employees, those involved in the Magna EPIC program can be further immersed in the evolving trends that are changing the way cars are built today.

Magna understands that no matter how fast its industry evolves, it will meet that velocity by elevating its people and will lead the automotive industry for decades to come.

Chapter 16

Uber:
Uber Pro

Tanya moved to the U.S. mainland from Puerto Rico with her family and immediately set up shop as an Uber driver. She also juggles two additional part-time jobs. Her husband Luis works full-time at an hourly position. Despite this hard work, the economics of their situation can still prove challenging at times. It's because their youngest daughter has a rare disease, and her care has led to a significant stack of medical bills. As parents, Tanya and Luis are fighting hard for the health of their daughter.

Both parents experience staggering worry, and every night after their kids are tucked in, they fret about what's coming, what's next, how they could get ahead and whether they should go back to school. They know that if at least one of them could work a full-time job with benefits, they could easily cover their daughter's medical bills and avoid falling further into debt. In this mix, Luis has intimated his vision for getting a college degree and becoming a social worker, but the funds, time and resources just are too out of reach.

For right now, Uber is Tanya's primary source of income. She takes it very seriously and holds herself to a high standard when she drives. She routinely receives high tips. While she's aiming for a promotion to manager at her other part-time job, she has seriously advanced within Uber's career path for drivers, earning Platinum Status.

One morning as she checked her phone en route to her first rider pickup of the day, she received an alert about a new Uber program known as Uber Pro. It offered an opportunity to provide drivers and delivery people the chance to achieve their long-term goals. Embedded within Uber Pro was Uber's C-Spark: an opportunity for top-performing drivers or their eligible family members to attend college tuition-free.

Tanya immediately texted Luis. He noted that the program was entirely digital, and best of all, a social work degree was available. Upon arriving at home, Tanya accessed her Uber portal to see if she qualified — sure enough, her mileage and excellent customer service gave her entrée to Uber Pro. Over the next week, Luis submitted transcripts from a college he briefly attended and applied. Within two weeks of inquiring, applying and planning, Luis was fully enrolled. His dream and the future of the entire family gained traction.

Upon earning his degree, Luis will become a full-time social worker, which means a salary and full benefits. Tanya was eventually promoted to full-time manager at her previous part-time gig. With their income future fortified, their daughter's health also began to improve. This family was on its way, and Tanya and Luis were deeply grateful to Uber for making this happen.

In doing so, Uber is the $68 billion company that continues to show itself as one of the most prominent digital disruptors of the last decade. With nearly 70% of the rideshare market and almost a quarter of the food delivery market, Uber is at once formidable and vulnerable. The C-Spark became a key strategic tool that coincided with Dara Khosrowshahi's hire, Uber's new CEO. Khosrowshahi has spent the last three years refocusing the business, placing emphasis on safety and creating an opportunity for attracting and retaining the right type of drivers to be the face and life's blood of the Uber physical experience. It's all a part of Uber's plan to become a global company and a local "super app."

He told CNBC's Squawk Box that "these apps provide all kinds of services to the consumer, are incredibly sticky and are the [hallmark] of business with incredibly high market caps."

Between its super app rhetoric and plans for autonomous vehicles, millions of drivers are still the face of the brand and crucial to advancing the adoption of the company's many innovations. They're also pivotal in Uber's effort to fend off aggressive competitive threats while remaking its image after a series of unfortunate, driver-related incidents. Its Uber Pro strategic priorities focused on attracting and retaining talent, corporate citizenship and the brand.

Uber had to find a way to retain their best drivers like Tanya while providing motivation to all prospective and existing drivers. Extending a driver by a year or two in Uber's world is an eternity, and it knew that by offering the education opportunity to entire families, the company would keep its drivers committed to the brand. It also knew that given its scale, offering undergraduate degrees for family members would make a lasting impact in the community.

Soon, more than a quarter of a million drivers and, with family member eligibility, more than a million people had access to the C-Spark through Uber Pro, validating the program as a centerpiece of its environmental, social and governance approach. Seen as part of its continued commitment to driver and delivery person well-being, Uber Pro is meant to innovate benefits and protections for workers in the gig economy. Uber Pro has been so successful and began having such a ripple effect on growth and impact in communities that it expanded the program beyond Platinum Level Drivers to its Gold and Diamond Levels. As such, Uber Pro is removing huge education barriers for millions of adults who can't typically afford to go to college. Along the way, it's a prime example of how social impact can be a driver of corporate growth and the bottom line.

As for its brand, Uber Pro is delivering proof that Uber is committed to its drivers within its culture, impacting overall esprit de corps. It's also creating a more dynamic and positive experience for consumers as top drivers are eager and loyal ambassadors for the brand. Additionally, as with Tanya's experience, Uber alumni will be proud standard bearers for the company in their support for the difference it made in their lives. Along the way, its brand has made a firm commitment to expanding access to lifelong learning to more people and offering a path forward for personal and professional advancement in the 21st century.

Central to the program's incredible response was the diversity of strategic education paths for the working adults co-created by Uber and InStride. A decision was made to offer more than 100 degree programs, making it ultimately useful and accessible to the company's vast, diverse pool of drivers. It led to three key paths for entry: 100 percent tuition coverage for undergraduate degree programs and skill-building courses, nondegree certificate courses for specific skills, or access to earned admission, which allowed students to start earning credit before starting a degree program. These strategic paths allow a driver community the size of Uber's to accommodate all walks of life in terms of any driver's previous education and their needs. Prior to the full-scale C-Spark, Uber piloted the program in eight cities. It was also very outspoken and intentional about the fact that Uber Pro came with no strings attached in terms of employment bonds or mandates.

By taking the C-Spark to an entire community of drivers and their families, Uber Pro is a game changer, building fierce loyalty and pride of purpose throughout its ecosystem. CEOs who work in parallel industries that rely on non-full-time independent contractors or franchisees who rely on part-time hourly workers, take notice. Uber has just given you a template for inspiring, motivating and activating your network of hired help.

In his 1991 independent film *Night on Earth*, an up-and-coming director named Jim Jarmusch depicted five cab rides from five drivers across the world: New York, Rome, Paris, Helsinki and Los Angeles. In it, Winona Ryder plays the Los Angeles cab driver Corky. In dialogue with her rider, she says with no small amount of sarcasm:

"I'm a cab driver, this is what I do. I have everything planned out. Everything is going just right for me now."

For Uber drivers like Tanya, Corky's self-deprecating humor is now an earnest statement of fact.

PART IV

Norwegian Grete Waitz was a groundbreaking middle- and long-distance runner in the late 20th century. In October of 1978, she was a total unknown when she strode to the starting line of the New York City Marathon. There were three elite contenders that year — a woman from Germany and two others from the United States. However, as the gun sounded, a fourth, Waitz, mysteriously emerged. As *Runners World* described it, "a tall woman with pigtails, with an unlisted bib number, was building a huge lead. She wore a plain white top and red shorts, and she had run with the favored athlete to 13.1 miles — looking as if she found the pace easy — then went past into the lead."

Waitz had never run more than 12 miles in her life. She was a world-class track athlete, having secured medals at 1,500- and 3,000-meter events in European championships. Her husband suggested she try the marathon as her track career appeared to have stalled. When she crossed the finish line that day, Waitz had broken the marathon world record by more than two minutes, running it in under two hours and 33 minutes. Between that day and 1988, Waitz would go on to win nine consecutive New York City Marathons. She also won the New York Mini 10k five times, twice in world records.

If you're a marathoner or a distance runner of any sort, you understand the majesty of these feats. Preparing to run in the middle of the pack, let alone among the elites, takes serious preparation. You spend weeks or months preparing. You log base mileage, long runs, speed work, and engage in rest and recovery. You sacrifice time with friends and family. You work out a perfect hydration and refueling solution as the miles clip by. Getting to the starting line is often the first victory en route to finishing a race.

Congratulations, dear CEO! You're at the starting line. The gun has sounded. You've ignited the C-Spark in a masterful and loud way. What's next? Time to win the race! Time to keep igniting the C-Spark over and over again, making it a backbeat of your brand. Importantly, time to use the power of your voice to call others to action. These calls are essential. They will win you allies in the journey to make strategic workforce education standard operating procedure.

The calls flow into four domains. It begins with your workers — C-Spark.me — and the call to action as they enter a new dawn of living, learning and working. It progresses to C-Spark.edu and the elements you should advance among your higher education coun-terparts. It dives into C-Spark.gov, where you can harness the energy and activity of policymakers keen on education reform to see, advance and solidify the C-Spark's place in America's new *Age of And*.

Finally, it comes back to you, dear CEO, as we make last calls to you and your colleagues as you're poised for the C-Spark.com colinear flywheel that will offer maximum thrust.

Chapter 17

C-Spark.me:
Calling the Workforce to Adventure

El Capitan rises into Yosemite National Park, an upsurge of granite that, along with Half Dome, lends the Yosemite Valley a cathedral-like quality. The Spanish translation of its name — The Chief — was derived from the indigenous Miwok language. Its sheer rise of 3,000 feet was famously captured many times by landscape photographer and environmentalist Ansel Adams. His mystical black-and-white depictions of the rock lend to its majesty and give it an almost waterfall-like quality.

Because it is a rock, it is climbed. This is the nature of humanity, whether that humanity is aged two, nine or 39 years old. This urge to climb originates for several reasons. Curiosity. Awe. Self-determination. A competitive fire in the belly. A love of nature and seeing and experiencing something up close.

No one (yet) has climbed El Capitan like Alex Honnold. One morning in 2017, Honnold rose, had a bowl of cereal and then, at 5:28 a.m., began his ascent of the rock. With no safety equipment — no ropes, no nets, no parachute — and simply using his body, he free-climbed a 2,900-foot section of the wall in just a little under three hours. The method is called "free soloing." It's obviously the most dangerous form of climbing in the world. It's a feat that has been classified as the athletic equivalent of the moon landing or the moment that Roger Bannister broke the four-minute mile. Trusting his body and with the mental acuity to find toe and finger holds, Honnold became an instant legend, propelled by an Oscar-winning documentary titled *Free Solo* that followed the lead-up and fulfillment of the triumphant event.

That lead-up truly began when Honnold was introduced to his sport at age five. He scaled rock climbing walls at a local gym. Then he began climbing internationally. For the El Capitan summiting, he prepared at locations in China, Europe, the United States and even Morocco. Honnold has built his entire life around his craft. He often lives out of a van because he loves nature and loves traveling to the places he climbs. He has created a pathway to make this happen — to do what he loves, to get paid doing what he loves and to continually push himself to do more. Understanding that he is unique — an athlete of once-in-a-lifetime skills is beside the point. A flame was lit inside at a young age; he believed it and took to the path, and El Capitan became his latest, decisive moment. Career and life have become one. He has implicitly and decisively answered the query of poet Mary Oliver when she asks, "Tell me, what is it you plan to do with your one wild and precious life?" For the worker, and this includes you dear CEO, what does this question mean in the *Age of And*?

The Lancet, a medical journal, published research that concluded a child born in the United States has a greater than 50% chance of living beyond the age of 100. Wild and precious lives are extending. That means careers are extending, too. Therefore, alongside digital and global change, there is another shift afoot, and it centers on the paradigm around work and life. Since the 19th century, when agrarian culture gave way to the Industrial Revolution, life has generally traveled a three-act journey.

Act 1 begins within the first few years after birth when the formalized educational phase of your life begins in a preschool or elementary school setting. Once in this first act, it extends for at least 12 to 15 years and culminates with high school education. For some of you, it extended to technical school, college and/or graduate school, which takes between two years or, if you pursue doctoral work, 10 to 15 years.

Act 2 can begin during the educational phase, but it is taken most seriously when the curtain is drawn on Act 1. It's called career, and on this phase of the path, you engage in a livelihood for money that you seize upon, gain proficiency in and extend across the decades with one or more employers.

Act 3 is retirement. The years of culturally defined work are over, and in the old days you would draw upon a pension or, ideally, you saved through a 401(k)-retirement plan or some other investment regimen and live off the fat of your prior earnings through to passing from this life. *Fast Company* described this as the Old American Dream: "If you work hard and save money, you can have enough for your kids to then work hard and save money; the end game for one generation is golfing, and for the next, to repeat the cycle."

This paradigm appears to be crumbling with speed. Traditional notions of retirement are dead. It began with the demise of the pension and extends to new views on the detrimental effects of Act 3. Sociologically and psychologically, retirement in the traditional sense has led to feelings of alienation and loneliness. The Institute of Economic Affairs found that compounding the isolation is a tendency toward individual inactivity and immobility that speed physical deterioration. If there is not a vibrant social and family life complemented by a community of faith, hobbies and other forms of work, artistry or craftsmanship that the retiree cherishes, a significant identity crisis ensues. Cognitive decline can accelerate. Reaching "Millionaire Acres" in the Game of Life is no longer the ideal. The changes are part and parcel of a historic force known as the fourth Industrial Revolution.

Bryan Penprase, dean of faculty, Soka University of America (California), breaks down the fourth Industrial Revolution (FIR) by defining its previous three phases. The initial Industrial Revolution is traced to 1884 when steam power and technological know-how fueled economic and social transformation. The phenomenon of Industrial Revolution was well underway when the term was coined in Arnold Toynbee's "Lectures on the Industrial Revolution of the 18th Century in England." Within it, Toynbee dissected how this new power was met with a "political culture which was receptive to change which included shifts in financial arrangements as well as other social progress."

Electricity marked the beginning of the second Industrial Revolution that predominated the latter half of the 19th century. The third Industrial Revolution emerged through personal computing technology and internet connectivity. The fourth is driven by Moore's Law and the speed and thoroughness of digital transformation — what Penprase describes as:

> the result of an integration and compounding effects of multiple "exponential technologies," such as Artificial Intelligence, biotechnologies, and nanomaterials. One example of the emerging reality within the FIR might be the development of

synthetic organisms (life from DNA created within computers and "bio-printed") manufactured using robotic assembly lines, where nano-materials provide immense improvements in the efficiency of production. The FIR extends the paradigm of Industrial Revolution into a future when many of the elements of what we might consider "industry" — fixed and centralized factories, massive labour forces within large corporations — will no longer exist.

It's a mouthful and mind-blowing, but Penprase's scholarly prophecy unfolds ideas of Raymond Kurzweil and others who say we are headed toward a "phygital" reality — the merging of digital and physical reality into "singularity," which will provide "untold benefits to humanity, as humans 'transcend biology.'"

For your workforce, dear CEO, it's time to challenge and call them to adventure — one that requires courage, persistence, presence, and consistent and real-time learning, called forth over decades galvanized by the beauty, grandeur and quest of the moment. At a point when concepts of retirement, lifelong learning, variety in career opportunity and the love of work, along with the continued engagement with society, are evolving, it's time to begin thinking about how lifelong learning plays a big role in fueling an ongoing, century-long sense of purpose and passion.

A 2020 *Forbes* article reported that this type of posture might not be an option. It cited an IBM report that projected that nearly 120 million people would need to upskill or reskill in the next five years. Its conclusion is swift: for those who love lifelong learning, you're on your way. For those who don't, necessity will become the mother of invention, and you will need to dig deep and invent a lifelong learning path for yourself. As we progress inexorably toward that tipping point, here are some core questions you should be asking your people as individual learners *AND* workers.

Are Your Workers Ready for Rapid and Iterative Changes in the Employment Landscape?

By 2030, automation will have affected more than 60% of all current jobs on the market. Legal administrators, fast food retail workers, telemarketers, fishermen, jewelers, lumberjacks, athletic officials/referees, mail carriers, bank tellers — virtually any job that appears in Richard Scarry's children's classic picture book *What Do People Do All Day* — will be replaced by automation. (Sorry Huckle Cat.) Call them blue collar. Call them white collar. Any collar of job can be displaced or overhauled, and with both, the need for constant learning, constant adaptation and agility and constant reorientation will continue accelerating in urgency and depth.

Broadsiding jobs is the constant, ongoing disruption of markets. Hotels? Meet Airbnb. Taxis? Meet Uber. Cable? Meet streaming. These aren't long-form erosions of an industry — the likes of which we've seen with Kodak or Borders bookstores. These are now known as disruptive "big bangs" that alter an entire market segment overnight. And the pace is quickening.

In this new environment of persistent change, your workers will need to prepare for a shifting role, a shifting career or a job shift and, more than likely, all three. In a way, this isn't new or controversial — just look at previous generations. Your father or mother may have held a position or set of positions within a single company for their entire careers. You and your workforce have probably already held more than five, and you're not done. The new average over a work life is ten. And remember, that's just today.

As jobs and markets are disrupted with increasing frequency, hiring emphasis will be placed on what a Taylor & Francis research study called "nonroutine cognitive tasks." An assembly line is routine. A health care provider, professional services consultant, scientist, technical services professional, educators and creators of curriculum — these are a tiny sampling of jobs that are nonroutine and will grow in opportunity and high-velocity skill evolution (that means skills will have a shorter half-life and need constant refreshment).

Skills. Let's pause on that word. As you begin offering your people ways to navigate the footholds and cracks in their granite slopes that offer the most leverage, this is the word that you must tell them will win the day. They will need to accrue, refresh, develop and consistently foster newer, better, more diverse skills. These activities require them to be forward-thinking. They will need to undertake fervent analysis of your company's needs and strategic direction against the backdrop of their own evolving career path and then make interdisciplinary leaps through both job performance and skill acquisition. For example, if they're an IT lead today, they should begin identifying other roles within your organization for tomorrow that will serve their career, such as a leap into research and development.

Remind them that where they work and where they learn might also change, and that's yet another variable to integrate. COVID-19 fast-tracked the decentralization of work life and education. Thankfully, the technology was there to meet the crisis.

Microsoft's own internal research on the impact of COVID-19 on the nature of work began uncovering the efficiencies and power of working from home, leveraging video-based meetings and the managerial, technical and social implications of the shifts in work environment. The upshot is still being measured, but Microsoft believes that:

> new trends in business decision-making, resource allocation and flexible or fluid work arrangements . . . carry complex implications for the future of corporate structures. And we have uncovered ways that COVID-19 and the unintended consequences of the rapid, global shift toward remote work have contributed to imbalances in well-being and access to opportunity.

Education is no different. "Traditional university students" undertook entire years of remote learning. Globally, before COVID-19, 13 out of 92 countries used to provide distance learning regularly or often, and after COVID-19 began that number jumped to 46 out of 92.

Dear CEO, jobs are changing, and your employees need you to express this and show that you understand. Whole industries are thriving or dying with greater speed. Career pathways are morphing. The workplace geography is hybridizing.

Are Your Workers Prepared to Work to Learn?

It's time to remind your workforce that they're not alone when it comes to change. A recent BCG report found that 1.3 billion people around the world have competencies that misalign with the work they perform. More than 53 million of those people are in the United States. *IndustryWeek* reported on findings from its survey that it depicts as having "carefully documented the manufacturing job shortages and the inability of America's flagship corporations to invest in the kinds of advanced training that would solve the problem. Instead, they opted for the short-term solutions of relying on immigration, outsourcing and automation, but not in advanced training." Tell your employees that you're committed to their future skill sets. It's an entry point for communicating how you are igniting the C-Spark for them, their family and the larger community. It will mean a lot.

Traditional higher education is also evolving before our eyes. A *Forbes* article headlined "Employer U" noted that "no one believes college graduates are well prepared for success in the workplace." Like NCAA "one-and-done" basketball players entering the draft early, some companies are even adopting a "Go Pro Early" model to lure bright talent from high school directly to the workplace and earn a degree on the job. When it comes to the worth of an education and when given two options for what they believe could launch a student's career out of high school more effectively, 60% selected a Google internship and 40% selected a Harvard degree. Universities are awakening to this fact. The BCG report also revealed the flip side of this coin: the learning lifecycle of workers today is subject to fragmentation because of frequent changes in employer. To combat this, universities are creating inroads to continuity for your employees, so that they can take advantage of educational career paths regardless of their place of employment.

These awakenings drive at the question by raising an important point. Your people work to earn a paycheck and, more than likely, health insurance. Remember, after the war, health insurance benefits were offered to lure the best and the brightest to the companies that wanted to succeed. Now they need to work to learn, and they need to evaluate and select their employers by considering whether employers like you are capable of supporting lifelong educational needs. If they have children, when their children are in high school, their conversation around education will soon come down to where are their children going to work so they can earn their education. If they expect and ask for more from you, be ready. Take it as a great sign.

Once they're learning on your company's dime, it's time to commit a proverb to memory. Peter Parker, also known as Spider-Man, gave us, "With great power comes great responsibility." In finding their superpowers as a learner, they need to remember that, "with great opportunity comes great responsibility." This mantra will resonate with anyone who put themselves through school with a side job. They couldn't drop the ball on that job as a student, and therefore as worker-learners, they can't drop the ball on their day job. This will require that as a company, you give them the support they need to learn and cultivate deeper time management skills. It means they will also have to give more of their time and energy to fulfill the dual journey of career and education. Tell them that in doing so, it will also eliminate years and up to hundreds of thousands of dollars of "good debt" embodied by the student loan.

This motivational proverb must also communicate with empathy that while they're learning, your people don't have to check their life at the door. Acknowledge the different pressures they face in their lives outside of work. Assure them there will be an emphasis on flexible options that work for them, which should include the "place of learning" and the time required to balance work, education and life beyond your building.

As they take advantage of the C-Spark, make sure you make them clearly aware of how it is a strategic tool in service to corporate and personal objectives. Dawn Lang, vice president for partnerships at the Council for Adult and Experiential Learning, has said that "Expanding awareness of — and access to — potential career pathways happens when people connect with the education and training that prepare them for in-demand roles." Offer them that awareness. Tell them to apply it and take advantage of working to learn.

Are Your Workers Prepared to Learn to Work?

Referencing BCG once more:

> Most members of the labor force are not involved in lifelong learning and continuous retraining. But skills are becoming obsolete at an increasingly fast rate — technical skills, for example, are outdated in two to five years — heightening the need for reskilling and upskilling. Many people lack motivation and accountability for personal development. Only 28% of respondents reported that they consider using self-service content for learning.

This is the gut-check moment for your employees' careers: are they willing to learn to work? To reskill and upskill? To leap? Many will be. That is, if you are able to consider their true needs and wants. An NPR story about what adult learners really want highlighted how the federal government's vocational training prioritized "the (immediate, changing) needs of the labor market over the needs and aspirations of adult students themselves."

An *IndustryWeek* survey affirmed this point. Adult learners don't want vocational training. Most (more than 70%) wanted to pursue a bachelor's degree. They want to "self-author" their journey and use undergraduate education in particular to rewrite their histories and mend past educational traumas such as having to drop out because of finances or academic performance. Importantly, among your millennial workforce, nearly 60% say that opportunities to learn and grow are extremely important to them when applying for a job.

In discussing learning to work with your people, underscore that it takes a keen level of discernment on their part as they look out for themselves, their family and their career. Be this honest and direct. Taking learning on is a big commitment. Therefore, what they choose to learn should be relevant to their career today and the talent marketplace of tomorrow. It should align with your industry relevance and ensure their employability.

Next, give them the guidance they need to initiate their process. Here's the recommended starting line: their manager and others in their company who are already on a learning pathway. After all, you need a human support system as well as a digital system to get the guidance and support you need (extra credit if you recognize this management function as a nonroutine cognitive skill). If education is an emotional decision, it's also a nonlinear decision that ebbs and flows and is impacted by your employees' workload and role (and the sick child they have to tend to this week). A manager will keep them on track and help guide your people through the process of connecting their learning aspirations with their career pathway.

Along that road, encouraging them to seek out an existing learning cohort — ones who have gone before them and yet are still aspiring to do similar things in pursuit of their goals — is of immense help. There, stories will be shared, understanding transferred and a learning path jumpstarted.

Finally, make sure that other key leaders within your organization are ready to dialogue about learning beyond the managerial layer. Infuse it into your mentoring program for employees. (Don't have a mentorship program? Get one. Everyone needs a mentor!)

The byproduct of human contact and accountability on your workforce's learning path is both a faster and clearer understanding of how their work and learning go hand in hand. It will further validate that they're not alone in the process, and they're not the only ones who are anxious or worried about the climb ahead. It can also help them more quickly crystallize outcomes and objectives of their education on the job. Most important, this is really a litmus test for your ability to meet them as an organization: are you synthesizing and sharing the information most relevant to them? Are you ever active in simplifying a complex process and showing your commitment to them? Are you invested? Learning to work should be a seamless and amazing experience that only fortifies their hunch about you as an employer.

National Geographic, reporting on Honnold's accomplishment, said that the climber embarked on:

a zigzagging odyssey that trace[d] several spidery networks of cracks and fissures, some gaping, others barely a knuckle wide. Along the way, Honnold squeezed his body into narrow chimneys, tiptoed across ledges the width of matchboxes, and in some places, dangled in the open air by his fingertips.

There are no promises that your workforce's journey will be any less challenging as the 21st century progresses. As the mystics say, somehow, we are carried across the sky. The truth of Honnold, though, is the truth of my question set, which when purified to a dharma-worthy query would elevate to something like, "When you stare down El Capitan, can you get your employees to embrace the gift of 'their one wild and precious life?'" For that is what's at stake. I'm going to lean into William Ernest Henley's poem, "Invictus," as I call you to motivate and inspire action on education through C-Spark.me among your team: *I am the master of my fate, I am the captain of my soul.*

In the world of work that is upon us, your people will have to take charge of their education through their lives — no one else will do it, and they must also take a holistic long-term perspective about their lifelong education. They need to heed the call of Stephen Nachmanovitch, violinist and author of *The Art of Is* and *Free Play*, who said, "If we operate with a belief in long sweeps of time, we build cathedrals; if we operate from a fiscal quarter to quarter, we build ugly shopping malls."

Chapter 18

C-Spark.edu:
Calling the Academy to Self-Disruption

It's 1996. The momentum of personal computing and internet connectivity — albeit painfully slow — is blossoming into the information age. IBM's Deep Blue beats Garry Kasparov in a chess match. The dot-com era is picking up steam. America Online (AOL) leads that charge. Its CD-ROMs offering a free month of internet service to experience the adrenaline rush of "You've Got Mail" are ubiquitous. Yahoo! has surpassed eXcite as the definitive search engine. AskJeeves launches to compete with it. There is no Google. Social media doesn't exist unless you count chat rooms and online forums as its precursor. Amazon.com is known exclusively as the World's Largest Bookstore. There is a clumsy race to see what will work in "cyberspace." It's a true frontier, and over the next four to six years, the still-awkward moments of the World Wide Web will mature into the high-speed center of everyone's life. No one knows where it's going exactly. Still, Forrester Research, The Gartner Group, Jupiter Communications, *WIRED* Magazine, Silicon Alley's New York New Media Association and *The Wall Street Journal's* Walt Mossberg all assured us it was big, it was next, and it was now.

The moment was unpredictable, but the internet's adoption into the fabric of global life seemed inevitable, and no corporation or institution could overlook it. In the early part of that year, a venerable institution decided to take destiny into its hands and make a bold move. In the media, signs of disruption emerged beyond AOL. A small company in Northern California sought to become a one-stop shop for major metropolitan centers in the United States. It was called Citysearch.com, and it began hiring freelance editorial staff to become a centralized hub or portal into a town, offering news, culture, events and business listings. Microsoft was doing the same thing, having begun a new project called "Cityscape" that had what *New York Magazine* called a "war chest of $500 million." It launched as "Sidewalk."

"Especially vulnerable to this new-media onslaught are newspapers," wrote *New York Magazine* columnist David Bennahum. "Last year, 88 percent of their ad dollars came from local advertising, generating approximately 30 billion for their industry. This includes classified ads, which have particular computer-friendly potential."

The article noted that most newspapers were toying with the idea of going online, which it said was "gambling precious revenue on an untested idea [that] is a perilous proposition." After all a "garden variety website" at that time cost "$1.3 million per year to launch and operate."

Still, *The New York Times* on the web launched in January 1996. It ran a front-page story discussing how the new "service hopes to build a relationship in cyberspace." It was a moment when website launches were still newsworthy, detailing features of the web presence that included most of the print edition's content, "reporting that does not appear in the newspaper and interactive features including the newspaper's crossword puzzle." Its launch proved successful, and its web presence endured for the next 15 years, but like many established institutions of its ilk, the digital version remained a stepchild to the print edition. In 2012, that changed.

The paper was facing a significant erosion in readership. Advertising revenue was down. When it hired former BBC Director General Mark Thompson as CEO to innovate its offering and retool it for digital and global expansion, the company had recently posted a loss of $88 million. You might know how this story ends, especially if you're still a reader or listening to its podcasts or accessing its cooking app while laboring in the kitchen. In 2020, its digital revenue exceeded print for the first time at more than $185 million. That is not the point. The point is how it got there — how an institution in a business built around glacially paced evolution came to shapeshift toward market relevance when the print media industry was beginning to look apocalyptic.

James Citrin, consultant and leader of the CEO practice, Spencer Stuart, was integral to discovering and advancing Thompson as a candidate for the position:

> So here he is in a position that requires him to transform *The New York Times* Company, and it was a tough position to be in. It was a company really resistant to change, and one [that's so massive and] where you don't actually hold all the levers when you're in power. So, he did two things that are about the most effective things I've ever seen. Number one, rather than have himself or the strategy group create the digital transformation game plan, he selected a small team of next-generation journalists from the newsroom to do a study on what the future of journalism should be and what the future of *The New York Times* should therefore be.

Citrin likened the organization to a university, wherein the newsroom, like a faculty, held both the intellectual fuel and cultural capital within the organization. That hand-selected team knew what had to happen. They knew the financials of the company. According to Citrin, they were brilliant:

> They created this manifesto called *The New York Times Innovation Report*, and it somehow was shared publicly. It was of such high quality that it told the world, "Oh my God, they're serious." So now they have the cultural acceleration of change from within. The second most effective thing — Thompson had the group come up with a strategic statement based on the report. It's only four words, and it's guided everything.

It was simple, purposeful and pragmatic:

Journalism Worth Paying For.

This single phrase signaled that the team understood shifting from print to digital would not, from a business model perspective, be driven by digital advertising. Citrin pointed out that this acknowledgment of the shift also foregrounded a generally poor user experience:

> They knew what they needed in order to make this whole thing work. They needed to have millions of subscribers that are willing to pay for world-class journalism delivered through world-class digital products. So that was the story, and it was

also the strategy. They set a goal of 10 million digital subscribers by 2025. At the time, it seemed ludicrous.

At the time, the digital edition had well under a million digital subscribers. With seven million as of 2021, it's on a fast track to exceed its objective.

"Again, those two things: transformation from the inside out and the strategic statement that is so clear that drives everything. Powerful," said Citrin.

Dear CEO, it is time for you to challenge your CEO.edu counterparts to go deep within to discover a new stroke of genius that unifies and empowers their campuses to shift from a model and a target audience that has remained largely unchanged since the 18th century. It is time, like the migrating readership, for them to more thoroughly address their migrating demographic — one that is moving from campus-dedicated, four- to five-year undergraduates in their late teens to intergenerational working adults and the companies that employ them. As Arizona State University President Michael Crow puts it, right now, "The circles are too small."

In the encounter leading up to a Starbucks-ASU partnership, Crow recognized the common philosophical thread between how Howard Schultz thought about the corporation and how Crow thought about the university. It came down to having a bigger vision in terms of workforce and student population, in terms of social impact and competitive advantage and in terms of partnership in the *Age of And*:

Howard's view of the corporation and my view of the university was that the circles were too small so you couldn't draw the circle of the university, just the students on campus. And if you did, you'd have no social impact or insufficient social impact, and if you drew the circle of the company just around its 30,000 stores, and you made that the totality of your view, in the long run you would be driven out of business by some other competitor who had a circle bigger than your circle.

In your dialogue with CEO.edu ask, "Are you content squabbling over or endeavoring to dominate a shrinking or, at best, a barely growing market segment in a cut-throat endgame with your competition? Or are you ready to draw a bigger circle? Are you ready to rearticulate how your legacy student population will contrast with the learner population over the next half-decade? Are you ready to make a bolder mark for your institution as a knowledge enterprise poised to become an agent of corporate partnership *AND* social impact?" If the answer to the first is no and the rest are yes, it's time to delve into the following, deeper queries.

Is CEO.edu Prepared with a Go-to-Market for Corporations and Working Adults As Customers?

The current university go-to-market approach still prizes a 300-year-old market segment that continues to drive campus posture and recruiting — teenage into young-adult learners who become magically minted through an academic-meets-social-meets-service-oriented powerhouse. In four to five years, CEO.edu hopes that these young people will emerge as equipped, compassionate, hard-driving, eager and intellectually curious leaders for tomorrow, ready to embark on a career. It's well-worn and templated. Drop in on campuses in the

Ivy League, the Southeastern Conference, the Mountain West or the Patriot League, and it would look the same: "Come to campus. Look at all we offer. Select your program. Go with the flow. We've thought through everything, and we do it at scale for a new batch of you every year on a semesterly or term-by-term basis."

John Rogers, partner and sector lead for education, TPG's The Rise Fund, believes that higher education's equivalent to the corporate mantra "our people are our greatest asset" rests in the term "life-long learners."

"Institutions could do a better job of seeing their students as lifelong learners," he said. "And that's not just in order to continue to serve them with education."

Rogers believes a new understanding and definition of lifelong learning must reframe the institution from the inside out. Think of it this way: continuing education, professional development and training, degree completion and online learning are "bolt-ons" to a quickly antiquating business model — tactical, adjunct efforts to seize more learners, grow new revenue streams and remain relevant. They are not up to the task of helping you reassess and rearticulate your posture in a world of *And*. Rogers talks about this in terms of how his alma maters — Yale, Stanford and Penn — approach him.

"[I] have attended some academic institutions that do have a lot of power in the labor market, but frankly, they're not following up with me," said Rogers. "They're just not thinking about me in that [lifelong learner] way."

Rogers believes it's time for academic institutions to understand their current and former students as, yes, customers, and also stakeholders in the advancement of a new mission — growth and social impact driven by a knowledge enterprise built for the terrain of the 60-year career and learning pathway.

"I think it's been more, 'if you build it, they will come,'" said Rogers. "It's always been done this way, but really understanding the student as customer and stakeholder is something I think academic institutions have been slow to do."

ASU's Michael Crow is one CEO.edu moving to the beat of a different drum and a voice calling in the wilderness, particularly about going to market. He has assessed this current model as inadequate to the moment — a moment wherein COVID-19 offered a crisis that illustrates global complexity and has delivered a negative shock to the system. Michael Crow told Ellie Bothwell in a World University Rankings interview:

The 21st century is going to be increasing in speed in terms of acceleration of change, globalization, and disruption of all types — social, economic, technological, biological. And you tell me whether the average college [where] faculty sit around in rooms and [wear] dark robes [is] going to be the best way to educate in a full-scale democracy going forward. I would say it's a necessary but insufficient modality. We need new modalities, new ways of teaching, new ways of creating learning environments. COVID-19 has now brought all this to the forefront in real time. We bring students to these faculties, but only certain students can go, and you can only go when you're 17, 18, 19 years old. What I think we're seeing now is that [through] technology [there is] is a way to take the same faculty and the same learning environment and to expand it, to project it.

While offering a window into Crow's "bigger circle" thinking, this thinking also points to a market segment that must be tended to: you. Here, the traditional "come and see" must shift to "go and learn." Therefore, as you connect with CEO.edu, make sure they engage with you in ways that are conversant in your world and meet your highest expectations.

Look for these institutions to bring a deep understanding of what you and your business are navigating in terms of opportunities and challenges. Query them about your external-facing market presence and product or service set, including your marketing and sales approach, distribution model and customer service sensibility. See if they understand and have a working knowledge of your internal-facing operation, including a breakdown of your current workforce — its demographics and its educational levels by position from the frontline and back office to the executive suite, and the career paths it offers those employees. Gauge whether they have a working knowledge of your corporate values and culture, your recruiting posture and any data or anecdotes on your impact within the communities you serve.

See if they come to your campus to listen. When that happens, do they begin with their universities' resplendent credentials, spilling their unique offerings without first hearing and understanding your objectives and the core challenges you're confronting to meet those objectives? Do they ask questions and take notes? In conversational tones, are they prepared to respond to your strategic opportunity and challenges with their own strategic workforce education framework outlined in a customized and contextualized way? Does their solution connect directly to your objectives and does it power growth and social impact?

Once they have come, watch for their ability to truly get corporate campus engagement. Do they have a proactive listening and response rhythm built into their go-to-market recruiting cycle? Do they spend the requisite six to 12 months to move this customized conversation forward to partnership? In pursuing all of the above, does the institution in question move you through a clear "business development" infrastructure and remain responsive to you, as if you're their sole client?

In reality, any university worth its salt will bring the best practice of a leading consulting firm or business-to-business enterprise to the fore and demonstrate their scalability to service multiple clients like you. Ideally, they will have a partner who can open doors and have conversations with CEOs like you. At InStride, this approach was taken and an advisory board was built that includes former Cardinal Health Chair and CEO George S. Barrett; former Citibank North America CEO Barbara J. Desoer; former KPMG Chair and CEO Lynne Doughtie; former Ford Motor Company President and CEO Mark Fields; former Regal Entertainment Chair and CEO Amy E. Miles; former Michaels Companies, Inc., Chair and CEO Chuck Rubin; former Walt Disney Company COO Tom Staggs and former eBay, Hewlett-Packard and HPE CEO Meg Whitman. Universities that are represented by esteemed groups such as this should ease your mind because you see there is industry credibility in play.

Do they nurture a relationship with you as they would with a high-profile donor? In doing so, do they seem like they've been there before? Do they create a sense that they see how the two of you can cultivate a long-term partnership over decades?

When they ask your advice on how to transform their go-to-market approach (and they will), let CEO.edu know that it is incumbent upon them to have a deep and current working knowledge of the strategic priorities of CEOs at large organizations and the implied workforce education imperative. Of course, you can also recommend a boundary-spanning strategic partner like InStride.

As you encourage CEO.edu to retool their go-to-market, invite them to reposition the university as a knowledge enterprise that transcends but includes the past while reframing lifelong learning and how it applies in corporate environs.

Does CEO.edu have an Online Learning Infrastructure to Support Large, Global Organizations, at Scale?

A refined customer lens and go-to-market strategy don't mean anything unless the rhetoric that fuels them is supported by a structure that demonstrably makes the impact sought by you (and the learners either in or bound for your company). That structure must ably meet learners where they are, carrying a breadth and depth of online offerings molded to customer needs that include high school, associate, undergraduate, graduate, boot camps and earned admission.

McKinsey reported on a complete reimagining of higher education to make this happen, contending that if universities could turn on a dime to meet the digital needs of virtual learners during COVID-19, they could build on that experience and fully reimagine the next five to ten years. It called for a strategic exercise to reevaluate institutional differentiators, services that should stay or go, scrutiny of the business model under which they operate and the opportunities their school has to challenge higher education conventional wisdom.

Here are some ground-zero strategic questions that you can use in dialogue with CEO.edu to ignite the C-Spark.edu. Do they have the resources and opportunity to seize upon short-form courses that are less profitable but nonetheless profitable versus the full-boat, high-profit degree program? Can they establish a data-grounded, market-based program design à la ASU that is achieved through a needs analysis versus an academic committee? Can they serve clients at the scale and complexity of large, global organizations operating in industry such as IT, programming, data science, energy and climate science that are rapidly changing? And as they serve those industries, how do they ensure they're constantly up to date and relevant? How will they handle that moment when the nontraditional student becomes the majority? What happens when online learning is mainstream and on-campus learning is a luxury?

Universities must also think about building a structure that can fully unfold and unbundle higher education for the corporate sector, repackaging industry-backed credentials, micro-credentials, pathways, stackable credentials, subscription models and the like. A similar phenomenon occurred in music (full recording, single song and streaming subscription purchase opportunities) and video (cable, streaming subscription and on-demand purchase options). Ryan Craig has thought extensively about this term (unbundling) and the configurations that map to it. In a *Forbes* article titled "The Great Unbundling of Education Starts Now," he recounts a skiing trip with his three boys who, by the end of the day, were executing jumps:

> On the chairlift, confidence begat cockiness and Zev began commenting audibly on other skiers' garish skiwear. Then Hal and Leo dreamed up what appeared to be mountain-focused constructive criticism: "Hey you . . . you're overskiing."

Or "you'd turn better if you didn't underski." More than a few skiers yelled back "What do you mean?" Another said "Thank you!" The overskiing/underskiing schtick kept us entertained as daylight waned, although it undoubtedly mystified a few actually competent skiers.

College in the pandemic-meets-post-pandemic world, he says, will be like overskiing/underskiing:

> The value of [a] college bundle sounds plausible but is actually meaningless. Despite unbundling in other industries, five years ago the value of the college bundle — what higher education charges for tuition and fees — remained plausible and meaningful, albeit precarious.

Craig breaks the bundle into two dimensions, temporal (a core, four-year commitment for a bachelor's degree) and spatial (on campus with a bunch of services most learners don't need and a bunch of fees that shouldn't apply to all students). He pulls both through the established university model. In doing so, he reinforces how the pandemic shines a light on the bundle, revealing the "man behind the curtain," and "the chasm between price and value is already clear to the casual observer." Craig warns that in the post-pandemic period, "presidents, provosts and trustees will try to put Humpty back together again. At all but the most selective institutions, they will fail."

He then points to three key ways to unbundle right now. Run with these as you meet with educational partners. First, encourage them to offer new industry-recognized credentials. Google is already doing this through its Google Career Certificates (GCC) program. It takes about six months to finish and offers foundational skills job seekers can leverage to find a job and begin a career. In an *Inc.* article on the program, Kent Walker, senior vice president of global affairs at Google, said that the company initiated the GCC because:

> college degrees are out of reach for many Americans, and you shouldn't need a college diploma to have economic security... We need new, accessible job-training solutions — from enhanced vocational programs to online education — to help America recover and rebuild.

Second, demand honesty about on-ramps. Craig points to certain nonselective institutions encouraging students who would otherwise seek loans to head to community college for their first two years, thereby making the last two years at a four-year school affordable.

Third, provide off-ramps. Talk to the institution about how, like a great athlete, some students who get a job offer through discovery programs should be encouraged to become professionals. Finally, tell CEO.edu to cultivate "last-mile training program" partners. Here, Craig foregrounds the University of North Florida's partnership with staffing and consulting firm Optimum Healthcare IT wherein Optimum hires and pays apprentices from UNF from day one.

Unbundling must also be accompanied by the institution re-thinking, redefining and expanding learning modalities in ways that can ever-increase the size of the circles. Michael Crow's ASU has reenvisioned itself in terms of five modalities — or what Crow calls "five realms of learning." The realms are arranged around a core of knowledge:

> Everything we know. Every theory. Every algorithm. Every computation. Every topological geometric mathematical vision of how the universe actually works. Every political theory. Every chemical molecular structure. Everything we know is in that core of knowledge. And as a major research university, we have thousands of faculty members that are engaged in that core of knowledge. They're updating theories. They're proving new things, doing new things and creating new things. They're taking from and adding to the core of knowledge.

The faculty is then organized into a university that offers five realms of entry at ASU. Realm one, closest to the core, is full campus immersion or a full campus digital sync, which offers what Crow calls "normal college." Daily, set class schedules are executed in real time via on-site and digital mediums.

Realm two is digital immersion online through technology enhanced learning. It's composed of online degree programs pursued by tens of thousands of students who are receiving "Star Trek-level asynchronous digitally immersive degrees."

The third realm is termed "digitally immersive, massively open learning." It means ASU offers courses at unlimited scale to millions of students globally who can take them at any time and at their own pace.

"Education through exploration" defines realm four. Learners use an avatar, virtual reality and augmented reality to pursue knowledge of a discipline outside the classroom. It's designed to motivate learners to go deep in a nontraditional setting. Through it, "students are learning science or other complicated subjects through the act of exploration."

Realm five, the outer realm, is "infinitely scalable learning" that is massively distributed, personalized and adaptive learning. Says Crow, "it's designed to be about whatever you need to learn, whenever you need it to enhance your life, protect your life or to move your life forward."

ASU's approach echoes Craig's sentiments. A nonselective school, it has spearheaded the destruction — not the reconstruction — of Humpty-Dumpty, and it has already moved on from a single-modality or dual-modality design around how it delivers education.

Is CEO.edu Prepared for the Corporate "Clock Speed"?

At every available opportunity, discuss with CEO.edu the need for more clock speed. University clock speeds move out of sync with the rest of the world. Mircea Eliade's definition of ordinary and sacred time is in full effect. Time on campus is sacred — a part of a holy rite for the university's traditional market segment. Therefore, energy, time and culture dedicates itself to that rite. No matter how agile, a typical university is moving at a different and significantly slower pace, whether that's the speed of service, commerce, healing or partnership.

It's because university time is most often broken into chunks of hours in specific days (with notable exceptions) that run across semesters over nine to ten months and sliced into four-year increments. This academic calendar is practically universal, liturgical and ultimately predictable. Corporate America has increasingly global interests that require movement at nanoseconds over 24-hour days, nearly all year, every year, with predictability that at times looks like an 8.0 earthquake on a seismograph. This incongruity makes steering a traditional university in rapid response to corporate America thoroughly tricky, sometimes impossible and often makeshift.

This fact alone is why, if you were to view, read or listen to a compendium of conversations, speeches, books, white papers, articles and interviews with Michael Crow since 2011, you'd see a phrase repeatedly flowing through his vernacular: clock speed. Often it will appear as the phrase "changing an institution's clock speed."

In 2011, Crow sat down with McKinsey and discussed the genesis of the clock-speed issue. To Crow, it's more than just adjusting the pace within the current university structure. Instead, it rests in changing how universities perceive their mission and how that adjustment transforms the way a university views, interacts with and operates in space and time:

> When you think about change inside a university, I think the most fundamental thing that I've worked on is being an institution measuring itself based on its inputs — you know, what's the selectivity of the students? You certainly have to have students who are qualified. But somehow that's [become] the measure of success. That, of course, has nothing to do with what you do once students come to the university. And so we've flipped it on its head, and we said, now the university will be measured by what we are able to achieve — what's the quality of the learner that we're producing, what's the speed capacity of the learner that we're producing. And so once you

are able to focus on that, then change comes from this change in mission, change in direction. Once you have a change in mission and a change in direction, then you can focus on change in routine. And you start tearing down the routines that are standing in the way of actually achieving the institution's actual goal. How do you do all of that and still be efficient? It means you have to fundamentally go back and look at the fundamental model of the curriculum, the nature of the semester, the clock speed of the institution — all of those things.

Fast forward to Crow's book *The Fifth Wave* a decade later and clock speed proves integral to building the university of the future. Central to the "Fifth Wave's" definition is another time-motion reference:

The Fifth Wave in American higher education is represented by a league of colleges and universities unified in their resolve to *accelerate* positive social outcomes through the seamless integration of world-class knowledge production with cutting-edge technological innovation and institutional cultures dedicated to the advancement of accessibility to the broadest possible demographic representative of the socioeconomic and intellectual diversity of our nation.

Within this call to accelerate, who composes Crow's "broadest possible demographic?" They're walking the halls, the warehouses, the factory floors and the retail locations of your company, and they need help. They deeply desire an education, and institutions within higher education have everything your people need. But because your people don't look or sound like a legacy student body of the past, the university in its current state cannot readily see or apprehend the opportunity. When you combine your speed, the challenges your workforce faces, a constant state of flux in the markets you serve and the unique requirements of your learners, most universities can't catch up to the levels of agility and velocity you desperately need for your future.

Therefore, the solution to preach among colleges and universities is "You must change clock speed." How?

At a high level, it means fostering a level of dexterity to pivot in ways that enable universities to serve at a scale and a complexity of a large, global organization like yours, particularly in fields that are changing rapidly, such as IT, programming, data science and energy. It also means universities seeking to partner with you must remain consistently up to date and relevant in your industry. And it means viewing the relationship and your needs as a corporation as the centerpiece for when, how and what your educational partners deliver: clock speed at the granular level that could include the time horizon of study or the length of a course.

Take Netflix as a hypothetical example — a company with educational needs based on an evolutionary arc grounded in relentless change. If a university's agility and clock speed could have allowed for it, they could have met Netflix early in the 21st century, educating its workforce in supply chain and logistics excellence for its growing DVD rental business — perhaps for a seven-year chunk of an initial partnership with their business school. Then, as it moved to streaming as the core of its business, it needed educational support for its next-wave workforce in online streaming/IT skills from a school of computer science and data science over another seven years. Finally, as it decided to undergo a significant overhaul in business model that shifted to original content creation for a global audience, Netflix needed education to support it with yet another new wave of employees in production- and business-of-production relevant skills — another seven-year initiative with a film, communications and business school. Such a partnership would represent more than two decades of a collaboration, thousands of employees and invaluable social impact. It would have also demanded from the university a wholly different structure to accommodate learning that would remain flexible for 21 years. All the while, the university would have leveraged an entirely different revenue model.

Netflix is just one example. There are hundreds of companies that share this need. There are hundreds of Ubers seeking to recruit and retain workers on the promise that they and their loved ones can get a college degree. There are hundreds of Starbucks that begin with a college degree program that grows such that when facing a racial bias crisis, for example, ask their university partner to help them in developing meaningful and relevant anti-bias training. Or, when they have a specialized hardware issue, engage their university partner's technology center, which solves the challenge in 90 days, handing over prototype devices ready for testing. There are hundreds of healthcare organizations like the pet hospital attempting to grow its geographic footprint and profitability month to month by offering new and established employees the chance to become a veterinarian through veterinary school. These companies simply scratch the surface of strategic workforce education scenarios that exist right now that play so well to college and university strengths, but only if those colleges and universities take steps to reorient their institution, calibrating their clock speed in time with your business. If this can happen, it will change American society for good, and institutions will do more than survive the higher education Hunger Games. They will thrive.

With these calls and questions in hand, you're equipped to ignite the C-Spark.edu. It's time to remind CEO.edu at leading universities that they have a business school teaching courses such as "design thinking," "creative destruction," and "strategic planning." It's time to encourage CEO.edu to walk the talk and demonstrate leadership in an industry increasingly mirroring technology in terms of "winner takes all." *Inside Higher Ed* estimates that within five years, higher education will consolidate from 5,000 online institutions to 50. In this historic moment, if CEO.edu can successfully reassess your audience, design with care and hone its ability to respond rapidly to a corporate sector that deeply needs its expertise, it can lead its university through the turbulence, and the rewards will be great.

And what exactly is that reward? Under CEO.edu's leadership, its institution will have found a way to offer a debt-free education to gainfully employed learners, solving the tension that currently exists between the two options and resolving the issues around mounting student debt that can never be repaid. It will have also found a way to ensure that corporations fund and support education, solving the issue of dismissing learners because they are unable to pay. It will have found a way to fully erase the line between notions of the academy and the extension school or continuing education program, solving for the artificial boundary between what constitutes an education and lifelong learning. And finally, it would have found a sustainable way to exponentially expand the circle of its institution's mission to employers, employees and their communities.

As CEO.edu considers this, briefly take them back to the 20th century. In 1996, there's a good chance that the university had its first .edu presence online. There's a chance that like *The New York Times*, it's online or distance learning programs were fair to middling in 2012. So, like former *Times* CEO Mark Thompson, challenge CEO.edu to turn in word to the people who stand to be disrupted the most. Push them to find the best and brightest inter-disciplinary minds within their institutions to create their own report on innovation. And then challenge CEO.edu to find their strategic why. What is their "journalism worth paying for?" In addition to growth and social impact, reassure CEO.edu they will learn a lot along the way.

Chapter 19

C-Spark.gov:
A Call to Save a Nation

At the turn of the 19th century, educational experimentation and the idea of universal schooling spread across America as child labor was frowned upon and the idea of a patriotic, educated citizenry gained steam. Horace Mann's idea of a common school set in motion the foundations of best practice that have endured to this day, including how educators are educated. Women began finding careers in teaching during this period, and states began involving themselves in the education conversation. It was in this era that American education began emerging as a golden ticket to the dream of freedom and self-determination. During this time, the secondary school ultimately rose to become a universal opportunity for learners.

In their book, *The Race Between Education and Technology*, Harvard economists Claudia Goldin and Lawrence F. Katz emphasize this latter development as the period's most significant breakthrough. By extending and advancing a high school education for all, America was questing for an informed citizenry and an educated workforce. Later in the century, history repeated itself as the GI Bill (1944) and the National Defense Education Act of 1958 fueled more profound educational opportunities by expanding college access. The act created a nation where personal income grew, and income inequality shrank. America became the world's most prosperous nation.

Then in the last few decades of the century, educational attainment slowed. High school graduation reached its peak in the early 1970s. And in 1980, growth in average educational attainment went from one year per decade, a consistent metric since the 1930s, to less than a year over the next quarter-century. Concurrently, technology's growth accelerated. So did economic inequality. John Rogers, partner and sector lead for education, TPG's The Rise Fund, says *The Race Between Education and Technology* offers a critical window into why education is such an essential priority for the 21st century:

> The single most powerful thing we could do to restore the American dream would be to equalize opportunity by investing in education for all. That includes working adults who have families [and] who need to be able to consume educational content in nontraditional ways, [which] require a method to reach and cultivate learners. To me, that's the rocket ship for the moonshot quest we need right now.

The rise and fall of educational attainment are in direct proportion to government intervention, and within that, dear CEO, you are arguably the most vital player. In the early 2020s, momentum in public policy circles around student loan forgiveness gained steam. Second only to home mortgages as a source of debt carried by Americans, it's in the national political dialogue. Legislation was also introduced to make community college free for all students, and four-year public and private minority-serving colleges free for those making under $125,000 yearly. Senator Bernie Sanders (Vermont) and Representative Pramila Jayapal (Washington) sought to double

Pell Grant awards to nearly $13,000. These types of proposals offer you an opening to bend the conversation toward strategic workforce education. It's a conversation that must happen at the federal and state level. Your power in this arena is unmatched in esteem and influence. As governor of Mississippi from 1988 to 1992, Ray Mabus made workforce education a statewide mandate, responding to CEOs like you:

> We invested a whole lot into training, into upskilling and into making sure that our workforce could meet the requirements of businesses. In four years, Mississippi, which then had a population of about 2.8 million, had a net increase of nearly 100,000 jobs. A lot of that increase was due to that effort. Our philosophy held that there were no more jobs for strong backs and weak minds, and to lure businesses in, we needed to show that our workforce was on point to do whatever jobs were required. The social impact was huge. Fewer people moved out of Mississippi. We were keeping more of our very talented people from migrating to Atlanta or Chicago or Los Angeles, and the jobs coming in were not low-paying, low-skill jobs that could move overseas. They were high-skill, more per-manent jobs with benefits. I was simply implementing what I heard from CEOs as I tried attracting them to Mississippi. When I would ask them, "What could Mississippi do to en-courage you to either set up a branch or a headquarters here," it was the same answer: "You can train your workforce. You can give them the skills that you need now and for the future."

Since Katz and Goldin's book was written, digital transformation has taken hold. Income inequality has taken off. Access to quality education has taken a nosedive, with many graduates considered unemployable from day one. Bipartisan support for education is strong and getting stronger. Still, a C-Spark.gov is required because the information it has access to and the structure of government intervention is inadequate for the *Age of And*.

A recent Pew Charitable Trusts report titled "How Governments Support Higher Education Through the Tax Code" explains why this might be the case. It inventories a tapestry of government spending and tax incentives in the United States. It concludes that at a state level, policymakers aren't provided a solid dashboard from their respective states to fully understand how their state supports higher education — the implication: there is no ground zero for intelligent dialogue and decision-making. At the federal level, there is the lack of a unified approach to packaging spending and tax provisions as a single category. Therefore, policymakers have no clear way to gauge and modulate support of higher education.

Therefore, dear CEO, you alone are uniquely positioned and qualified to ignite C-Spark.gov. Are you prepared to light up the phone of your legislators and other key contacts in high seats of government? Are you ready to join as peers to advance incentives and other critical policies that jumpstart a more immediate transition to the *Age of And*? Do you genuinely believe in strategic workforce education as a tool for your workforce, and believe it's time to band together with other like-minded CEOs? Will you make the voice of a united CEO front heard through a multi-spark campaign, just as the Business Round-table, SHRM and others are doing with the American Upskilling and

Retraining Assistance Act? If so, you need to be asking three questions of policymakers and influencers throughout the government.

In the Short Term, Will You Advocate for Permanently Raising the $5,250 Employer Education Program Tax Credit Ceiling?

With the workforce education crisis in flames, an immediate solution for addressing it in the short term rests in tax code IRC 127. It's a provision that allows your employees to exclude corporate tuition reimbursements from gross income under your "educational assistance program," whatever its flavor. Yet, the maximum deduction is $5,250 per calendar year. This sum amounts to a lose-lose for you and your learners.

Against the backdrop of full tuition, $5,250 is minuscule, and companies have little incentive to activate it. Even with it in play, the workforce must often take on debt to pursue their education. Worse, companies that contribute more than the deductible amount put the learner in the predicament of paying tax on any reimbursement exceeding $5,250. Importantly though, it does have the attention of lawmakers.

During COVID-19, the CARES Act took IRC 127 and morphed it into a symbolic gesture of loan forgiveness. Employees could leverage the same amount of tax-free reimbursement and put it toward legacy student loans, even if they accrued those loans before working for their employer. Again, it's a drop in the bucket for anyone who has taken on a student loan.

New bipartisan legislation known as the Upskilling and Retraining Assistance Act currently in committee offers a ray of hope for IRC 127. It seeks to raise the limit to $12,000 over the next two years.

It's a C-Spark-worthy number and a dollar amount that you could deploy immediately in service to implementing strategic workforce education at scale. As it stands, IRC 127 is a meager government assist that requires permanent reform to prove meaningful. Your voice is vital to catalyzing this adjustment in the short term.

In the Midterm, Will You Advocate for More Corporate Incentives for Workforce Education?

Face it, at a high level, many of you no longer believe that government can keep pace with corporate America when it comes to national rallying points for future-facing, leading-edge initiatives. Daniel Casse, managing partner, High Lantern Group, and president, G100, validates this assertion:

> I think the federal government — and this is true of state governments, too — for lots of complex reasons have become less relevant to American business. Where would I go today if I wanted to influence education? Khan Academy or the U.S. Department of Education? If I wanted to influence transportation? Tesla or the U.S. Department of Transportation? I get that they do two different things, but over the last 30 years, leadership is increasingly coming from private sector companies. The federal government does a good job on basic research and writing checks, but I don't think it's the place you look to for innovation.

It's a fair assessment, and yet what of the workforce caught in *The Race Between Education and Technology* conundrum? It's in crisis, and there is little to no incentive for you to invest in it other than your own ROI calculations, which have received a significant upgrade by your thorough read of this book. Still, it can be hard to justify to shareholders. Government and policymakers provide the daylight you need to scale the C-Spark across your company. Working from the posture of incentives also eliminates the need for either a tax code labyrinth or tax-funded workforce education.

Deloitte, in its report on *Employment Credits and Incentive Services*, offers you the inroad you need to take action. Through its surveying of CEOs and CHROs, it found that skill acquisition among the workforce isn't fast enough. This lack of speed is due to the drastic reevaluation and changes taking place around corporate learning — everything we've discussed so far tied to employee expectations; lifelong learning opportunities; flexible, on-demand and self-directed opportunities; etc. Deloitte concludes that "incentives can potentially help by enabling businesses to offset a portion of their investment in employee learning and training. Benefits, including state and local subsidies, can potentially offset 33 to 66% of qualified training expenses."

As you sit with this and call your peers, here are some incentive-focused ideas to initiate dialogue. To begin, what if you advocate that for every dollar you spend on a career-related workforce education program, you would get a 50-cent tax credit? That would mean that the tax credit would, in essence, deliver a two-times multiplier on your strategic workforce education program. Again, that's probably a lot more efficient than a lot of other forms of tax spending.

Better yet, what if governments would match a corporate investment in employees dollar for dollar? Therefore, instead of state and local governments engaging in bidding wars to see who can invest in and offer the most attractive tax incentives to companies, what if they instead decided to match corporate investment in employees at varying rates? In other words, the government matches every dollar a company invests in an employee.

There is a precedent for this type of match. In the 1990s, Canada began luring production companies from the United States with the promise of filmmaking that offered less onerous tax burdens on what were already multimillion-dollar budgets. States became wise to this, and now many offer tax credits. If you move your film from California to New Mexico, a film can save money on taxes owed or receive other monetarily significant financial perks for the location shoot. It requires that you as a film company invest in a percentage of local crew to complete your production. States bank on the boost to local economies in the short term, and over the long haul, shoot locations can be transformed into tourist destinations. While moviemaking is a sprawling team sport that includes various layers of workstreams, the tax credit structures are pretty straightforward. They most often include movie production incentives and film tax credits covering a portion of income tax owed to the state. Cash rebates for a percentage of what the production company spends get reimbursed at the end of production, with grants, sales tax exemptions, lodging exemptions and fee-free locations (meaning you don't have to pay for a shoot permit to leverage said location).

You don't have to look to film as an exact parallel, and furthermore, there is a lot of published thinking that lays the groundwork for advocacy on this front. The American Enterprise Institute (AEI) outlines how you are not alone in your concern about the impact of an unskilled, untrained workforce. Its report offers a reminder that "the skills gap costs the U.S. economy $160 billion annually in terms of unfilled labor output, reduced productivity, and depressed earnings." Further, skills gaps result in poor quality. Poor quality costs you directly. The American Society of Quality estimates that poor quality has far-reaching impacts costing as high as 15 to 20% of sales revenue and 40% of total operations.

AEI goes on to say that, "if the goal is to increase the number of job seekers that participate in high-quality training programs, more can be done to improve the coordination between the Department of Labor and these groups." It then offers a series of recommendations for enhancing federal workforce development identifying, analyzing and rooting out inefficiencies in the current system.

It then offers an invitation to you, CEO, by foregrounding the fact that "policymakers continue to seek ways to create opportunities for individuals to access training and education that translate to jobs and careers, all while meeting the labor demands of an evolving economy."

Over the Long Term, Will You Campaign for a Regulatory Mandate for Strategic Workforce Education?

Because of our belief in the strategic depth and value of workforce education, this paragraph represents the one time you will see it favorably equated to a workforce benefit. However, as a strategic tool across the six strategic priorities, the actual *Age of And* will only be realized when the C-Spark is scaled nationwide — just like the Atomic Age, Space Age and Information Age. For that, employer-sponsored healthcare provides the ideal model.

You, dear CEO, benefit from a healthy workforce that now expects and selects employers based in part on the type and depth of healthcare coverage offered and grounded in law. You will benefit equally from a C-Spark-fueled, strategically educated workforce that is also grounded in law. It is time to assert yourself in making this visionary call, following through on working with policymakers to create a regulatory framework for SEE. You're probably thinking, "No way. That's for CEO-next!" As Dominic Casserley, former senior partner, McKinsey & Company, says, in this way, you are prisoner to your clock speed. It demonstrates a lack of personal agency among CEOs of every ilk:

> I think it's probably lack of knowledge of the potential effectiveness [of strategic workforce education], but also more and more, I think, a sense of timeframe. CEOs are faced with needing to make a difference in the next six months. In public corporations or a big private equity operation, time frames are short. So, you tell me as a CEO that I'm going to invest in workforce education, and I will see a difference. I sit here knowing what I know of workforce education in the first place, and I think it will be marked by a gradual improvement that leads to a bigger difference in the next two or three years — that's probably the prevailing CEO perception. They're going to say, "I haven't got the time," right?

ASU's Michael Crow delivers the counterargument to this short-term thinking:

What if all companies were doing this and the entire work-force emerged substantially enhanced, and the acquired additional assets from such a greatly enhanced workforce, in general, would benefit everyone? It's correlative to economist Mancur Olson's logic of collective action. There is real value in the collective action of enhancing human capital. We recognize it most when it doesn't happen. When the factory town shuts down, and a whole populace is skilled for a particular warehouse or candy factory or tractor factory. The factory leaves, the people are still there, and the skillset doesn't transfer. The [skills] haven't been developed, and somebody will say, well that's the role for schools. No. Schools take care of people before they're 18. After 18, we all have to think about this together.

To Crow, this is about taking all of it to a new level in a new way:

So, if you look at this net/net, there's a net benefit to everyone by upgrading the entire human capital framework to a higher level of performance that then would benefit every company rather than relying on slow, cumbersome bureaucratically designed public schools that peaked around 1970. And we've got to have some way to add to the learning outcomes of all these people.

"All well and good," you might be thinking, "but this is a long-term grind. What's a real incentive I have to take up such a disruptive cause?"

Workforce education and the inequality gap are moving toward becoming legacy-rich, white-hot issues for policymakers. Think of them as data and data privacy. Trust that you do not want workforce education to end up in the same place as data and data privacy. Without a regulatory framework around it, forged through public-private sector dialogue, it's a debacle — a patchwork that includes the California Consumer Privacy Act, the European Union's General Data Protection Regulation and shifting cyber law costing you millions in legal, risk management, vendor management, breach cleanup and lawsuits. Wade in now, seize the agenda, start the dialogue and make sure the C-Spark is mandatory.

Keep in mind that in the healthcare journey, employer-sponsored programs were not always mandatory, but when it began, employer-sponsored healthcare was a 100% corporate tax deduction. Employer-sponsored healthcare set the tone, created the texture of its delivery and shaped a good portion of policy and legislation, including ERISA, COBRA, HIPAA and the ACA. Yet upon earning the total weight of regulation, healthcare has become a given and public good for those working full time. Workforce education is awaiting this same path. A regulatory mandate will solidify and standardize the C-Spark in ways that will quickly stimulate the *Age of And*, additionally solving for the agency problem.

What does first-mover status look like on advocating for a regulatory framework tied to workforce education? Climate offers a great model. What if, like carbon emissions, the government worked alongside corporations to set specific goals for workforce education investment totals that phased in over time, across decades? What if there was the equivalent of buying carbon offsets that forced companies not meeting the goal in a given period to pay into an education fund?

First-mover status also looks like serving as a C-Spark educator. Policymakers are eager about the issue of workforce education, and as you may already know, they come to the table with some bias. Like all first movers, you'll need to mitigate that bias, armed with the power of C-Spark thinking to educate them. From the land of CEO.edu, the American Association of State Colleges and Universities has said that "governors and legislators want to ensure that state residents are prepared for the ongoing transition to the knowledge-based economy. Investments in certificate and two-year programs that align with state workforce needs remain popular in state capitals."

Of course, you now know that these short-term solutions, though politically adored, affect just a thin sliver of the strategic workforce. Also, often, short-form credentials are narrow and relied upon too heavily as a workforce education policy answer. Your workforce needs learning pathways connected to career pathways matched to an appropriate mix of workforce education opportunities across a 60-year arc. New America, an organization dedicated to "renewing the promise of America by . . . honestly confronting the challenges caused by rapid technological and social change," has pointed out that half of working adults who earn such credentials earn poverty-level wages, and most adults who earn them are not employed.

It's yet another powerful example of why you need to have a loud, consistent and significant voice in this conversation early and often.

In 1972, the Business Roundtable was formed by the CEOs of Alcoa, GE, U.S. Steel and the Labor Law Study Group. It was joined by the CEOs of General Motors Corporation, DuPont and Exxon. Over its nearly 50 years of work, it has lobbied mightily on behalf of corporate America. In 2010, *The Washington Post* called it President

Barack Obama's closest ally in the business community. The C-Spark. gov needs this type of nonprofit bloc of CEOs to take up the mantle of workforce education in a focused, diligent and aggressive way. One voice or one corporate citizenship initiative will not make a dent, dear CEO. C-Spark.gov will require many of you banded together to leverage policy to end the workforce crisis and manifest the *Age of And*.

Chapter 20

C-Spark.com:
A Call to Double Down

Margaret Wheatley, an organizational consultant, philosopher and researcher, offers this description of how your ability to lead your people is inexorably linked with your ability to believe in your people:

> Sane leadership is the unshakeable faith in people's capacity to be generous, creative and kind. It is the commitment to create the conditions for these capacities to blossom, protected from the external environment. It is the deep knowing that, even in the most dire circumstances, more becomes possible as people engage together with compassion and discernment, self-determining their way forward.

Wheatley is well known for her groundbreaking work on organizations as living systems. Using a combination of quantum physics, chaos theory, biology, sociology, anthropology and ancient spiritual practices, she has offered wisdom around organizational dynamics since the 1990s. In periods of change, writes Wheatley, "any organization that distances itself from its employees, and refuses to cultivate meaningful relationships with them, is destined to fail."

Brad Smith, executive chairman, Intuit, takes this idea a step further and applies it to the whole of the stakeholder ecosystem that you deal with day to day, leaning deeply into biology at the intersection of Maslow:

> Employees are first, customers are second and shareholders are third. And if we describe a corporation as a biological entity with a hierarchy of needs represented by these three groups to thrive and stay alive, each serves a specific hierarchy of life-giving purpose.

Within Smith's analogy and hierarchy, employees are first because they serve as the air a company breathes. Without it, a body will not last more than approximately three minutes. Customers and community are second. They are like water. Without water, the body will make it roughly three days before it begins shutting down. Shareholders are third; they are like food. Without food, the body can make it up to three weeks before it perishes:

> You don't get this arbitrary choice to not take care of any one of these categories, but you have to know in which order actually to do it. And the quote from Thomas Edison that a vision without execution is merely hallucination is true. You can have the greatest idea to help a customer, but if you don't have employees to help build it and bring it to life, it's just a hallucination. So that's why we start with employees first. There's a lot of debate across industries about this. Many would ask, why wouldn't you be customer-centric when you

list customers first? It's a mindset that gets in people's way —
it's flawed. The reason being that you can't do anything for
customers without great employees.

Smith believes the second flawed mindset views money spent on
employees as an expense and not an investment. He says some leaders
will worry about investing in the employee, and then the employee
doesn't stay — a short-term liability. He believes you have to look at
employees as long-term assets, even if they choose to leave:

> At the end of the day, you've instilled in them the capability and
> the belief that you cared enough to invest in them, and they
> were a top priority for you such that they will speak positively
> about you — be a positive promoter after they leave and help
> you build your brand. And the more alumni you have that go
> out and run companies, then, you know, the more successful
> you've become as well. So, I think the two mindsets that must
> be corrected are the prioritized order of the stakeholders and
> viewing this as an investment, not a liability, up to and includ-
> ing, even if you put investment in someone and they choose
> to leave. Even if they do, that is still a great thing.

Dear CEO, what does your hierarchy look like today? Is it aligned
with Smith's? If not, what does it cost you? What's the cost of a disengaged software developer writing careless code that creates a security
vulnerability and leads to a devastating hack? What's the cost of an
untrained or intellectually underdeveloped sales representative of-
fending and losing a customer? What's the cost of someone unable

to succeed in your company and telling the world via Glassdoor and social media? What's the price of your competitor hiring the right talent that can adapt and grow?

These costs are mounting. In manufacturing, a 2018 *Industry-Week* survey — the sixth in the last 30 years — "carefully documented the inability or unwillingness of America's flagship corporations to invest in the kinds of advanced training directly that would solve the problem. Instead, they opted for the short-term solutions of relying on immigration, outsourcing and automation, but not in advanced training."

According to BCG, "on average, a worker holds upwards of ten different jobs before the age of 50, and that number is likely to rise, according to the U.S. Bureau of Labor Statistics. As a result, employee learning is subject to fragmentation and a lack of continuity in the learning life cycle."

It stands to reason that the migratory nature of employees is in direct proportion to their place in the hierarchy and the level of investment made in them. This fact drives the major reflection exercise of this last chapter, dear CEO. Are you the visionary who sees your workforce as the air of your organization — the life's breath that drives its success? Do you seek to execute on the phrase "we put our people first?" If yes, following are the core questions you must ask yourself as you advance the C-Spark ever deeper into corporate America (and beyond).

Are You Prepared to Emphatically and Visibly Ignite the C-Spark?

It has been asked of you a lot in this book; yet, it's vital to query you one last time. The future of the workforce is in your hands. The future of workforce education is in your hands. No longer sequestered or delegated or a thing that is nice to have, it is a strategic tool of power that you either wield or yield, dealing with the natural consequences of that choice. The air, water and food equivalents of your stakeholder set understand this. In particular, shareholders are hardening their stance on your ability to deliver on it.

Paul Lundstrom, CFO, Flex, observed in a *Financial Times* article on the business case for staffing that there had been a new and apparent curiosity by investors during the pandemic, and they are asking "very specific questions on things like continuing education, training, workforce development and diversity. There's way more focus on that than what we've seen before."

Lundstrom's words underscore the C-Spark's upshot: corporate growth and social impact don't exist in some ideal future once you've handed off the workforce education decisions to your CHRO, CFO or a willing and bright business unit leader. It has already happened. You're living in it, and the ground has shifted under your feet. Now it's up to you to connect the dots and use your smarts and reserves of creativity to marshal the C-Spark.com — from its outcomes, people and pathways to partners, delivery and launch.

As you've also come to recognize, it's not just a single C-Spark. It's a multifaceted ignition that occurs inside and outside your organization. It's among your .me people, among your customers and shareholders and among your peers in the highest levels of .edu and .gov.

No one else can do it. No one else can own it. It's your last reminder, dear CEO.

Are You Prepared to Hard-Code the C-Spark into Your Corporate DNA?

May you never forget the colinear flywheel generated by the C-Spark. It offers the balance that will maximize thrust for your organization in the quarters and years to come. Your ignition means that it has a shot to engrain itself within your organization and integrate fully into your corporate DNA. The shifting ground you have recognized beneath your feet is the shifting ground of the American worker. It is ground that had to shift because of those from your lineage with whom you share chief executive power.

The Society of Human Resource Management (SHRM) has chronicled the timeline of the American workforce. In the early 20th century, careers and career paths were grounded in "tradition, socioeconomic status, family and gender." Men followed in the footsteps of their fathers. Few women had a course, and work was limited to home and the oppressive strictures of the culture.

At the end of World War II, corporations "became the driving force in U.S. business. Both employers and employees operated under an implied contract: employees would be loyal, and in turn, employers would provide employment until retirement."

In the late 20th century, "boom and bust cycles" of the U.S. economy drove the way you, dear CEO, looked at employees and treated them. Layoffs, restructuring, industry consolidation and mergers and acquisitions put a clear emphasis on commodifying the worker and eroding the trust of the implied contract. The worker lost a choice in the matter and quickly seized the terms of a DIY career journey. As in any evolutionary cycle, workers have become at ease with creating newly implicit rules of the game. With the traditional route gone, they exist as free agents out of which they demand flexibility, enrichment and professional development.

Within this environment, employees can only envision a path directly proportional to your ability to define that path in ever-widening holistic terms. They require a permanent C-Spark that is continuously celebrating, relaunching and reinventing itself to maximize eligibility, awareness, adoption and graduation. They need a C-Spark linked to a career pathway and woven into their managerial relationships up and down the organization.

Since the environment in which both of you work is moving so quickly, they must also become trusted collaborators and co-creators. A Gartner study found that the number of skills for a single job increases by 10% year over year. One-third of the skills that appeared in an average job posting in 2017 will disappear in 2021. It represents nearly one billion jobs globally, and to successfully adapt, you must share responsibility. With this in mind, the career path and learning path, now fused, must be an object of partnership with a consistent and intentional feedback loop. That loop must extend beyond your corporate campus and onto the campus of .edu and the domain of .gov, consistently tweaking and deepening your relationship with educational partners, who deliver the goods, and the policymakers, who can bake that delivery into law.

When the C-Spark refracts in all directions and takes on this collaborative flavor, you know that it's becoming hard-coded into your company's DNA. Proactivity will increase as your culture fully apprehends and embraces how education provides a fast track to personal and corporate growth and social impact. Your strategic priorities — revenue, agility, recruitment and retention, DE&I,

corporate responsibility and your brand — feel the lift. Your customers see and respond to the difference. Your shareholders experience the return as you paint that return narrative more thoroughly and forcefully within the context of the *Age of And*.

Are You Prepared to Champion the C-Spark with Investors and Stakeholders?

The day the tide turns among a few visionary investors who see human value in your worker has arrived, and yet it's still leading edge. Along with Wall Street, many investors will remain C-Spark skeptics. Therefore, you must be willing to formulate the "why" of your C-Spark story every day among core audiences and make it a part of your topline messaging.

George Barrett, former chair of the board and CEO, Cardinal Health, Inc., acknowledges the challenge of defending the C-Spark to your investors while making it imperative:

> I think most CEOs should say that what they're looking for is a workforce that believes they have the opportunity to grow to be their best, and when that [happens], it creates an environment for serving all stakeholders. We serve our shareholders because our workforce will perform more effectively. We serve our customers because our workforce will be more excited about their work and therefore more excited to deliver on the promise we make to customers, right?

Barrett says that the C-Spark becomes a touchstone for a higher-level identity within an organization:

It's a statement — a statement of commitment, and the implicit goal I think is that in return, you're going to get more commitment from your workforce. They have a greater identity with the mission, and you'll realize greater retention. Ideally, you'll also begin to enjoy increased advancement from within. That's a spectacular and rewarding thing.

Barrett's sentiments at the 20,000-foot level provide the requisite visionary take on the "why." You must also cultivate a superior ground game. It begins with costs — costs of igniting the C-Spark, which are sometimes hard to demonstrate, and for shareholders and analysts, tough to grasp. In this struggle, you have a secret weapon: your unique take on the universal strategic priorities. Is a lack of skill, productivity and execution on the part of your workforce directly affecting your revenue and profitability? Is massive change that leaves your workforce in need of upskilling costing you the corporate agility you need to advance new opportunities and more market share? Can you recruit enough workers to grow — what does it cost you to miss out on the right talent? Can you retain them once you've recruited them, and how much does it cost if you don't? In both cases, what does your DE&I posture look like, and how much will it cost you if you don't get it right soon? How are you perceived as a corporate citizen, and how much is that costing you per share? How does the brand — internally and externally — fare without the C-Spark, and what's the cost in terms of internal culture and external halo?

Dominic Casserley, former senior partner, McKinsey & Company, believes the C-Spark can be foregrounded in this way to illustrate long-term value creation and more:

If it is focused on things that are relevant to the vision, mission, and strategy and operations of the company, strategic workforce education is going to add that. It may not do so next quarter, and I'm sorry Mr. or Ms. Analyst, but if it's done right, if it's tailored, structured and strategically relevant, it will clearly add value. Oh, and by the way, on top of that it's building skills in the workforce, it's relevant in general.

Casserley's colleagues at McKinsey extend this logic through the upshot of the COVID-19 pandemic. They write:

Imagine a crisis that forces your company's employees to change the way they work almost overnight. Despite initial fears that the pressure would be too great, you discover that this new way of working could be a blueprint for the long term. That's what leaders of many companies around the globe are finding as they respond[ed] to the COVID-19 crisis.

McKinsey demonstrates that through the pandemic, more than the working environment has changed. So, too, has the learning environment, which has created a landscape that "foster[s] teaching new skills to employees, wherever they may be. COVID-19 has accelerated the adoption of fully digitized approaches to re-create the best of in-person learning through live video. This transformation makes it possible to scale learning efforts more cost-effectively and permits great personalization."

Then they bring it home, offering you ample talking points that you can take directly to the street: "Companies can't be resilient if their workforces aren't. Building your reskilling muscle now is the first step to ensuring that your organization's business model is a success."

Amy Miles, former chair of the board and CEO, Regal Entertainment Group, says good CEOs understand there is a quarter-by-quarter view of their business, but it's not the only view:

> As a good CEO, you have to be able to communicate why your strategy makes sense for the long term. Wall Street might say that's a necessary evil, but that's not a good answer for a corporation. I think as you continue down the path from now to year ten, you've got to hit performance criteria along the way. Investors will want to see that, but ultimately, I think that as CEO, you can't get so caught up in that quarter by quarter you start making short-term decisions. You have to stay focused on the long-term good. You have to have the short-term results that support that long-term good and long-term vision, and you have to have the broader story that supports that long-term good and long-term vision. Investors will usually come along with that.

What does this story look like when the long term is considered even as it moves at a quarter-by-quarter pace? Starbucks is once more the beacon. Kevin Johnson, its CEO, has reorganized its corporate strategy around becoming profit positive, people positive and planet positive. In its annual global social impact report, Johnson discusses these three components of the company's work:

Decades ago, Starbucks developed an agenda of global social impact priorities. In broad strokes, our investments have centered around balancing our role as a for-profit company to better people and the planet. That means we invest in people — especially our partners — so they, in turn, can support people in the communities we serve. It also means we recognize healthy human lives depend on healthy ecosystems, so we work to better the health of our natural resources. As a result, we now have a long-term aspiration to be a resource-positive company — storing more carbon than we emit, providing more clean freshwater than we use, and eliminating waste.

To Johnson, the "pursuit of profit is consistent with the pursuit of doing good," and as Starbucks continues to evolve, Johnson said, "We must stay true to our heritage and what we stand for: people positive, planet positive and profit positive, working as partners to create a different kind of company for the next 50 years."

Dear CEO, you can envision, communicate and orchestrate the whole of your business around the C-Spark that will build buzz, excitement and the right kind of visibility among investors and Wall Street for your organization.

Most important, the colinear flywheel set in motion will solidify the value you see as you walk into your buildings every day: the people who work for you. They are your air, made up of brilliant, diverse, eager, hungry, grateful, messy and sometimes frustrating people. Because of you, dear CEO, you can make a difference in their lives and ensure they produce lifegiving O_2 for years to come. Your vision now can impact the life of your business AND the life of a new generation.

And with that, the theoretical and practical exploration of the C-Spark and the *Age of And* is complete.

Brad Smith has a parting parable that was foreshadowed at the very beginning of the Introduction. It's a valuable touchstone as you reflect on the type of CEO legacy you seek to leave through SEE. He discovered it via Bill Campbell, the management coach to many of Silicon Valley's most significant leaders. It goes like this:

There's a person in a ditch. A traveler passes by and sees the person, asking, "What's wrong?"

The individual replies, "I've been in this ditch for hours, and I can't get out."

The first traveler throws money in and says, "There you go," and then leaves. The person is still stuck in the ditch.

A second traveler passes by and asks, "What's going on?"

The person answers, "I'm stuck in this ditch, and I don't know what to do."

The second traveler says, "Oh, I believe in you. You're one of the most talented people I've ever seen. I know you have it in you. I bet you'll be able to get out." The traveler leaves.

The person thinks, "Great. I feel spiritually and psychologically supported, but I'm still in the ditch."

The third traveler comes along and asks, "What's wrong?"

The person says, "I'm stuck in this ditch."

The third traveler suddenly leaps into the ditch with the person.

The person says, "I can't believe this. You've jumped in here with me, and now we're both stuck."

The third traveler says, "No, I know the way out."

Now that you are equipped with the C-Spark and have full

understanding of the *Age of And*, will you be the third traveler, dear CEO? Are you willing to get in and lead your people out of the workforce ditch that has become the crisis of our time? Will you take up the mantle of the C-Spark, ignite it definitively and repeatedly, leverage it strategically, embed it into your corporate DNA and advocate for it and advance it among your investors for the good of your own growth and social impact?

My sincerest hope (and belief) is that you have or will say yes to all of these questions. If so, this book was a great start, and as you leverage it in pursuit of the *Age of And*, I wish you well.

Notes

Introduction

Michael Crow and Steve Ellis quotes appear courtesy personal interview.

Part I
Chapter 1

Depictions of the first atomic bomb explosion were adapted from the *Current Biography Yearbook, 1964*, H. W. Wilson, p. 331.

For more on the engineering behind the initial Apollo Missions rockets, visit https://history.nasa.gov/SP-4206/ch4.htm#110 and https://www.nasa.gov/topics/history/features/f1_engine.html. Accessed May 2021.

Chandler, David L. "Behind the Scenes of the Apollo Mission at MIT." *MIT News*, July 18, 2019. Accessed May 2021. https://news.mit.edu/2019/behind-scenes-apollo-mission-0718.

CTBTO Preparatory Commission. "Manhattan Project." Accessed May 2021. https://www.ctbto.org/nuclear-testing/history-of-nuclear-testing/manhattan-project/.

Duffin, Erin. "Percentage of the U.S. Population with a College Degree, by Gender 1940-2019." *Statista*, June 11, 2021. Accessed June 2021. https://www.statista.com/statistics/184272/educational-attainment-of-college-diploma-or-higher-by-gender/.

Encyclopaedia Britannica. "Manhattan Project." Accessed May 2021. https://www.britannica.com/event/Manhattan-Project.

Fain, Paul. "Higher Education and Work Amid Crisis." *Inside Higher Ed*, June 17, 2020. Accessed May 2021. https://www.insidehighered.com/news/2020/06/17/pandemic-has-worsened-equity-gaps-higher-education-and-work.

"Gartner Says Only 20 Percent of Employees Have The Skills Needed For Both Their Current Role And Their Future Career." *Gartner*, September 6, 2018. Accessed May 2021. https://www.gartner.com/en/newsroom/press-releases/2018-09-06-gartner-says-only-20-percent-of-employees-have-the-skills-needed-for-both-their-current-role-and-their-future-career

Knapp, Alex. "Apollo 11's 50th Anniversary: The Facts And Figures Behind The $152 Billion Moon Landing." *Forbes*, June 20, 2019. Accessed May 2021. https://www.forbes.com/sites/alexknapp/2019/07/20/apollo-11-facts-figures-business/?sh=458a1c433771.

McCarney, Rhys. "How the Apollo Program Gave Silicon Valley a Jump-Start." *Medium*, July 1, 2019. Accessed May 2021. https://rhys-mccarney.medium.com/how-the-apollo-program-gave-silicon-valley-a-jump-start-4a69cb3bd0ca.

McKinsey Global Institute. *Solving the Productivity Puzzle: The Role of Demand and the Promise of Digitization*. McKinsey & Company. Accessed May 2021. https://www.mckinsey.com/~/media/McKinsey/Featured%20Insights/Meeting%20societys%20expectations/Solving%20the%20productivity%20puzzle/MGI-Solving-the-Productivity-Puzzle-Executive-summary-February-22-2018.pdf.

Rice University. "How Houston Became 'Space City, USA.'" Rice and NASA. Accessed May 2021. https://www.rice.edu/nasa.

Rizvi, Saad, Katelyn Donnelly, and Michael Barber. "An Avalanche Is Coming: Higher Education and the Revolution Ahead." *IPPR*, November 11, 2013. Accessed May 2021. https://www.ippr.org/publications/an-avalanche-is-coming-higher-education-and-the-revolution-ahead.

Scaruffi, Pierro. "Part 5: The Integrated Circuit and the Arpanet." *A Brief History of Electrical Technology*. 2016. Accessed May 2021. https://www.scaruffi.com/science/electric.html.

Shedden, David. "Today in Media History: The First Commercial Web browser, Netscape Navigator, Is Released in 1994." *Poynter Institute*, October 13, 2014. Accessed May 2021. https://www.poynter.org/reporting-editing/2014/today-in-media-history-the-first-commercial-web-browser-netscape-navigator-is-released-in-1994/.

Thompson, Hunter S. *Fear and Loathing in Las Vegas: A Savage Journey to the Heart of the American Dream*. New York: Vintage, 1989.

University of Arizona. "UA Expertise Key in Mapping Moon's Surface." University of Arizona News, June 4, 2019. Accessed May 2021. https://news.arizona.edu/story/ua-expertise-key-mapping-moons-surface.

Chapter 2

David Hoverman quotes appear courtesy personal interview.

For more on the Business Roundtable redefinition of corporate purpose, visit https://www.businessroundtable.org/business-round-table-redefines-the-purpose-of-a-corporation-to-promote-an-economy-that-serves-all-americans. Accessed May 2021.

For more on the *2019 Edelman Trust Barometer*, visit https://www.edelman.com/sites/g/files/aatuss191/files/ 2019-05/2019_Edelman_Trust_Barometer_CEO_Trust_Report.pdf. Accessed May 2021.

Friedman, Thomas L. *Thank You for Being Late: An Optimist's Guide to Thriving in the Age of Accelerations*. New York: Farrar, Straus and Giroux, 2016.

Hutchinson, Lee. "45 years After Apollo 13: Ars Looks at What Went Wrong and Why." *Ars Technica,* April 16, 2015. Accessed May 2021. https://arstechnica.com/science/2015/04/apollo-13-the-mistakes-the-explosion-and-six-hours-of-live-saving-decisions/.

Pelosi, Peggie. "Millennials Want Workplaces with Social Purpose. How Does Your Company Measure Up?" *Chief Learning Officer,* February 20, 2018. Accessed May 2021. https://www.chieflearningofficer.com/2018/02/20/millennials-want-workplaces-social-purpose-company-measure/.

Richards, John, and Chris Dede. "The 60-Year Curriculum: A Strategic Response to a Crisis." *EDUCAUSE Review,* October 26, 2020. Accessed May 2021. https://er.educause.edu/articles/2020/10/the-60-year-curriculum-a-strategic-response-to-a-crisis.

Silverstein, Amy, Debbie McCormack, and Robert Lamm. "The Board's Role in Corporate Social Purpose." *The Harvard Law School Forum on Corporate Governance* (blog), July 20, 2018. Accessed May 2021. https://corpgov.law.harvard.edu/2018/07/20/the-boards-role-in-corporate-social-purpose/.

Chapter 3

Harris, Jasmine. "In the Name of 'amateurism,' College Athletes Make Money for Everyone except Themselves." *The Conversation*, April 5, 2019. Accessed May 2021. http://theconversation.com/in-the-name-of-amateurism-college-athletes-make-money-for-everyone-except-themselves-114904.

Lederman, Doug. "Professors' Slow, Steady Acceptance of Online Learning: A Survey." *Inside Higher Ed*, October 30, 2019. Accessed May 2021. https://www.insidehighered.com/news/survey/professors-slow-steady-acceptance-online-learning-survey.

Whitford, Emma, "Public Higher Education Funding Has Not Recovered from 2008 Recession." *Inside Higher Ed*, May 5, 2020. Accessed May 2021. https://www.insidehighered.com/news/2020/05/05/public-higher-education-worse-spot-ever-heading-recession.

Chapter 4

Jason Baumgarten, Lynn Doughtie and Chuck Rubin quotes appear courtesy personal interview.

Part II

Opening

Smith, Brad, and Carol Ann Brown. "The Day the Horse Lost Its Job." *Microsoft Today in Technology* (blog), December 21, 2017. Accessed May 2021. https://blogs.microsoft.com/today-in-tech/day-horse-lost-job/.

Chapter 5

Barbara Desoer, Sean Flynn, David Hoverman, Tsun-yan Hsieh, Amy Miles, Phil Regier and Tom Staggs quotes appear courtesy personal interviews.

To access Deloitte's *2019 Report on Human Capital Trends*, visit https://www2.deloitte.com/content/dam/Deloitte/us/Documents/public-sector/us-2019-government-perspectives-human-capital-trends-report.pdf. Accessed May 2021.

To access Spencer Stuart's 2020 Annual Board Index visit: https://www.spencerstuart.com/research-and-insight/us-board-index. Accessed May 2021.

To learn more about Henry Ford's philosophy of business and the workforce, visit http://projects.leadr.msu.edu/makingmodernus/exhibits/show/henry-ford-assembly-line/impact-on-detroit. Accessed May 2021.

To access *The New York Times* article covering news of Henry Ford's shift to a five-day workweek, visit https://timesmachine.nytimes.com/timesmachine/1926/09/26/100002542.html?pageNumber=1. Accessed May 2021.

For a complete discussion of digital transformation at the intersection of Moore's Law and globalization, access my previous book *WIREFRAMED*, available at https://www.amazon.com/WIRE-FRAMED-Simplifying-Digital-Innovation-Business/dp/1735622311.

For more on flywheels, visit https://www.britannica.com/technology/flywheel. Accessed May 2021.

Bobkoff, Dan. "IBM: When Corporations Took Care of Their Employees." *Marketplace*, WVTF, June 13, 2016. Accessed May 2021. https://www.wvtf.org/post/ibm-when-corporations-took-care-their-employees#stream/0

Martineau, Kim. "Toward Artificial Intelligence That Learns to Write Code." *MIT News*, June 14, 2019. Accessed May 2021. https://news.mit.edu/2019/toward-artificial-intelligence-that-learns-to-write-code-0614.

Musto, Julia. "Black Staffers Urged Nike to Own Up to Equality Issues Before Diversity-Themed Ad Campaign." *Fox Business*, August 5, 2020. Accessed May 2021. https://www.foxbusiness.com/economy/workday-during-covid-19-pandemic-is-48-minutes-longer-has-more-meetings-and-emails.

O'Brien, Sarah. "Study Warns the Digital Talent Gap Is Widening—Here's What You Can Do." *LinkedIn Talent Blog* (blog), October 26, 2017. Accessed May 2021. https://www.linkedin.com/business/talent/blog/talent-strategy/study-warns-digital-talent-gap-is-widening.

Porter, Michael E., and Nitin Nohria. "How CEOs Manage Time." *Harvard Business Review* (July-August 2018). Accessed May 2021. https://hbr.org/2018/07/how-ceos-manage-time.

Savitz, Eric. "Apple CEO Tim Cook: Live from the Goldman SachsConference." *Forbes*, February 14, 2012. Accessed May 2021. https://www.forbes.com/sites/ericsavitz/2012/02/14/apple-ceo-tim-cook-live-from-the-goldman-sachs-conference/?sh=6fad87505955.

Simonite, Tim. "Google's Learning Software Learns to Write Learning Software." *WIRED*, October 13, 2017. Accessed May 2021. https://www.wired.com/story/googles-learning-software-learns-to-write-learning-software/.

Chapter 6

Jason Baumgarten, Mark Fields and Chuck Rubin quotes appear courtesy personal interview.

For more on *Midnight Diner*, visit https://www.imdb.com/title/tt1882928/. Accessed May 2021.

For more on VC investment in fintech, visit https://www.
businesswire.com/news/home/20210222005993/en/VC-In-
vestment-in-Fintech-More-Than-Doubles-in-Second-Half-of-
2020-%E2%80%93-Expected-to-Remain-Strong-Into-2021-Accord-
ing-to-KPMG%E2%80%99s-Pulse-of-Fintech. Accessed May 2021.

For more on PwC'S look at customer experience, visit
https://www.pwc.com/us/en/services/consulting/library/
consumer-intelligence-series/future-of-customer-experience.html.
Accessed May 2021.

Retail data appear courtesy InStride.

Financial services data appear courtesy Deloitte, *Finextra*, *Forbes*
and nCino.

Food production and consumer packaged goods data appear
courtesy Inside Higher Ed, The Lumina Foundation, Marsh and
McLennan, University of California at Davis, The United Nations,
The United States Bureau of Labor Stastics (BLS).

Healthcare data appear courtesy BLS, EL, Nursing Solutions, Inc.,
PwC Health Research Institute and Relias.

Industrial/manufacturing data appear courtesy The American Society for Quality, The National Association of Manufacturers, The Society for Human Resource Management (SHRM) and Tooling-SME. Technology data appear courtesy *Fortune*, Deloitte, *IndustryWeek*, Gallup, *Harvard Business Review*, McKinsey & Associates and the Unites States Equal Employment Opportunity Commission (EEOC).

Loprest, Pamela, and Kelly S. Mikelson. "Frontline Workers in the Retail Sector." *Urban Institute*, August 2019. Accessed May 2021. https://www.urban.org/sites/default/files/publication/100769/frontline_workers_in_the_retail_sector_1.pdf.

Chapter 7

Michael Crow, Steve Ellis, Phil Regier and Michelle Westfort quotes appear courtesy personal interview.

For more on the ASU-Starbucks Center for the Future of People and the Planet, visit https://stories.starbucks.com/stories/2021/starbucks-announces-new-planet-and-people-positive-research-facility-in-partnership-with-arizona-state-university/. Accessed May 2021.

For more on the Columbia University and U.S. Marine Corps partnership visit https://www.military.com/education/getting-your-degree/leadership- scholar-program.html. Accessed May 2021.

For more on the CUNY and JetBlue partnership, visit https://sps. cuny.edu/jetblue-crewmembers-earn-your-masters-degree-online. Accessed May 2021.

For more on the Starbucks Technology Center and Arizona State University, visit https://news.asu.edu/20180108-solutions-star-bucks-interns-digital-experience-skysong. Accessed May 2021.

For more on the University of Pennsylvania and Intel partnership, visit https://newsroom.intel.com/news/intel-works-university-pennsylvania-using-privacy-preserving-ai-identify-brain-tu-mors/ #gs.0olkov and https://www.pfizer.com/news/press-release/press-release-detail/pfizer_inc_and_the_university_of_pennsylva-nia_announce_15_million_partnership. Accessed May 2021.

For more on the University of Virginia and U.S. Navy partnership visit https://www.darden.virginia.edu/executive-education/for-organizations/military-partnerships/navy. Accessed May 2021.

For more on the University of Wisconsin-Madison and Aldevron partnership, visit https://news.wisc.edu/aldevron-expands-manufacturingcapabilities-in-madison/. Accessed May 2021.

Fine, Charles H. *Clockspeed: Winning Industry Control in the Age of Temporary Advantage*. New York: Basic Books, 1998.

Hatch, Joshua, and Brian O'Leary. "Where Does Your Freshman Class Come from?" *Chronicle of Higher Education*, July 23, 2020. Accessed May 2021. https://www.chronicle.com/article/where-does-your-freshman-class-come-from/?cid=gen_sign_in.

Lederman, Doug. "Online Is (Increasingly) Local." *Inside Higher Ed*, June 5, 2019. Accessed May 2021. https://www.insidehighered.com/digital-learning/article/2019/06/05/annual-survey-shows-online-college-students-increasingly.

Chapter 8

Jonathan Lau quotes appear courtesy personal interview.

For more on Kevin Johnson's take on the Starbucks SCAP program, visit https://www.youtube.com/watch?v=k1Pheh2yoP4 (as of May 2021). Accessed May 2021.

Barzun, Jacques. *From Dawn to Decadence, 1500 to the Present: 500 Years of Western Cultural Life*. New York: Harper Perennial, 2001.

Charan, Ram, and Geri Willigan. *Rethinking Competitive Advantage: New Rules for the Digital Age*. New York: Currency 2021.

Volzer, Deb, Jessica Burgess, and Andrew Magda. *Reimagining the Workforce 2021: Closing the Skills Gap through Education.* Louisville, KY: Wiley Edu. LLC, 2021. https://edservices.wiley.com/wp-content/uploads/2021/02/202102-ReimaginingtheWorkforce2021-report-WES.pdf.

Chapter 9

Steve Ellis, Teri McClure, Ray Mabus and Ron Sugar quotes appear courtesy personal interview.

For more on Howard Schultz comments at the Starbucks SCAP launch visit https://aipcommercialrealestate.com/starbucks-fulfilling-company-conscious/. Accessed May 2021.

Ripley, Amanda. "The Upwardly Mobile Barista." *The Atlantic* (July/August 2021). Accessed May 2015. https://www.theatlantic.com/magazine/archive/2015/05/the-upwardly-mobile-barista/389513/.

Chapter 10

Lynne Doughtie and Tom Staggs quotes appear courtesy personal interview.

For more on Kevin Johnson's take on the Starbucks SCAP program, visit https://www.youtube.com/watch?v=k1Pheh2yoP4. Accessed May 2021.

Part III

Chapter 11

Dan Aja and Brian Garish quotes appear courtesy personal interview.

For more information on the Australian Cattle Dog, visit https://www. akc.org/dog-breeds/australian-cattle-dog/. Accessed May 22, 2021.

Chapter 12

Bach, Natasha. "How Carvana Is Transforming the Car Buying Process." *Campaign Live*. Haymarket Media, December 16, 2020. Accessed May 22, 2021. https://www.campaignlive.com/article/ carvana-transforming-car-buying-process/1702931?utm_source= website&utm_medium=social.

Dignan, Larry. "Carvana Scales Its Auto Purchasing Amid Triple Digit Q3 Growth, Partners with Lyft." *ZDNet*, November 7, 2019. Accessed May 22, 2021. https://www.zdnet.com/article/carvana-scales-its-auto-purchasing-amidtriple-digit-q3-growth-partners-with-lyft/.

Morrison, Lauren. "Car Vending Machine." *MotorWeek*. Accessed May 22, 2021. https://www.motorweek.org/features/fyi/car-vending-machine/.

Naughton, Nora. "Growth in Online Shopping and Used Cars Lifts Carvana, Attracts Competition." *Wall Street Journal*, August 10, 2020. Accessed May 22, 2021. https://www.wsj.com/articles/growth-in-online-shopping-and-used-cars-lifts-carvana-attracts-competition-11597060148.

Chapter 14

For more on the *2021* Fortune/*IBM Watson Health 100 Top Hospitals*, visit https://fortune.com/2021/04/27/100-top-hospitals-2021-ibm-watson-health/. Accessed May 2021.

For more on *Fortune's* Top Healthcare Leaders, visit https://www.forbes.com/sites/robertreiss/2021/05/24/10-ceos-transform-ing-healthcare-in-america/?sh=38517c3c4b7d. Accessed May 2021.

Healthcare data appear courtesy Bureau of Labor Statistics, EY, Nursing Solutions, Inc., PwC Health Research Institute and Relias.

Chapter 15

For more on Henry Ford, visit https://henryfordchangingtpm.weebly.com/social-impact.html and https://www.thehenryford.org/. Accessed May 22, 2021.

For more on *Night on Earth*, visit https://www.rottentomatoes.com/m/night_on_earth. Accessed May 22, 2021.

Irwin, John. "Magna More Than Doubles Q1 Net Income, Improves 2021 Forecast." *Automotive News*, May 6, 2021. Accessed May 22, 2021. https://www.autonews.com/suppliers/magna-more-doubles-q1-net-income-improves-2021-forecast

MacDonald, Chris. "Forget Tesla! Magna Stock Is the Way to Play the EV Space." *The Motley Fool*, January 24, 2021. Accessed May 22, 2021. https://www.fool.ca/2021/01/24/forget-tesla-magna-stock-is-the-way-to-play-the-ev-space/.

Magna International Inc. "Sustainability Report 2019." Accessed May 22, 2021. https://www.magna.com/docs/default-source/sustainability-policy/magna-intl-annual-information-form---sustainability-report-(online-version)---clean-pdf.pdf?sfvrsn=c57a97d6_0

Chapter 16

To watch Dara Khosrowshahi's CNBC Squawk Box segment, visit https://www.cnbc.com/video/2021/05/06/uber-ceo-dara-khosrowshahi-we-think-we-can-be-the-local-super-app.html. Accessed May 22, 2021.

Part IV

For more on Grete Waitz and her emergence on the New York running scene, visit https://www.runnersworld.com/news/a24419569/grete-waitz- anniversary-nyc-marathon/. Accessed May 22, 2021.

Chapter 17

For more on Stephen Nachmanovitch, visit https://www.freeplay.com/. Accessed May 22, 2021.

Brownstein, Joseph. "Most Babies Born Today May Live Past 100." *ABC News*, October 1, 2009. Accessed May 22, 2021. https://abc-news.go.com/Health/WellnessNews/half-todays-babies-expected-live-past-100/story?id=8724273.

Busteed, Brandon. "'Employer U' Is Here, And It's Here to Stay." Forbes, February 7, 2020. Accessed May 22, 2021. https://www.forbes.com/sites/brandonbusteed/2020/02/07/employer-u-is-here-and-its-here-to-stay/?sh=744e8542c45c.

Busteed, Brandon. "The Really Good and Really Bad News on Lifelong Learning." *Forbes*. February 17, 2020. Accessed May 22, 2021. https://www.forbes.com/sites/brandonbusteed/2020/02/17/the-really-good-and-really-bad-news-on-lifelong-learning/.

Collins, Michael. "Where Will Manufacturing Get Highly Skilled Workers for the Digital Revolution?" *IndustryWeek*. September 14, 2020. Accessed May 22, 2021. https://www.industryweek.com/leadership/article/21141889/where-will-manufacturing-get-highly-skilled-workers-for-the-digital-revolution.

"Invictus." Poetry Foundation, 1875. Accessed May 22, 2021. https://www.poetryfoundation.org/poems/51642/invictus.

Jansen, Eric. "Traditional Retirement Is Dead." *CNBC*. November 1, 2017. Accessed May 22, 2021. https://www.cnbc.com/2017/11/01/traditional-retirement-is-dead.html.

Kamenetz, Anya. "What Adult Learners Really Need (Hint: It's Not Just Job Skills)." *NPR Ed* (blog). NPR, April 18, 2018. Accessed May 22, 2021. https://www.npr.org/sections/ed/2018/04/18/600855667/what-adult-learners-really-need-hint-its-not-just-job-skills.

Kolko, Jon. "The New American Dream Is Just as Unattainable as the Old One." *Fast Company*, August 7, 2020. Accessed May 22, 2021. https://www.fastcompany.com/90476099/the-new-american-dream-is-just-as-unattainable-as-the-old-one.

Penprase, Bryan. "The Fourth Industrial Revolution and Higher Education." Soka University, December 3, 2018. Accessed May 22, 2021. http://sites.soka.edu/faculty/bpenprase/wp-content/uploads/2018/03/bpenprase.fourth.industrial.revolution.article.ver_.Dec_.3.sorted.refs_.pdf.

Puckett, J., Ernesto Pagano, Tyce Henry, Tobias Krause, Pashmeena Hilal, Arianna Trainito, and Abigail Frost. "Call for a New Era of Higher Ed – Employer Collaboration." *BCG Global*, July 7, 2020. Accessed May 22, 2021. https://www.bcg.com/publications/2020/new-era-higher-ed-employer-collaboration.

Ra, Sungsup, Unika Shrestha, Sameer Khatiwada, Seung Won Yoon, and Kibum Kwon. "The Rise of Technology and Impact on Skills." *International Journal of Training Research 17*, no. sup1 (July 5, 2019): 26–40. Accessed May 22, 2021. https://doi.org/10.1080/14480220.2019.1629727.

Scarry, Richard. *What Do People Do All Day?* New York: Random House, 1968.

Synnott, Mark. "Exclusive: Alex Honnold Completes the Most Dangerous Free-Solo Ascent Ever." *National Geographic*, October 3, 2018. Accessed May 22, 2021. https://www.nationalgeographic.com/adventure/article/most-dangerous-free-solo-climb-yosemite-national-park-el-capitan.

Teevan, Jaime, Brent Hecht, and Sonia Jaffe, eds. *The New Future of Work: Research from Microsoft on the Impact of the Pandemic on Work Practices.* 1st ed. Microsoft, 2021. Accessed May 22, 2021. https://www.microsoft.com/en-us/research/uploads/prod/2021/01/NewFutureOfWorkReport.pdf.

Chapter 18

James Citrin, Michael Crow and John Rogers quotes appear courtesy personal interview.

For more on Mircea Eliade, visit https://www.britannica.com/biography/Mircea-Eliade. Accessed May 22, 2021.

For more on InStride's Advisory Board, visit https://www.instride.com/leadership-advisory/. Accessed May 22, 2021.

For more on Ryan Craig's "A New U: Faster + Cheaper Alternatives to College," visit https://www.insidehighered.com/digital-learning/article/2018/08/22/qa-ryan-craig-author-new-book-faster-cheaper-college. Accessed May 22, 2021.

To access McKinsey's interview with Michael Crow, visit https://www.mckinsey.com/~/media/McKinsey/Industries/Public%20and%20Social%20Sector/Our%20Insights/Innovating%20US%20higher%20education%20Arizona%20State%20Universitys%20Michael%20Crow/Innovating%20US%20higher%20education%20Arizona%20State%20Universitys%20Michael%20Crow.pdf. Accessed May 22, 2021.

Bennahum, David S. "City of Bytes: High Tech Giants Are Invading the Local-News Business with Expensive 'City Sites' — Which Probably Means More Bad News for Newspapers. *New York Magazine.* September 30, 1996.

Craig, Ryan. "The Great Unbundling of Higher Education Starts Now." *Forbes*, July 24, 2020. Accessed May 22, 2021. https://www.forbes.com/sites/ryancraig/2020/07/24/the-great-unbundling-of-higher-education- starts-now/?sh=2ff92a346ed2.

William B. Dabars. *Designing the New American University.* Baltimore: Johns Hopkins University Press, 2015.

Crow, Michael and William B. Dabars. *The Fifth Wave: The Evolution of American Higher Education*. Baltimore: Johns Hopkins University Press, 2020.

Kroger, John. "10 Predictions for Higher Education's Future." *Leadership in Higher Education* (blog). *Inside Higher Ed*, May 26, 2020. Accessed May 2021. https://www.insidehighered.com/blogs/leadership-higher-education/10-predictions-higher-education%E2%80%99s-future.

Lewis, Peter H. "*The New York Times* Introduces a Web Site." *New York Times*, January 22, 1996, sec. Business. Accessed May 22, 2021. https://www.nytimes.com/1996/01/22/business/the-new-york-times-introduces-a-web-site.html.

Sheffield, Hazel. "Thompson Has Digital Cred But Faces Challenges at NYT." *Columbia Journalism Review*, August 16, 2012. Accessed May 22, 2021. https://www.cjr.org/behind_the_news/mark_thompson_has_digital_cred.php.

Walker, Ken. "A Digital Jobs Program to Help America's Economic Recovery." The Keyword (blog), July 13, 2020. Accessed May 22, 2021. https://blog.google/outreach-initiatives/grow-with-google/digital-jobs-program-help-americas-economic-recovery/.

Chapter 19

Daniel Casse, Dominic Casserley, Ray Mabus and John Rogers quotes appear courtesy personal interview.

For more on *The Race Between Education and Technology*, visit https://inequality.hks.harvard.edu/race-between-education-and-technology. Accessed May 22, 2021.

For more on the CARES Act and IRC 127, visit https://www.natlawreview.com/article/stimulus-bill-extends-availability-student-loan-forgiveness-us. Accessed May 22, 2021.

For more on The College for All Act, visit https://www.nasfaa.org/news-item/25370/New_Bill_Would_Make_Community_College_Free_for_All_Double_Maximum_Pell_Grant_Award (as of May 22, 2021).

For more on the American Upskilling and Retraining Act, visit https://www.congress.gov/bill/116th-congress/senate-bill/4408/all-info. Accessed May 22, 2021.

To access the American Enterprise Institute's *Improving Skills Through America's Workforce Development System*, visit https://www.aei.org/research-products/report/improving-skills-through-americas-workforce-development-system/. Accessed May 22, 2021.

To access the American Association of Colleges and Universities report, *Higher Education State Policy Issues for 2020*, visit https://www.aascu.org/policy/publications/policy-matters/Top102020.pdf. Accessed May 22, 2021.

To access Deloitte's report on *Employment Credits and Incentive Services* visit https://www2.deloitte.com/content/dam/Deloitte/us/Documents/Tax/us-tax-employment-services-brochure.pdf. Accessed May 22, 2021.

To access the Pew Charitable Trusts report *How Governments Support Higher Education Through the Tax Code*, visit https://www.pewtrusts.org/~/media/assets/2017/02/how-governments-support-higher-education- through-tax-code.pdf. Accessed May 22, 2021.

Ositelu, Monique O. "Five Things Policymakers Should Know About Short-Term Credentials." *New America*, last modified March 2, 2021. Accessed May 22, 2021. https://www.newamerica.org/education-policy/reports/five-things-policymakers-should-know-about-short-term-credentials/.

Six Sigma. "The Cost of Poor Quality: Why Quality Is the Most Important Success Metric." *Six Sigma Daily* (blog), July 23, 2020. Accessed May 22, 2021. https://www.sixsigmadaily.com/quality-most-important-success-metric/.

Chapter 20

George Barrett, Dominic Casserley, Amy Miles and Brad Smith quotes appear courtesy personal interview.

Margaret Wheatley quote appears courtesy https://margaretwheatley.com. Accessed May 22, 2021.

For more on Gartner's study of the workforce, visit https://www.gartner.com/en/newsroom/press-releases/2018-09-06-gartner-says-only-20-percent-of-employees-have-the-skills-needed-for-both-their-current-role-and-their-future-career. Accessed May 22, 2021.

To access SHRM's Developing Employee Career Paths and Ladders Toolkit, visit https://www.shrm.org/resourcesandtools/tools-and-samples/toolkits/pages/developingemployeecareerpathsandladders.aspx. Accessed May 22, 2021.

Agrawal, Sapana, Aaron De Smet, Sébastien Lacroix, and Angelika Reich. "To Emerge Stronger from the COVID-19 Crisis, Companies Should Start Reskilling Their Workforces Now." McKinsey & Company, May 7, 2020. Accessed May 22, 2021. https://www.mckinsey.com/business-functions/organization/our-insights/to-emerge-stronger-from-the-covid-19-crisis-companies-should-start-reskilling-their-workforces-now.

Collins, Michael. "Where Will Manufacturing Get Highly Skilled Workers for the Digital Revolution?" *IndustryWeek*, September 15, 2020. Accessed May 22, 2021. https://www.industryweek.com/leadership/article/21141889/where-will-manufacturing-get-highly-skilled-workers-for-the-digital-revolution.

Johnson, Kevin. "A Message from Starbucks CEO Kevin Johnson: Our 2019 Impact." Starbucks. June 24, 2020. Accessed May 22, 2021. https://stories.starbucks.com/stories/2020/a-message-from-starbucksceo-kevin-johnson-our-2019-impact/.

Murray, Sarah. "Pandemic Boosts Business Case for Investing in Staff." *Financial Times*, January 10, 2021. Accessed May 22, 2021. https://www.ft.com/content/98939b68-d246-40b2-be74-63e75683b3ec.

Puckett, J., Ernesto Pagano, Tyce Henry, Tobias Krause, Pashmeena Hilal, Arianna Trainito, and Abigail Frost. "Call for a New Era of Higher Ed – Employer Collaboration." *BCG Global*, July 7, 2020. Accessed May 22, 2021. https://www.bcg.com/publications/2020/new-era-higher-ed-employer-collaboration.

Wheatley, Margaret. "When Change Is Out of Our Control." *Human Resources for the 21st Century*. New York: Wiley, 2003.

About the Author

VIVEK SHARMA has extensive experience building and growing profitable businesses through the application of technology and data. He is the CEO and Co-founder of InStride, helping CEOs of large organizations usher in the *Age of And* through strategic workforce education. Vivek previously held leadership roles at The Walt Disney Co., Yahoo! and McKinsey & Company and is an independent board director and technology committee chair for JetBlue Airways. A graduate of the Indian Institute of Technology, he also teaches data science at the University of Southern California. Vivek's first book, *WIREFRAMED — Simplifying Digital Innovation for Business Leaders*, explains how digital technology is shifting commerce, the workplace and the geopolitical landscape. He is an active member of the Indian-American community and lives in Southern California with his wife and two children.

CPSIA information can be obtained
at www.ICGtesting.com
Printed in the USA
LVHW012005170921
698124LV00003B/4/J